Policy Studies Institute

D1076582

Black and White Britain

Policy Studies Institute

Black and White Britain

The Third PSI Survey

Colin Brown

 Heinemann · London

Heinemann Educational Books Ltd
22 Bedford Square, London WC1B 3HH

Heinemann Educational Books Inc
70 Court Street, Portsmouth, New Hampshire 03801

First published 1984
Reprinted 1984

British Library Cataloguing in Publication Data

Brown, Colin, *19-- —*
    Black and white Britain: the third PSI survey.
    1. Blacks—Great Britain—Social conditions
    I. Title   II. Policy Studies Institute
    305.8'96'041   DA125.N4

    ISBN 0-435-83124-0
    ISBN 0-435-83125-9 Pbk

Printed in Great Britain by
Biddles Ltd, Guildford, Surrey

CONTENTS

LIST OF TABLES

ix

xiii

NOTES ABOUT THE TABLES

(1) In the tables, the following conventions are used. An empty cell (zero per cent) is denoted by a dash, (-). A percentage greater than zero but smaller than 0.5 is denoted by an asterisk,(*). If the unweighted base of a percentage is less than 50, the percentage is given in brackets.

(2) Percentages are rounded to the nearest whole number.

(3) Some tables refer to the individual samples, others to the household samples. The difference between these is explained in the introduction.

(4) The base for the percentages is the 'weighted base' given at the foot of most tables. This is a base which is statistically corrected for different sampling probabilities. The 'unweighted base', also given at the foot of the table, shows the actual number of interviews on which this is based. This is explained further in the introduction.

(5) Unless otherwise stated, all tables are based on the data collected in the PSI survey.

Preface and Acknowledgements

This report is based on a project sponsored by a number of bodies. The core funding was provided by several government departments, headed by the Home Office; the others were the Department of the Environment, the Department of Health and Social Security, and the Department of Employment together with the Manpower Services Commission. Further funding was provided by the Greater London Council, the Calouste Gulbenkian Foundation, the Hilden Charitable Trust, the Joseph Rowntree Charitable Trust and the Wates Foundation. Any opinions expressed are those of the author, and do not necessarily represent the views of any of the funding bodies.

We are very grateful for the guidance and encouragement given by the project's Advisory Group, which met at key stages of the project. The Advisory Group members were:

Lord Briggs (Chairman)   Mr R Langham
Dr Muhammad Anwar   Dr Janet Lewis
Mr Neil Atkinson   Mr N Nagler
Mr Dennis Brooks   Mr Herman Ouseley
Mr S F J Butler   Ms Usha Prashar
Mr J Croft   Dr Dipak Ray
Mr George Greaves   Mr G Sutton
Cllr P S Khabra   Mr Keith Thorpe

The survey fieldwork was conducted by Research Services Limited and by the Social Survey Division of the Office of Population Censuses and Surveys; I am indebted to their staff, who helped a large and complicated project to run smoothly at every stage. In particular, Roger Thomas of OPCS and Pym Cornish of RSL made vital contributions to the survey. Our special thanks go to the hundreds of interviewers who showed great skill and perseverance, often in appalling weather conditions.

The survey could not have taken place without the techniques developed during the pilot project (also funded by the Home Office and the Department of the Environment) in which Social and Community Planning Research played a large part. My thanks go to Jane Ritchie who organised the work at SCPR.

I am also grateful to Abdul Matin of the Commission for Racial Equality, who helped to organise the questionnaire translations; to Quantime Limited, whose computer programs were used for the data analysis; and to C.A.C.I. for their rapid processing of Census statistics.

I wish to thank my colleagues at PSI for their assistance during the project; Naomi Connelly, Bill Daniel, John Pinder and Ken Young all gave especially useful advice and constructive criticism. I am grateful to Clare Pattinson and Stephanie Maggin for the skill and patience they have shown whilst typing and setting successive versions of the report. My biggest debt is to David Smith, who was responsible for many of the better features of the project's design and execution, and who gave me help and advice throughout; in the end, it was he who made everything work.

Finally, my thanks go to the thousands of people who voluntarily gave up their time to answer our questions. I hope those who see this report will think it was all worthwhile.

1 Introduction

This is the report of a survey investigation into the circumstances of the British black population. Through individual interviews we have collected the personal details of a sample of adults of different ethnic origins throughout the country; these interviews are all based on the same questionnaire, and this enables us to make reliable comparisons of the characteristics of different ethnic groups. The main focus of our research is on inequalities in the distribution and quality of housing and employment, but the survey data extend to other topics such as household structure, household income, education and attitudes towards race relations.

The PEP/PSI surveys

This is the third of a series of survey investigations carried out by the Policy Studies Institute and its predecessor, Political and Economic Planning(PEP). The first PEP survey of racial minorities was carried out in 1966, in six towns in England, as part of a group of projects to investigate the extent of racial discrimination and its effect on immigrants from different parts of the New Commonwealth(1). The second PEP survey was carried out in 1974 as part of a programme of research which had a wider focus than discrimination alone: the aim was to study the extent to which racial minority groups tended to suffer disadvantages in British society, whether or not those disadvantages were the result of direct racial discrimination against them(2). This was a national survey, although its sample excluded black people living in areas of very low density of immigrant residence. This third survey, carried out in 1982, was also a national survey, and it included black people living in areas of low density.

At the time of the first PEP survey in 1966 the New Commonwealth immigrant population in Britain was about 900,000. Most of these people had migrated during the late 1950s and 1960s, and they were therefore relative newcomers to Britain. The main factors that prompted the migration were the search for work on the part of the migrants and a shortage of labour in Britain's

1

expanding post-war economy. In the 1950s there were no restrictions on the entry of Commonwealth citizens, but in 1962 the first Commonwealth Immigrants Act was passed and this, together with further immigration legislation in 1968 and 1971, has been the most important determinant of the rate of immigration over the past twenty years. By the time of the second PEP study, in 1974, the New Commonwealth immigrant population, together with British-born descendants, numbered about a million and a half, but the overall trend of the immigration rate was downwards, and the character of the migration had changed radically: large numbers of the early migrants were young workers, predominantly men, who came here without dependants, but the later migrants were more often women, children and older dependants. Family roots were being put down in Britain, and it was no longer correct to refer to British blacks as an immigrant population: over a third had been born in this country. By 1982, New Commonwealth immigration had declined further and was almost entirely made up of dependants of people already settled here; the population with New Commonwealth origins had grown to about 2.2 million, of whom about four-fifths were black. The black population is now over 40 per cent British-born and over half of those who are immigrants have lived here for more than fifteen years.

The successive PEP/PSI surveys have therefore addressed a question of racial equality and justice which has gradually changed its character between 1966 and 1982, from a concern about the position and treatment of immigrant workers to a concern about the circumstances of the black members of the British population.

The 1966 PEP study revealed that racial discrimination existed on a substantial scale, but the programme of research centred on the 1974 survey demonstrated that there were other factors that resulted in the unfair treatment of black people in Britain, factors that were not just the result of intentional acts of racial discrimination: the policies and practices of employers and other organisations were found often to work against the interests of black people, even though those policies and practices had developed when there were few black people in Britain. This, along with direct discrimination, was brought under the umbrella term 'racial disadvantage'. A legal distinction was made, in the 1976 Race Relations Act, between indirect discrimination and direct discrimination. Direct discrimination had been made unlawful in the 1965 and 1968 Race Relations Acts, but the 1976 Act went on to outlaw individual acts and organisational practices that worked to the disadvantage of identifiable racial groups, regardless of the way they were described or formulated, and regardless of the motive.

One purpose of this type of survey is to obtain information on the total impact of racial disadvantage on the black population.

2

This requires a detailed survey because it is important that our comparisons between white people and black people take into account the other differences that presently exist between them: for example, in this study the analysis of job levels can be adjusted for any differences of qualifications and English fluency. It is also important to understand from the outset that no direct evidence of racial discrimination is available from a survey like this, except in the reports of individuals who have reason to suspect that they have been its victims. For objective evidence about the levels of discrimination we must look to other studies, and in particular to the research carried out by making test applications to employers and other bodies and observing the responses to black and white applicants(4).

The 1982 survey has many features in common with the 1974 PEP survey. We have aimed wherever possible to make valid comparisons between the two sets of results by maintaining continuity of question wording and by ensuring that people living in similar areas are being compared. It is these comparisons over time, coupled with the informants' own accounts of changes in their jobs, housing and other aspects of their lives, that give this survey its particular value.

Because of practical considerations described later in this chapter the 1974 survey excluded from its sample of black people those living in areas of very low densities of black residence. As a result, the survey was representative of about 76 per cent of Britain's population of Asian and West Indian origin; the remaining 24 per cent lived in areas where the population was almost exclusively white. The 1982 survey was able to include black people from these areas, thus giving a nationally representative sample. However, because the black population in these areas has different characteristics from those of the black population in the denser areas (there is, for instance, a larger proportion of self-employed black people in these areas), any comparison between the two surveys that aims to detect change over time has to exclude this group. In the comparison tables we therefore leave out from the 1982 results all informants living outside the areas defined as eligible for the 1974 survey. It should be noted that when we talk of the '1974 areas' in the 1982 survey, these are not the same actual fieldwork areas, but areas that would have been eligible for inclusion in that survey(3); the 1974 survey was conducted in a sample of districts specially selected on a representative basis from all eligible districts, and the 1982 survey was conducted in a freshly selected set of districts. More details of the 1982 sampling scheme are given later.

Even after making this geographical adjustment, we need to be careful about the meaning of comparisons between the 1974 and 1982 survey results, for the black population in 1982 is not the

3

same group of people as it was in 1974. Over this period the British black population has grown by over a third; this growth has been the result of natural increase and immigration, in roughly equal proportions. Also during this period many young black people have grown up and established their own households, and some large households have divided into two or more smaller ones. Our analyses try to distinguish changes in the circumstances of individual adults and households from changes that are related to the appearance of the new adults and new households.

The population studied
The terms used in this report to refer to different ethnic groups need to be defined. In any discussion of race relations there is a danger that words may carry unintended meanings that alter the sense of an argument or imply a particular political standpoint. In Britain this problem of language is particularly acute because recent considerations of citizenship, nationality and immigration are overlaid on older arguments about racial categories, their scientific validity and their relationship with national and ethnic origins. It is not our intention to discuss any of these issues except to make clear our own usage of terms. From their beginning the PEP and PSI studies have been primarily concerned with the position in British society of the dark-skinned immigrants who came to Britain from various parts of the New Commonwealth after the end of the second world war. When our research included other immigrant groups, such as Cypriots, Hungarians and Italians, the results showed that the problems of prejudice and discrimination faced by the 'coloured' immigrants were of a far greater magnitude than those faced by other immigrants, and this finding convinced us that our focus on the treatment of the 'coloured' group was the right approach. In recognition of the fact that members of this group - whether their family origins are in the West Indies, in the Indian sub-continent or in Africa - are all vulnerable to the prejudice and discrimination based on skin colour, we refer to them in this report as a single group, as black people. We use the term 'family origins' because with the passing of time an increasing proportion of black people in Britain are British-born, rather than immigrants; we include these British-born people because they are also subject to the effects of discrimination based on skin colour. Our choice of the work 'black' in preference to 'coloured' and 'black and brown' is simply in line with current usage.

There are, however, very good reasons to make distinctions between the groups within the black population; groups with different cultural backgrounds have different needs and different characteristics, and any account of the position of minority groups in British society must analyse these differences. For this reason, most of the survey results are split not only between black people and white people, but also between the main groups within the black population: those with family origins in the West Indies and those with family origins in the Indian sub-continent. Our first preference is to refer to these groups respectively as 'of West Indian origin' and 'of Asian origin'; they are intended to include black people with family origins in these areas regardless of where they were born. However, these terms are clumsy and we therefore often abbreviate them to 'West Indian' and 'Asian', with no intended difference of meaning. It is worth stressing this point; our use of an adjective based on area of family origin is not meant to carry any implication about birthplace or nationality, and is merely to distinguish between different groups within the black population. Because of further differences between the groups from different areas of the Indian sub-continent we also split those of Asian origin into groups according to country of origin (India, Pakistan, Bangladesh); those of Asian origin who were resident in Africa prior to coming to Britain are also classified separately, as of 'African Asian' origin. Otherwise, people with recent family origins in Africa have not been included in the survey. The exclusion of Africans from the black sample is because of the small size of this group in relation to the rest of the British black population. Less than one in ten black people in this country are of recent African origin (we use the term 'recent African origin' in order to make it clear we are not talking of the West Indian population, which of course has its more distant origin in Africa). To have included a large enough sample of them in the survey would have involved a considerable extension to the fieldwork; the exclusion is regrettable, because this group is in many ways distinct from the rest of the black population, but the extra work that would have otherwise been necessary was beyond the resources of the project.

The terms 'racial minorities' and 'ethnic minorities' are also used in this report to refer to the black population; despite the technical differences between the strict meanings of these terms, they are used interchangeably here. Our use of the term 'British' is in reference to people resident in Britain, and not to any category of British citizenship.

We should also make clear the way in which these definitions were used to determine eligibility for the survey. People of Asian or West Indian origin were defined as non-white people who were born in the Indian sub-continent or the West Indies, or whose families originated in these areas. This included 'African Asians', as their family origins are in the Indian sub-continent. People born in Britain to one or more parents of Asian or West Indian origin were also included. Households containing one or more persons of Asian and West Indian origin were included in this survey even if other household members were white or of other ethnic origins, but individual interviews were carried out only with people of Asian or West Indian origin. This group corresponds closely with that covered by Office of Population, Censuses and Surveys (OPCS) estimates of the population of 'New Commonwealth and Pakistani ethnic origin' originating from these areas. The OPCS definition is 'persons born in the New Commonwealth who are not of UK descent, plus children born in Great Britain to parents of New Commonwealth ethnic origin, including children with only one such parent (children of mixed unions).' Separate estimates are produced by OPCS for people within this definition who have origins in the Indian sub-continent and the Caribbean.

The comparison survey of white people covered the remainder of the population, excluding people of Chinese and South East Asian origin and people who were 'coloured' but not of Asian or West Indian origin; the most important of these exclusions was of people of black African ethnic origin. No white people living in households with people of Asian or West Indian origin were included in this survey: mixed households were included only in the other survey.

The design and execution of the survey
In the rest of this introductory chapter we give a description of the methods used to obtain the information presented in this report. Although we advise that some knowledge of the conduct of the survey is important for an understanding of its results, we acknowledge that some readers will wish to skip these paragraphs and move directly to the substance of the report. We therefore give here a very brief summary of the key points of the survey methodology:

(a)   The survey of black people comprises 5,001 interviews with individual adults from 3,083 separate households.

(b)   The comparison survey of white people comprises interviews from 2,305 adults, each from a separate household. In some cases information was only obtained in relation to the household, and individual details could not be obtained; the total white sample size for the individual adult data is 2,263.

(c)   Both surveys are designed to be nationally representative of their respective populations of England and Wales.

(d)   The samples for both surveys were obtained by first compiling comprehensive lists of households living within a nationally representative set of areas and then systematically selecting the informants.

(e)   For the survey of black people the interviewers were usually matched by ethnic group with the sampled individuals. Where necessary, Asian informants were interviewed in one of five Asian languages.

6

(f) The interviewing, the coding of questionnaires and the transfer of data to magnetic tape were all carried out by Research Services Ltd and by the Social Survey Division of the Office of Population Censuses and Surveys. The analysis of the data by computer was carried out by PSI.

Overall strategy

The aim of the survey was to obtain a large amount of information by personal interview from a nationally representative sample of five thousand black people of Asian and West Indian origin and a nationally representative sample of over two thousand white people. The technical problems confronting this endeavour were severe. As we shall see in detail in the body of the report, the British black population is not only a very small part of the whole population, it is also geographically distributed in a very clustered way. Also, there is no list from which we can draw the names or addresses of black people for a sample survey, as we can for the whole population using the electoral registers, rating lists or postcodes. We therefore had to start from scratch and locate a sample of black people using a variety of techniques, all of which relied entirely on the work of interviewers in the field to find potential informants. This kind of operation had been carried out before - for example, the 1974 PEP survey used door-to-door screening as its main tool for finding a sample of black people - but had not been attempted on a nationally representative basis. In areas of relatively concentrated Asian and West Indian residence it is a simpler proposition to carry out a survey of this sort than it is in the areas where very few black people live. The clustering of most of the target population, which makes it easy to find areas where many interviews might be obtained, leaves the remainder of the target population spread very thinly over a very large area of the country. To find a sample of these dispersed people, one cannot use a straightforward door-to-door screening method because the cost would be immense. The 1974 survey limited its coverage to areas of known immigrant residence; as a result it was representative of about 76 per cent of the British Asian and West Indian population. To have included the remaining 24 per cent would have involved making calls at 24,000 addresses to find every 100 eligible informants.

Whatever procedure we adopted for establishing a sample of people of Asian and West Indian origin, it would rely in part for its efficiency on prior indications of the concentration of ethnic minority residence in the geographical areas involved, because different allocations of field resources would have to be made in different areas: more field staff would be required in areas of high ethnic minority concentration than in other areas because of the larger numbers of persons eligible for interview. In practice this meant relying on the 1971 census small-area statistics, and therefore meant that the geographical boundaries of the areas covered by the survey had to fit in with those used in the census. This created a problem for the selection of the sample of white people because there exist no lists of the general population that are easily made geographically compatible with the small areas in the census.   There is no reason in principle why the census enumeration districts (EDs) could not be found within, say, the electoral registers, but there would be a very large amount of detailed clerical work involved.   Consequently, if the areas to be included in the survey were to be the same for the black and the white samples, the white sample could not be drawn conventionally from available lists.

In advance of the survey PSI carried out a review of the available methods for establishing a sample of black people, and carried out extensive field tests to determine the feasibility of sampling Asian people by name identification from the electoral registers and to test a new method of enumeration which is described below.   The conclusion of this development work was that electoral registers would prove to be too unreliable in a large number of areas, and that for both for Asians and West Indians the sample would have to be established by interviewers visiting the survey areas and using a variety of door-to-door methods(5).

The plan was therefore to select a sample of areas with boundaries as defined for the 1971 census enumeration and to compile, in the field, lists of Asian, West Indian and white households in each area, and from these lists select our sample. The fieldwork for the survey thus consisted of two phases: first an enumeration phase to establish the sample, and then the main interviewing phase.   During the enumeration (we also refer to this as the screening phase) the interviewers obtained details of the ethnic group, mother-tongue, English language fluency and sex of each adult in the households that contained people of Asian and West Indian origin.   In this way, not only could people be systematically selected for the sample of individuals, but arrangements could also be made to match, ethnically and linguistically, the interviewers to the selected informants.

The collaboration of the two survey organisations
The survey fieldwork was conducted by two organisations in collaboration.   Although the samples of black and white people were based on a common set of geographical areas, the different distributions of the two populations meant that the bulk of the white interviewing work was outside the areas where most of the black interviews took place; the white interviews were mainly organised and conducted by the Social Survey Division of the Office of Population Censuses and Surveys, while a commercial

8

research agency, Research Services Limited (RSL), was appointed to organise and conduct the interviews with black informants. For reasons of fieldwork efficiency, these functions were switched around in some areas. Thus, about 300 interviews with white people in inner-city areas were carried out by RSL, and about 100 interviews with Asians and West Indians, in areas of very low concentration of residence of black people, were carried out by OPCS. The most important aspect of the co-ordination between the fieldwork of the two organisations, however, was in the enumeration phase of the survey. In the areas expected to yield most black informants, RSL performed the enumeration work, and OPCS obtained from them lists of addresses of potential white informants; in the other areas OPCS used their white interviews as starting points for the enumeration of potential black informants. The actual procedures used are described below.

The sample structures and the enumeration

Over a thousand census enumeration districts (EDs) were selected systematically, by computer, from all the EDs in England and Wales. Scotland was excluded from the survey because few people of Asian and West Indian origin live there: according to the 1971 Census Scotland contains two per cent of the British population born in the West Indies or in the Indian sub-continent. The EDs were selected in such a way as to be grouped in about 260 geographical clusters: nearly all of these clusters comprised four EDs within a single electoral ward. The size of the area covered by an ED varies considerably, but on average each contains about 165 households. Within each ward cluster, the EDs selected for the survey were not necessarily contiguous: they were chosen systematically from a list of all the EDs in the ward. Those EDs which had a relatively high concentration of Asian and West Indian residents were given a higher probability of selection than others, to ensure there were more of these EDs in the survey, and therefore ensure that black informants from such areas were from a good geographical spread of areas. This meant that in the final sample of informants there was a larger proportion of black people from these high concentration areas than is the case nationally; to correct this the data was statistically reweighted, to restore the sample to a nationally representative one. This is why a 'weighted base' and an 'unweighted base' is given in the tables: the unweighted base gives the actual number of interviews on which the data are based, while the weighted base is a statistically processed version which incorporates adjustments for the different probabilities of selection. They are both stated in the tables because the weighted base is useful if a reader wishes to re-percentage the figures with different combinations of categories (for example, to obtain a percentage for all black informants where

9

only the separate Asian and West Indian figures are given), while the unweighted base is a better guide to the statistical reliability of the figures in the table.

We should stress here that both the ethnic minority and the white surveys are based on the same nationally representative set of areas, and that no bias towards any particular type of geographical area is built into the sample design. Both surveys can therefore stand on their own as sources of national statistics on their respective populations. The re-weighting of the survey data, as described above, compensated for any variation of the sampling probabilities between geographical areas.

The EDs and the ED clusters were classified according to estimates of the relative numbers of Asian and West Indian people within them, calculated from the 1971 Census. Although the 1971 Census was out of date, it was the only source of such data available; the 1981 Census results for EDs were not published at the time of our survey. On the basis of this classification, the enumeration fieldwork was organised in different areas as follows:

(i)   EDs where more than one in ten households were expected to be Asian or West Indian. An RSL interviewer listed all the addresses in the ED by walking round the area, using a map of the ED boundary; this produced a 'visual listing' of dwellings, identified only by their street names and numbers. The interviewer then called at each dwelling to enquire whether anyone of Asian or West Indian origin lived there; if they did, a short doorstep interview was carried out to obtain details necessary for the sampling procedure and for ethnic and linguistic matching of interviewers and informants.

(ii)   Other EDs in clusters in which more than one in two hundred households were expected to be Asian or West Indian. An RSL interviewer made a visual listing of dwellings, as described above. The interviewer then went to every sixth address on his or her list, and enquired if there was anyone of Asian or West Indian origin living there, then asked whether the informant knew if anyone in the five dwellings either side of theirs was of Asian or West Indian origin. Interviewers were specifically instructed not to ask for names or addresses; instead, if they were told that there was someone of Asian or West Indian origin in a gap between any of their initial calls, interviewers went to each of the five addresses in that gap to enquire about the occupants. In this way most of the black people in an area could be located with far fewer calls than would be necessary if every household in the area were contacted.

10

(iii)   EDs in other clusters
An OPCS interviewer made a visual listing of the dwellings in the area. From this list the households for the white sample were selected (nearly all addresses in these areas contain only white people); at the end of each interview the OPCS interviewer enquired whether there were any people of Asian or West Indian origin living at the ten addresses either side of the informant. On receiving a positive response, the interviewer followed the same procedure as described in (ii) above, calling at all ten addresses until the Asian or West Indian people were found. Because the white interviews were so spread out (fewer than three to an ED) it was necessary to make a call at one address in between each interviewed household to enquire about the presence of Asian or West Indian households in the surrounding group of addresses: most of the addresses in each ED were therefore covered by one form of screening or another.

In the development work for this project it was established that the new enumeration method, based on information obtained from people selected at fixed intervals along a street, was both efficient and accurate, even where there were complicated arrangements of dwellings, such as converted flats and blocks of flats. With this technique, the total number of calls necessary to find all the Asian and West Indian households in each area was reduced sufficiently to make a nationally representative survey possible, covering even the areas of low density ethnic minority residence.

The actual sample of Asians and West Indians was selected as follows. All of the households found to contain anyone of Asian or West Indian origin were included in the sample of households; from within them, a sample of adults was selected by systematically picking two adults from each household containing two or more adults, and all adults who were single-person households. The white sample was selected by systematically picking about one in every 60 of the addresses (excluding those known to contain black people) from the visual listings of the enumeration; at each address the resident household was included in the household sample, and one adult was systematically selected for the sample of adults. For both the black and the white samples these procedures gave a lower probability of selection to individuals living in larger households than to those in smaller households, and therefore further weights were applied during the analysis of the survey results to make them representative of all adults in all types of household.

11

Both the survey of Asians and West Indians and the survey of whites are, therefore, based on a nationally representative sample of households and also on a nationally representative sample of individuals.

The interview and questionnaires

At each selected houshold, the head of household was interviewed using a questionnaire that covered subjects such as household structure, housing tenure and costs, type and size of the dwelling, sources of household income and various others relating to the whole household and its accommodation. This part of the interview schedule was termed the 'household module'. A second questionnaire was used to interview the selected individuals within the houshold (up to two individuals in each Asian or West Indian household, and one individual only in each white household) about their own circumstances, experiences and views. This part of the schedule was termed the 'individual module'. A third questionnaire was used to extend the individual interview for half of all the selected Asian and West Indians, and this was termed the 'alternate module'. The reason for having such an elaborate arrangement was to balance the needs of the survey, in terms of the quantity and quality of information required, with the practical difficulties of keeping the co-operation of informants throughout lengthy interviews. The head of household was the best person to provide details of the household and dwelling, but information about the individuals could best be given by the individuals themselves. Within the Asian and West Indian survey it was therefore possible for three adults to be interviewed in the same household: the houshold head and two others. The early drafts of the individual module were too long to be used in these circumstances. To solve the problem, a number of questions were moved to a third module which would not be used more than once in each household. This procedure reduced the time the interviewer spent at each address, but for the questions on the alternate module it halved the sample size. However, in the white comparison survey, the individual module was short enough to administer to every informant in its entirety.

The questions were often based on those used in the 1974 PEP survey. Some changes were made as a result of the problems encountered during the 1974 survey, as a result of piloting work done in 1981, and in order to align our wording and definitions with those of other major national surveys, such as the House Condition Survey and the Labour Force Survey. One of the difficulties of work such as this is the diversity of question formats and definitions in use: it could only be overcome if each key question were repeated in several different forms and that would be impossible. Our particular difficulty was the need to be able to compare our results with contemporary national surveys and to be able to compare them with the 1974 survey. The final versions of the questions are the products of a long period of development and consultation with the government departments responsible for the national sources of data, in particular with the Office of Population Censuses and Surveys, and with the study's advisory group. Even after this we were left with some hard decisions over the final content of the questionaire.

For Asian informants who were not fluent in English we produced versions of the questionnaire with the questions and pre-codes printed in Gujarati, Urdu, Punjabi, Bengali and Hindi, alongside or underneath the questions in English. For these versions we tried to ensure accuracy and a correct 'level' of language by obtaining a draft translation and having the final version written out by another translator working from the draft; where possible we arranged for two independent first drafts to be available to the final translator. The aim was to maintain tightness of definition while adopting a relatively colloquial manner. This cannot be consistently achieved; the problems are mainly those of conceptual equivalence rather than of formal accuracy of translation, and they are particularly acute where the questions are about attitudes and beliefs. A number of solutions to the problem have been attempted over the years by those conducting cross-national surveys. At PSI we carried out a review of these techniques and some development work of our own in preparation for this survey, and concluded that, within a reasonable time-scale and budget, the method we adopted was the most hopeful. Even this technique proved to be very hard to organise at the time, and some of the questions on some of the Asian-language versions are direct translations by a single person; most, however, are the product of the method employing two or three translators.

Response

We give below the response rates obtained in the main survey fieldwork: these are the numbers of interviews shown as a percentage of households or individuals in each group selected for interview. As explained above, the white household sample was selected from lists of addresses compiled by interviewers making a visual inspection of the survey areas, while the sample of black households comprised those identified by the door-to-door enumeration interviews. Black households that were not identified by the screening were therefore absent from the sample approached in the main survey fieldwork. For this reason the response rates for the white and black samples are not directly comparable; in the case of the black sample there is a further (unknown) degree of 'non-response' (perhaps 'non-coverage' would be a more accurate term) that is not shown in these figures. Every

13

effort was made to ensure that this shortfall was kept to a minimum, both by careful piloting of the enumeration methods and by intensive field checks on the coverage of selected areas.

	Response Rate
Asian households	85%
Asian men	81%
Asian women	81%
West Indian households	76%
West Indian men	64%
West Indian women	70%
White households	83%
White adults	82%

The response rates for Asians and whites are at a similar, high level, but for West Indians they are lower. In the 1974 survey there was a similar gap between the response rates of Asians and West Indians in the main interviewing fieldwork. For the current survey the difference between the Asian and West Indian rates is made up both of refusals and failures to contact the selected person. The percentages of refusals and non-contacts for the three individual samples were as follows:

	West Indian		Asian		White
	Men	Women	Men	Women	
Non-contact	20%	15%	12%	12%	3%
Refusal	16%	15%	7%	8%	15%

It can be seen that the non-contact rate was higher for the Asian and West Indian samples than for the white sample. Refusal rates were, however, lower for Asians than for whites, and for West Indians were the same as for whites. However, because the black and white samples were obtained in rather different ways, there is only limited value in making direct comparisons of these specific categories of non-response between blacks and whites.

Notes
1. W.W. Daniel, Racial Discrimination in England, Penguin 1968.
2. David J. Smith, Racial Disadvantage in Britain, Penguin 1977.

3. These areas were census enumeration districts with Asian and West Indian immigrants making up more than 2.4 per cent of their population, in local authorities with over 0.5 per cent Asian and West Indian immigrants in their populations.

4. W.W. Daniel, Racial Discrimination in England, Penguin, 1968; M. Firth, 'Racial Discrimination in the British Labour Market', Industrial and Labour Relations Review, Vol. 34, No. 2, January, 1981, pp. 265-72; J. Hubbuck and S. Carter, Half a Chance?, Commission for Racial Equality, 1980; R. Jowell and P. Prescott-Clarke, 'Racial Discrimination and White-Collar Workers in Britain', Race, Vol. XI, No. 4, April 1970, pp. 397-417; N. McIntosh and D.J. Smith, The Extent of Racial Discrimination, PEP Report 547, 1974.

5. C. Brown and J. Ritchie Focussed Enumeration: The development of a method of sampling ethnic minority groups, PSI/SCPR, May 1981.

II Background

Ethnic group

The sample for the racial minorities survey is made up of black people of Asian origin and West Indian origin. The definitions used when designing the survey and in carrying out the interviewing fieldwork were discussed in the previous chapter, where it was also explained that our definitions match closely with those used by the Office of Population Censuses and Surveys in making estimates of the sizes of the different populations of New Commonwealth and Pakistani origin from 1971 Census figures and subsequent birth, death and migration statistics. At the beginning of the survey fieldwork, the latest figures available from OPCS showed that people of Asian and West Indian origin in Great Britain numbered 1,651,000 in 1980, representing just over three per cent of the population(1). It should be remembered that people of African origin (with the exception of the African Asians) are excluded from all these figures, and were not included in the PSI survey. OPCS estimated they numbered 123,000, less than a third of one per cent of the British population.

We give below a breakdown by ethnic group of the people covered by the PSI survey, and a comparison based on the OPCS figures. Separate PSI figures are given for the adults actually interviewed and the total population within the households where interviews took place; this is because the ethnic group profiles of these two samples differ as a result of the different numbers of children. It can be seen that there is a larger proportion of Asians within the PSI sample than would be expected from the OPCS estimates, and this is due to two separate factors. First we know that the response rates in the PSI survey were higher among people of Asian origin than among people of West Indian origin, and this must artificially change the proportions of the two groups. Secondly, there was a real change in the ethnic mix of the black population between the dates of the OPCS estimate (1980) and the PSI survey (1982), and this was in the direction of a larger proportion of Asians. This is because the residual immigration of dependants from the Indian sub-continent is far larger than that from the West Indies, and because fertility rates are presently higher among Asian women. The fact that the differences between the OPCS and PSI figures show a larger Pakistani and Bangladeshi group in 1982 reflects this movement: this group features prominently in the recent immigration of dependants and has the highest fertility rates.

Within the analysis of the PSI survey no attempt has been made to re-weight the data to account for the high proportion of Asians caused by different response rates. In most cases where this procedure would have affected the results for the black sample as a whole, we give the results separately for the Asian and West Indian groups, and this removes the need for such reweighting.

We have divided the Asian group according to their family's country of origin, and this categorisation will be seen in the report to show up important differences within the Asian community. Often, however, we have carried out additional analysis by Asian religion because this can make an equally important contribution to our understanding of complex ethnic variations. Table 2 shows that country of origin and religion are related to each other in the following way. Nearly all of the Pakistani and Bangladeshi informants are Muslims, while the other Asian groups have a wider spread of religious affiliation: over 40 per cent of the Indians are Sikhs, over 30 per cent are Hindus, and only 16 per cent are Muslims; sixty per cent of the African Asians are Hindus, 24 per cent are Muslims, and 11 per cent are Sikhs. Overall, six per cent of Asian informants have a faith other than Islam, Hinduism or Sikhism, most of these people being Christians of Indian and Sri Lankan origin. Very few Asians report that they have no religion: only one per cent give this specific response to the question, in contrast to 12 per cent of West Indians and eight per cent of whites.

Birthplace and date of settlement in Britain
In the previous chapter we mentioned the political dangers inherent in the classification of British people as Asians or West Indians according to their family's country of origin. As we are now describing the ethnic profile of the black people covered by our survey, it is important to stress that over 40 per cent of the people in this country whom we are labelling 'of Asian or West Indian origin' were born in the United Kingdom. Over half of the West Indians in the households within our survey were born in the UK, but, because of differences in the timing of the principal migration periods, the figure for Asians is under 40 per cent (Table 3). The UK-born section of the black population is made up largely of young adults and children, and therefore we find that a large majority of the adults interviewed in our survey were born

17

overseas, although there is again a marked difference between the Asian and West Indian groups: only four per cent of the Asians, compared to a quarter of West Indians, were born here. If we break down the adults sample into two age groups we see that among those aged 16-24, over 80 per cent of West Indians, and 15 per cent of Asians were born in the UK, while the figures for those aged 25 and over are three per cent for West Indians and under one per cent for Asians.

Table 4 shows the proportion of Asian and West Indian heads of households who were born in this country. Because mixed households are included in the survey sample, some of the UK-born household heads are white, so we give below a separate figure excluding households headed by a white person. Only one in a hundred Asian households is presently headed by a non-white person born in this country, compared with about one in ten West Indian households.

All informants who were immigrants were asked which year they came to this country. Nearly all immigration of black people from the West Indies and the Indian sub-continent has taken place since the second world war, but, as Table 5 shows, the timing of the migration has varied between the different ethnic groups and between men and women. These variations are due to a combination of factors: different social and political forces prompted the migration from different areas; the migrants came from a variety of societies, which produced different patterns of migration; and, above all, the numbers of black people moving into the UK have been controlled by the government since 1962 by a series of legal and administrative measures. Although it is beyond the scope of this report to attempt a thorough analysis of these factors, the table shows the various phases of the migration of men and women from the different ethnic groups.

The earliest migration was of West Indian men: one in six of the immigrant men now in Britain came here before 1956, and over two-thirds were here by mid-1962. The migration of West Indian women was a little slower, although over half of the immigrant women here today had arrived by mid-1962. The intake of both men and women from the West Indies slowed progressively in the 1960s, and a very small proportion of British West Indians arrived after 1972. The majority of Asian immigrant men came to Britain after the West Indian migration had begun to decline (that is to say after the 1962 Commonwealth Immigrants Act) but the pattern varies between the Asian groups: around ten per cent of the Indian, Pakistani and Bangladeshi men came before 1960, and about 60 per cent had come by 1968, but the bulk of the Pakistani migration was a little earlier than that of the Indians and Bangladeshis. After 1968 male immigration from these areas slowed progressively, but it is in this period that the majority of African Asian immigrants came to Britain: only 25 per cent of African Asian men in the survey came to Britain before April 1968. It can be seen from the table that Asian women migrated later than men, although the lag between the men and the women was far greater for Pakistanis and Bangladeshis than for Indians or African Asians.

Sex and age

Although the balance of the sexes among adults of West Indian origin is almost the same as among the white population, there is a relatively high ratio of men to women among Asians, and this is particularly the case for the Pakistani and Bangladeshi groups (Table 6). It should be noted, however, that the Asian sex ratio is moving towards that of the rest of the population. During the initial periods of immigration there was a considerable predominance of men, but with the passing of time they have been joined by women. The ratio of males to females is highest among the Pakistanis and Bangladeshis, but it can be seen from comparison with the 1974 PEP survey figures that the ratio is changing most rapidly for these groups.

Table 7 shows the age breakdowns for men and women of the ethnic groups in the surveys. White, West Indian and Asian adults have age profiles that differ radically from each other, and the explanation can again be found in the timing of the main phases of immigration. Considering men first, we see that when compared to the fairly flat age distribution of the whites, there is a bulge in the West Indian distribution, peaking in the 45-54 group, and a similar feature in the Asian distribution peaking in the 25-34 group. These peaks correspond to the main periods of primary migration of young male workers from the two areas: most of the West Indian men came to Britain in the 1950s and early 1960s, while Asian men came here over a longer period, in several phases during the late 1950s, 1960s and 1970s. There is among the West Indian men another peak in the age distribution in the 16-24 group, and this is mainly composed of people who were born here to first-generation immigrants. The absence of such a peak in the Asian distribution reflects the later migration and hence the later commencement of post-immigration childbearing.

The age distributions of women are similar to those of the men in the same ethnic groups, but there are fewer women than men in the older age groups: women tended to come to Britain later than men, but, in addition, relatively fewer middle-aged and older women than men from these age groups migrated - particularly in the case of West Indians.

While it can be seen that the adult ethnic minority population is much younger than the adult white population, a comparison of the age profiles of the entire populations, including children, shows an even greater difference (Table 8). More than half of the

19

population of Asian and West Indian origin, compared with about 35 per cent of the general population, is aged under 25. Looking at the ethnic groups separately, we see that 40 per cent of Asians are under 16 years old, compared with 30 per cent of West Indians and 22 per cent of the general population. There are greater proportions of children among the Asian and West Indian populations principally because more of the ethnic minority adults are in the child-rearing age groups, but also because they have tended to have larger families.

A good deal of the published policy-related discussion of the demographic structure of the black population has rightly stressed the significance of the relatively low average age. It is now worth noting, however, that sharply increasing numbers of people of Asian and West Indian origin will be reaching senior citizenship over the next twenty years; only 3 per cent of the black population are now of pensionable age, but a further 20 per cent of West Indian people, and 13 per cent of Asian people, are aged 45 or over.

Geographical distribution
Although a detailed analysis of the residential patterns of the black population is presented later, some basic facts have to be given at this stage to give a necessary geographical perspective to the other data in this report.

The British black population is not spread across the country in the same way as the white population; if it were, then each town would have a small black community making up about three per cent of its population, and this is not the case. In other words, a large proportion of the black population lives in a small number of local authority areas, and within these areas the black residents tend to be concentrated in a small number of electoral wards. This uneven distribution means that black people, although a tiny proportion of the national population, have been seen to be relatively numerous in some localities, and this has often contributed to very inaccurate perceptions of the total size of the black community in a town or city, and to some wild ideas about the national figures. It also means that in most areas of the country there are very few black people indeed. Half the white population in Britain lives in towns and rural areas(2) that have less than half of one per cent of their local residents coming from ethnic minorities. Table 9 shows that at the level of census emuneration districts (EDs) the pattern of concentration - and, consequently, segregation - is very sharp. Three-quarters of the black population lives in a set of EDs in which we find only a tenth of the white population.

The regional distributions of the white, Asian and West Indian populations are given for the PSI survey and for the 1981 Census, and these two sources show a close overall correspondence, but there are some differences of note in the separate Asian and West Indian distributions (Table 10). Whether these are differences of substance, resulting from the numbers of black people actually found in the Census and in the survey, or differences of classification, resulting from the definitions of ethnic origin used by PSI and OPCS, we cannot say without further analysis. Both sets of figures, however, show that there are dramatic differences between the regional distributions of white, Asian and West Indian people in this country. The importance of the Greater London area stands out immediately, with a third of all Asian people and a half of West Indian people (over a half, according to the Census) living there, as opposed to 11 per cent of white people; we also see that the West Midlands region accounts for a larger part of the Asian and West Indian populations than of the white population.

Chapter IV discusses these facts in greater detail, and takes up the issue of whether residence patterns have changed over the past decade.

Mixed marriages

Although the adults sample for the survey of racial minorities was composed entirely of black people, information on all people living in the household, regardless of ethnic origin, was collected by questioning the head of household. Using this data we can tell how many heads of household are partners in a marriage where one person is of Asian or West Indian family origin and the other is of UK family origin. Although this definition is imperfect - a small proportion of spouses of UK family origin may be black - this is unlikely to have a significant effect on the mixed marriage figures.

Of all the households in the minorities survey, six per cent are headed by a partner in a mixed marriage or mixed cohabiting relationship. As can be seen from Table 11, this figure is higher for West Indians, at nine per cent, than for Asians, at four per cent. For both groups it is more common for black men rather than black women to have a white partner. Because there are fewer married heads of household in the West Indian sample than in the Asian sample, the overall figures for mixed unions change somewhat if they are recalculated as a proportion of all marriages and cohabiting relationships, rather than as a proportion of all households: the Asian figure remains at four per cent, but the West Indian figure rises to 15 per cent. Mixed couples tend to be younger than others, although this is not a strong relationship. Mixed unions are most common in areas of low concentration of local black residence, as might be expected: in EDs with concentration of less than four per cent over a quarter of marriages within the West Indian sample are mixed, and the figure for the Asian sample is 11 per cent. In this analysis we have included informants who are 'living as married' in the married group. Only about 3 per cent of couples in the West Indian and Asian survey are living as married, but they account for 10 per cent of the mixed unions; 23 per cent of cohabiting couples are mixed, compared with seven per cent of officially married couples. Most of this difference lies within the West Indian sample, as nearly all of the mixed couples in the Asian sample are officially married.

Notes
1. These figures are taken from OPCS Monitor PP1 81/6, issued December 1981, and refer to the population in 1980. Estimates of the size of the population of New Commonwealth and Pakastani ethnic origin also exist for 1981, but these include groups other than Asians and West Indians, or are otherwise not comparable with the estimates we use here.
2. This calculation is based on the pre-1974 local authority areas. In 1974 the local government reorganisation reduced the number of local authorities from nearly 1400 to just over 420. Consequently, many of the new areas comprise several towns; the old areas are also used in the analysis elsewhere in this report.

Country of origin of Asians and West Indians: PSI survey and OPCS estimates compared

Column percentages

	PSI Survey, England and Wales		
	Individual Adults Interviewed (1982)	All Persons in Households within the Survey (1982)	OPCS Estimate, Great Britain All Persons (1980)
Ethnic Group:			
Indian	26	26	28
Pakistani	18	20	) 21
Bangladeshi	6	7	)
African Asian	16	13	12
Sri Lankan	1	1	(not available)
Total Asian	67	68	61
West Indian	33	32	39
Base:			
(weighted)	10358	19213	-
(unweighted)	5001	12843	-

Source of OPCS estimate: OPCS Monitor PP1 81/6, December 1981

23

Table 2:   Asians: Religion by country of origin

Column percentages

	All Asian	Indian	Pakis tani	Bangla- deshi	African Asian	Sri Lankan
Religion:						
Muslim	46	16	96	96	24	-
Sikh	20	43	*	-	11	-
Hindu	27	31	1	2	60	50
Church of England	2	3	1	1	*	11
Roman Catholic	3	4	1	-	3	25
Other Religion	1	1	-	-	*	10
No religion	1	1	1	1	*	2
No answer/ Don't know	1	1	1	1	2	2
Base: Adults						
(weighted)	6894	2672	1840	617	1634	132
(un- weighted)	3323	1241	935	336	743	68

24

Column percentages

	All	West Indian	Asian	Indian	Paki-stani	Bangla-deshi	African Asian	Sri Lankan
				Family Country of Origin				
Birthplace								
UK	11	26	4	7	3	1	*	-
West Indies	25	74	-	-	-	-	-	-
India	27	-	41	90	-	-	25	-
Pakistan	17	-	26	-	96	-	1	-
Bangladesh	6	-	9	-	-	97	*	-
Africa	12	-	17	-	-	-	73	-
Other	2	*	3	3	*	2	-	100
Base:								
Adults (weighted)	10358	3465	6894	2672	1840	617	1634	132
(unweighted)	5001	1678	3323	1241	935	336	743	68
Percentage of all adults and children in household (excluding whites) who were born in UK	43	54	38	43	42	31	24	33

25

Table 4:   Proportion of households with household head born
               in UK

All West Indian households	12%
West Indian households, excluding those with white head of household	9%
All Asian households	2%
Asian households, excluding those with white head of household	1%

Note: Households are classed as Asian or West Indian if they
        contain any adults of Asian or West Indian origin.

Table 5:   West Indian and Asian immigrants: Date of settlement in Britain

Column percentages

	West Indian		Indian		Pakistani		Bangladeshi		African Asian	
	Men	Women	Men	Women	Men	Women	Men	Women	Men	Women
Before 1956	16	6	6	4	2	*	2	–	1	–
1956–1957	22	20	7	3	9	2	8	–	2	*
1960–June 1962	32	28	11	6	20	3	9	*	2	1
July 1962–1964	9	15	13	11	13	8	30	4	5	4
1965–March 1968	8	12	22	22	22	15	11	9	15	11
April 1968– 1972	6	9	16	21	18	21	21	35	35	38
1973–1977	1	3	14	18	9	31	13	28	28	32
1978–1982	1	1	7	9	5	18	5	37	7	9
Don't know/ no answer	4	7	4	6	2	2	2	1	5	5
Base: Adults not born in UK (weighted)	1203	1362	1349	1139	1042	741	362	248	924	709

Table 6: Sex breadown by ethnic group, 1974 and 1982 surveys compared.

	White[1]	West Indian	Asian	Indian	Paki-stani	Bangla-deshi	Afri-can Asian
Per cent male in 1982	48	472	56	54	58	59	57
Per cent male in 1974	48	50	59	56	65		56

1. White figures from Census.
2. If the different response rates for males and females in the West Indian sample are taken into account, the 1982 figure becomes 50 per cent. There was no differential between the Asian male and female response rates.

Table 7:   Age breakdown by ethnic group (adults)

Column percentages

Age Group	White Male	White Female	West Indian Male	West Indian Female	Asian Male	Asian Female
16-24	19	17	29	28	19	23
25-34	19	17	13	20	30	34
35-44	16	15	15	22	20	24
45-54	15	14	23	21	19	13
55-64	14	14	15	6	9	5
65 and over	16	22	4	1	3	2
Average age	43.5	46.3	38.4	35.6	37.2	34.3

Base: Adults						
(weighted)	2567	2802	1630	1790	3870	3013
(unweighted)	1001	1262	781	876	1836	1484

Table 8:   Age breakdown by ethnic group (all persons)

Age Group	General population 1981 (England and Wales)		West Indian		Asian	
	Male	Female	Male	Female	Male	Female
0- 9	13	12	16	16	27	28
10-15	10	9	14	14	13	13
16-19	7	6	15	12	7	6
20-24	8	7	9	11	8	10
25-34	15	14	10	15	17	20
35-44	13	12	10	14	12	12
45-54	12	11	15	13	10	7
55-59	6	6	5	2	3	2
60-64	5	5	3	2	2	1
65 and over	12	18	2	1	2	2
Base: All persons						
(weighted)			2856	3030	6586	6120
(unweighted)			1857	1977	4470	4117

1. Source of general population figure: Census 1981. Sex, Age and Marital Status, Table 2

Table 9:   Distribution of households in areas of different
             concentration of ethnic minority residence, by
             ethnic origin

Cumulative column percentages

Percentage of households in Enumeration District found to contain people of Asian or West Indian origin	White	Asian	West Indian
Over 30 per cent	1	21	18
Over 12 per cent	4	49	48
Over 4 per cent	10	75	76
Over 2 per cent	14	84	86
Over 1 per cent	22	90	92
All areas	100	100	100
Base: Households			
(weighted)	2694	1834	2851
(unweighted)	2305	1189	1893

Notes: (1) Local concentration of ethnic residence derived from
       survey fieldwork.
       (2) An Enumeration District contains on average about 165
       households.

Table 10: Regional distribution of whites, Asians and West Indians in England and Wales.

Column percentages

Region:	PSI Survey				1981 Census — Population in households with head born in:			
	White House-holds	Asian and West Indian House-holds	West Indian House-holds	Asian House-holds	UK	Indian Sub-continent, East Africa Caribbean	Carib-bean	Indian sub-continent, East Africa
Greater London	11	40	49	34	11	41	56	33
Other S. East	23	13	8	17	21	12	9	14
E. Midlands	7	8	3	10	8	7	5	8
W. Midlands	10	15	16	14	10	18	16	19
N. West	12	7	8	7	14	8	5	10
Yorks/Humberside	13	9	3	14	10	8	5	9
Rest of England and Wales	24	8	13	5	26	6	5	6
Base: Households								
(weighted)	2694	4686	1834	2851				
(unweighted)	2305	3083	1189	1893				

Table 11:   Heads of households: incidence of mixed marriages

Column percentages

	West Indian		Asian	
	All Areas	E.D.s with concentration of blacks 4% and under	All Areas	E.D.s with concentration of blacks 4% and under
Households where head of household has mixed marriage or mixed cohabiting relationship				
Wife is white	7	13	3	7
Husband is white	2	6	1	3
Base: All households				
(weighted)	1834	440	2851	702
(unweighted)	1189	190	1893	318
Per cent of married and cohabiting household heads with mixed marriage	15	26	4	11

III Household Structure

In the previous chapter we compared, in broad terms, the demographic characteristics of the black and white populations, and in later chapters we shall see how the distinctive demographic features of different ethnic groups are related to their social and economic conditions. In this chapter we focus on a particular aspect of the demographic background - household structure - which has great importance because different types of household have different needs, are subject to different constraints and possess different opportunities, especially in the housing market. We shall see that there are many differences between the white, Asian and West Indian groups in respect of household size and structure.

Household definition
In this survey we defined a household as 'a single person or group of people living regularly at the address and sharing basic food and catering arrangements'. People who never ate together were treated as belonging to separate households. Thus, a household could be made up of more than one family, provided they lived together and shared their basic catering arrangements; conversely, a single family would be classed as two households in the same dwelling if their catering arrangements were kept entirely separate. In practice there were few 'borderline' cases, and very few cases in which this definition located more than one household at a single address.

Household size
Counting both adults and children, we find that average household sizes among the minorities are larger than among whites, although there is behind this simple statement a complex pattern of ethnic differences. Table 12 shows that the average number of people in white households is 2.6, while for Asians it is 4.6 and for West Indians it is 3.4. These averages are the products of very different distributions: while over 20 per cent of white households comprise

34

a single person, only 13 per cent of West Indian households and five per cent of Asian households contain one person; at the other end of the scale, there are only three per cent of white households with more than five people, while the figures for West Indian and Asian households are 11 per cent and 29 per cent respectively. Within the Asian group, the Pakistanis and Bangladeshis have very much larger households than the others (Table 16).

These findings are better interpreted if we refer separately to the numbers of adults and children in the households (Table 13). It can be seen that Asian and West Indian households frequently contain large numbers of adults when compared with white households, although only among Asians is there an absence of single-adult households: single-adult households are as common among West Indians as among whites, but we shall see later they are different types of household - among whites they tend to be lone pensioners, but among West Indians tend to be younger single people or lone-parent families.

Both Indians and West Indians have, on average, more children (persons aged under 16) in their households than whites, but there is a further order of difference between Asians and West Indians. Only 31 per cent of white households contain children, while the figure for West Indians is 57 per cent, and is much higher for Asians, at 73 per cent; nearly a third of the Asian households have more than two children resident, compared with 12 per cent of West Indian households and five per cent of white households. If we compare only the households that contain children, we see that the average number of children is almost the same for whites and West Indians (1.6 and 1.7 respectively) but much higher for Asians (2.6).

Household structure
Household structure can be looked at in several ways. One is the analysis of the numbers of family units within the household. A family unit is basically defined as a person or a married or cohabiting couple, together with their children who are unmarried and have no children themselves. Thus, a couple living with their 25 year old son would constitute a single family unit, but if he was married and remained with his parents, he and his wife would count as a second family unit, and if a grandparent moved in then the total would rise to three. The number of family units is a useful measure because it helps distinguish between large households made up of parents and several children and households with more complex structures.

About 90 per cent of West Indian and white households contain a single family unit, while the figure for Asian households is lower, at about 80 per cent; eighteen per cent of Asian households contain two family units, and over three per cent

35

contain more than two (Table 14). This shows that the Asian households, which we have seen are substantially larger on average than white and West Indian households, are more likely to have complex structures. Within the Asian category some ethnic and religious groups are particularly likely to have more complex households than others: twenty-five per cent of African Asian households and Sikh households contain more than one family unit, while the figure for non-Sikh Indians is under 15 per cent. Note that the predominantly Muslim Pakistani and Bangladeshi groups have large household sizes but are not more likely than the Asian group as a whole to have more than one family unit in the household; this fits with the fact that they have on average more children in the household - that is to say there is a substantial proportion of Muslim households made up of large families consisting only of a husband, wife and children.

Another way of looking at household structure is to analyse the vertical extension of the household - in other words the number of different generations resident. The simplest way to do this using the survey data is to classify household members by age group: Table 15 shows the proportions of households containing different combinations of people aged up to 15, 16 to 54, and over 54. As we would expect, the Asian and West Indian households more frequently contain a combination of adults and children than the white households, and black households comprising only people over 54 are relatively rare. It is very interesting, however, to see that despite the small proportion of black people aged over 54, households containing all three age groups are more common among blacks than whites: for Asians the figure is nine per cent, for West Indians it is four per cent, and for whites it is two per cent. Some of the households with all three age groups in fact contain only two generations of a family: these are families of parents and children where one or both parents are aged over 54. As a refinement to the analysis, therefore, we additionally show in the table the proportion of households that contain all three age groups but also contain more than one family unit; this removes the two-generation families, as they have, by definition, only one family unit. Despite the smaller numbers of these truly vertically-extended households, the differences between the ethnic groups remain (7 per cent of Asian households, 2 per cent of West Indian households and 1 per cent of white households).

Horizontal extension is also a useful concept when looking at household structure. If any members of the resident family are related to the head of household other than as husband, wife, child or grandchild, or if there is more than one family resident, we have called this a horizontally extended household. For example if two brothers live with their wives and children in the same household, this is classed as horizontally extended; if the two brothers were unmarried and living with their parents, the household would not be horizontally extended.

In Table 15 we see that this type of extension is more common among West Indians (8 per cent) and Asians (16 per cent) than whites (4 per cent). It is also more common among Pakistanis and Bangladeshis, and among Sikhs, than among other Asians (Table 16). A feature which is observable among the Bangladeshi group is the relatively high proportion of these extended households that exclusively comprise male adults: about one in five of them, compared to one in twenty of the other Asian households. These all-male households were also a common feature of the other Asian groups in the past, and played an important part in the settlement process after immigration. Often a group of men shared a dwelling while individually establishing themselves in this country, before the arrival of dependants. The persistence of this type of household among Bangladeshis is related to the timing of immigration of dependants to Britain: this process began later than for other groups. It is also interesting to note that the proportion of horizontally extended households that are all-male is nearly as high for West Indians as for Bangladeshis, although the reasons are unlikely to be the same, as the immigration of West Indian men and women took place much earlier.

Lone-parent households

Compared with white and Asian households, a high percentage of West Indian households consist of a lone parent with children under sixteen. Eighteen per cent of all the West Indian households are of this type, while the figures for Asians and whites are four per cent and three per cent (Table 17). Thirty-one per cent of all West Indian households with any children are headed by a lone parent, compared with five per cent and ten per cent of Asian and white households with children. It should be noted that these are figures for lone parent households, as opposed to lone parent families: other types of household may have one-parent families within them, and these are not included in these figures.

The relatively large proportion of single-parent households among West Indians and the fact that women outnumber men by a factor of eight to one in this group are indications of patterns of marriage and childbearing that differ from those of whites and Asians. West Indians tend to wait longer in life before setting up married or cohabiting partnerships: this is evidenced by the fact that overall about 40 per cent of West Indian households contain a single adult alone or a lone parent with children under 16. It is not uncommon for West Indian women to have children in their late teens and twenties and to wait until much later to establish a marital or cohabiting household. It would be wrong, however, to characterise lone parents as predominantly young. Four-fifths of West Indian lone parents are aged 25 or over.

Heads of household

Further illustration of the differences between ethnic groups in terms of their household structure is obtained from the characteristics of the head of household. In the survey we defined the head of household as the person in whose name the house or flat was held; if the dwelling was held jointly the head of household was taken to be the person who knew most about the housing costs and payments. This definition had been found to be most satisfactory during the pilot research for the project, and has the particular virtue of being independent of the person's sex: often in surveys there is in the head-of-household definition a preference for it to be a man. For instance, if a woman wholly owns a house, the General Household Survey will always take her husband as head of household if he lives with her. It was felt that sex should not be a factor in the definition used in this survey, particularly because the implied assumptions about gender roles may be more strained in describing some ethnic groups than in describing others.

A third of West Indian households are headed by women, compared with a quarter of white households and fewer than one in ten Asian households (Table 18). Over half of the white women who are heads of households are widows; further analysis shows that the West Indian women are more often lone parents, single women without children, or women living with their husbands. Only eight per cent of the West Indian female heads of households are widows. It is interesting to compare the extent to which white, West Indian and Asian women who are married or cohabiting are classed as heads of household: this is the case for four per cent of white couples, ten per cent of West Indian couples, and three per cent of Asian couples.

The heads of household age distributions differ radically between whites and blacks: nearly half of the whites are 55 or over, but only 18 per cent and 14 per cent of the West Indians and the Asians respectively are in this age group. The greater incidence of heads of household aged under 45 among Asians when compared with West Indians is because of the later timing of the main period of migration; it is, however, beginning to be balanced by the formation of new 'second generation' West Indian households, and this can be seen in the greater proportion of West Indian heads of households in the very lowest age groups: one in ten of West Indian households is headed by someone aged under 25, more than twice the proportion of white or Asian households.

The differences between ethnic groups in respect of age structure and household structure are reflected in the different marital status figures. Both Asians and West Indians have few

38

widow or widower heads of household because there are so few elderly black people, but in other respects the two groups are as distinct from each other as they are from whites. Ninety per cent of Asian households are headed by a married person, only four per cent by a single person, and only one per cent by a person 'living as married'. By contrast, only 55 per cent of West Indian households are headed by a married man or woman, but 20 per cent are headed by a single person, and seven per cent by someone living as married. The proportion of household heads who are divorced or separated is also very different: 15 per cent for West Indians, and two per cent for Asians. If the age difference is taken into account (that is, if the married and widowed groups are treated as one) the marital status pattern among the whites is rather similar to that of the Asians: despite other differences in household structure, it is clear that the married couple is the basic unit in the vast majority of cases, although marital ties are undoubtedly stronger among the Asians. While over half of the West Indian households are headed by married people, the high proportion headed instead by people without resident partners shows that it is not possible to think in terms of a single dominant household formation pattern as in the case of whites and Asians.

Household type classification

It is possible to put together a number of the contrasts between the household structures of the different ethnic groups in a composite classification of household types, with the aim of making other findings of the survey easier to understand. The classification we have adopted is as follows:

(1) Pensioner(s) only. Households containing one or more persons of pensionable age (defined as men aged 65 and over and women aged 60 and over), but no-one from any other age group. The term 'pensioners' is used here as shorthand for 'persons of pensionable age' and it does not necessarily imply they are drawing a retirement pension.

(2) Extended households. Households that fall into either of the 'vertically extended' or 'horizontally extended' categories, as discussed above.

(3) Lone parent with child(ren). Households that contain only a parent and her or his children, at least one of whom is under 16.

(4) Others with child(ren). Households that contain children under 16, not classifed in (2) or (3). Nearly all are just couples with children, so in the text we also refer to these households as 'nuclear families with children' but some may also contain grandparents aged under 55.

(5)   Lone non-pensioner adult. Households containing a man aged under 65, or a woman aged under 60, on his or her own.

(6)   Adults without children. This residual category contains non-pensioner couples without children (or with children aged over 16 only), and non-extended families without children under 16 (for example, a 70 year-old woman living with her two daughters aged 35 and 40).

Each ethnic group presently has a distinctive make-up of household types, as shown in Table 19. Among whites, three household types account for most of the population: pensioners (29 per cent), nuclear families with children (26 per cent) and adults without children (32 per cent). Among West Indians there are very few pensioner-only households, and although for the remainder there is some resemblance between the white and West Indian patterns, there is a much larger group of lone-parent households among the West Indians (18 per cent compared with 3 per cent), and a larger group of extended households (8 per cent compared with 4 per cent). Among Asians, over half of the households are nuclear families with children (56 per cent), and there is also a relatively large group of extended households (18 per cent); the proportion of adults without children is lower among Asians than among whites and West Indians, and there are very small numbers of pensioners, lone adults and lone parents. It should also be noted that in comparison with Indians and African Asians, very few of the Pakistani and Bangladeshi households are made up of adults without children (this category does not include horizontally extended adult-only households).

Even within these categories we can still see substantial differences between West Indian, Asian and white households. Table 20 shows, for example, that very few of the Asian adults living alone are women (8 per cent, compared with about 30 per cent for whites and West Indians), that few of the heads of West Indian pensioner households are married or co-habiting (8 per cent, compared with 37 per cent for whites and 60 per cent for Asians), and that there are in almost every category more heads of household aged over 54 among whites, and more heads of household aged under 25 among West Indians.

Household structure, occupational class and geography
Among Asians there is a tendency for households headed by people with lower job levels to be larger than others: the average size of households headed by non-manual workers is 4.1, compared with 4.9 for those headed by skilled manual workers and 5.2 for those headed by semi-skilled and unskilled manual workers. Among West Indians this relationship is also evident, but it is weaker: the corresponding figures for non-manual, skilled manual, and semi-

40

skilled/unskilled manual workers are 3.2, 3.7 and 3.6 respectively. Among whites there is no consistent, linear relationship between occupational class and household size. The strong relationship among Asians also shows in the proportion of extended households in the different occupational groups: 18 per cent of non-manual workers head extended households, compared with over 30 per cent of semi-skilled and unskilled workers. The link between household structure and occupational class among Asians can be largely explained by the fact that the various Asian ethnic groups, which presently have different household sizes and structures, tend to be found in different types of job, as we shall see in Chapter VI; for example, only a fifth of Pakistani men have non-manual occupations, compared with nearly half of African Asian men, and as the average household sizes of these groups are respectively 5.2 and 4.2 it can be seen how these differences lead to a relationship between class and household size. There is also a relationship between the local concentration of black households (the number of black households per hundred households in the area) and the strength of the differences between black and white household sizes and structures. The relationship is not the same for Asians and West Indians. In areas of higher concentration, Asian households are larger, both in terms of the number of children and the number of adults. They are also more complex: horizontal extension and vertical extension become more frequent as higher concentration areas are considered, and the presence of more than one family unit in the household becomes more frequent. West Indian average household size falls a little as local black concentration rises. This is due to a slightly lower proportion of households without children in the more concentrated areas; average numbers of adults remain fairly constant, but this is the result of the balance between a larger proportion of households with only one adult and a larger proportion with more than two adults. Lone parent households are more common among West Indians in areas of higher concentration.

The population of Asian and West Indian origins is heavily, though not exclusively, concentrated in urban areas, and particularly in inner-city areas. There are differences between the types of household found in the inner cities and the rest of the country, and these differences are greatest among the white popultion. Households living in the inner cities are less likely than others to be nuclear families; among Asians this difference is not large, but among West Indians there is a substantially larger proportion of lone-parents in the inner cities: in the inner areas of London, Birmingham and Manchester taken together, lone parents account for 22 per cent of West Indian households, compared with 14 per cent in the rest of the country. Among the white population the contrast between the inner-cities and other areas is rather different: in the inner areas the main reason for the lower proportion of nuclear families is the much higher proportion of households that contain only pensioners - 42 per cent, compared with 28 per cent elsewhere.

Household structure - trends over time
Table 21 compares summary statistics from the 1974 and 1982 surveys, to outline differences between the Asian and West Indian population in comparable geographical areas at the two dates. It is clear that household sizes have fallen considerably over a short period of time. White household sizes have also fallen, but at a slower rate: in the 1971 census the average household size in England and Wales (for all the population) was 2.9, while in the 1981 census it was 2.7, and this compares with a fall from 4.3 to 3.4 for West Indians and from 5.2 to 4.8 for Asians, over a period two years shorter.

The decline in the average size of West Indian households has been entirely due to the fall in the average number of children; in fact the average number of adults has actually risen, from 2.2 to 2.4. The fall in the number of children is very large indeed, and it is due to reductions in both the proportion of households containing any children and the numbers of children in these households. By contrast, the fall in the average size of Asian households is made up of equal reductions in the average numbers of adults and children. The proportions of West Indian and Asian household containing children were similar to each other in the 1974 survey, at 76 and 79 per cent respectively, but now the West Indian figure has fallen to 54 per cent whereas the Asian figure has remained relatively large at 74 per cent.

It is this fall in the proportion of households with any children which is responsible for the fall in the average number of children in Asian households overall; among households that do contain children there has been hardly any change in the average number. The overall stability of this figure is in fact the result of an increase among Pakistanis and Bangladeshis and a decrease among Indians and African Asians. The reasons for this are easy to understand: there is an underlying trend towards a decrease in the fertility of British Asian women, but as a result of the later migration of Pakistani and Bangladeshi women, more couples in these groups are presently in the family-building stage of their lives.

Despite the fall in the numbers of children, the number of households with members representing all three age groups has risen among Asians and West Indians. This is a reflection of the growing numbers of elderly people. By contrast, we see no growth among Asians of the proportion of horizontally extended households, and the proportion of those that are made up exclusively of men is now smaller.

The proportion of lone parents has grown in both the West Indian and Asian populations, although the figure for the latter is still half that for the white population. The increase among the West Indians is very large: in the comparable areas the percentage of households with children that are headed by a lone parent has risen from 13 to 36 in the period between the two surveys.

<u>Table 12:</u>　　　<u>Household size by ethnic group</u>

Total of adults and children in household	White	West Indian	Asian
1	23	13	5
2	34	20	10
3	16	23	15
4	17	21	23
5	7	12	18
6 or more	3	11	29
Mean number of persons	2.6	3.4	4.6
Base: Households			
(weighted)	2694	1834	2851
(unweighted)	2305	1189	1893

Table 13: Numbers of adults and children resident in household by ethnic group

	White	West Indian	Asian
Average number of adults in household	2.0	2.3	2.7
Per cent with only one adult	25	26	7
Per cent with more than three adults	6	17	22
Average number of children in household	0.5	1.0	1.9
Per cent without children	69	43	31
Per cent with more than two children	5	12	31
Base: Households (weighted) (unweighted)	2694 2305	1834 1189	2851 1893
Households with children: average number of children	1.6	1.7	2.6

Table 14: Number of family units in household, by ethnic group

Number of family units in household	White	West Indian	All Asian	Indian	Pakis-tani	Bangla-deshi	African Asian	Muslim	Hindu	Sikh
1	89	89	79	82	77	77	74	78	79	75
2	11	10	18	16	20	16	22	18	18	23
3	*	1	3	2	3	5	4	3	2	3
4 or more	*	1	1	1	*	2	*	1	1	*
Base: Households (weighted)	2694	1834	2851	1150	751	277	604	1339	748	520
(unweighted)	2305	1189	1893	726	518	197	411	937	481	349

Table 15:   Vertical and horizontal extension of household

Column percentages

	White	West Indian	Asian
Household contains:			
People aged 55+ only	37	7	3
People aged 16-54 only	22	27	18
People aged 16-54 and 55+, but none under 16	10	8	6
People aged 16-54 and under 16, but none 55+	28	52	64
All three age groups	2	4	9
All three age groups and more than one family unit	1	2	7
Household is horizontally extended	4	8	16
Base: Households			
(weighted)	2694	1834	2851
(unweighted)	2305	1189	1893

Table 16: Household size and structure: comparison of different Asian groups

	All Asian	Indian	Pakis- tani	Bangla- deshi	African Asian	Muslim	Hindu	Sikh
Average number of persons in household	4.6	4.3	5.2	5.0	4.2	5.0	4.0	4.8
Per cent with 6 or more persons	29	22	43	44	20	39	16	31
Average number of children in household	1.9	1.6	2.5	2.6	1.3	2.3	1.2	1.9
Per cent without children	27	29	17	18	38	20	39	22
Per cent with more than one family unit in household	21	18	23	23	26	22	21	25
Per cent horizontally extended	16	13	19	19	17	17	16	18
Base: Households (weighted) (unweighted)	2851 1893	1150 726	751 518	277 197	604 411	1339 937	748 481	520 349

Table 17:   Lone parents

Column percentages

	White	West Indian	Asian
Female lone parent with child(ren) under 16	3	16	3
Male lone parent with child(ren) under 16	*	2	1
Base: Households			
(weighted)	2694	1834	2851
(unweighted)	2305	1189	1893
Lone parents with child(ren) under 16 as a percentage of households with children under 16	10	31	5

Table 18: Characteristics of heads of household

Column percentages

	White	West Indian	Asian
Male	74	67	93
Female	25	33	7
Married	66	55	90
Living as married	2	7	1
Single	7	20	4
Widowed	18	4	4
Divorced/separated	7	15	2
Age:			
16-19	*	1	*
20-24	4	9	4
25-34	16	20	32
35-44	16	22	27
45-54	16	27	23
55-64	18	15	10
65+	30	3	4
Base: Households			
(weighted	2694	1834	2851
(unweighted)	2305	1189	1893

Table 19: Household type

Household type:	White	West Indian	All Asian	Indian	Paki- stani	Bangla- deshi	African Asian
Pensioner(s) only	29	2	2	2	*	*	3
Vertically or horizontally extended household	4	8	18	15	21	18	21
Lone parent with child(ren) under 16	3	18	4	4	3	7	3
Others with children under 16	26	36	56	56	63	61	43
Lone adult (not pensioner)	6	11	4	3	5	8	3
Adults without children	32	25	17	20	9	6	27
All Households (weighted) (unweighted)	2694 2305	1834 1189	2851 1893	1150 726	751 518	277 197	604 411

51

Table 20   Head of household characteristics by type of household by ethnic group

	White						West Indian						Asian					
	Pensioners	Extended	Lone parents	Others with children	Lone adults	Others	Pensioners	Extended	Lone parents	Others with children	Lone adults	Others	Pensioners	Extended	Lone parents	Others with children	Lone adults	Others
Per cent with female head of household	50	33	87	3	33	11	(59)	34	94	10	30	22	(31)	9	68	2	8	8
Per cent with head of household married or living as married	37	49	7	98	2	89	(8)	50	5	98	4	81	(60)	86	42	100	21	91
Per cent with head of household aged																		
- under 25	-	7	7	4	10	6	(-)	21	21	6	14	5	(-)	6	7	'3	11	6
- over 54	100	42	5	3	25	46	(100)	24	3	8	22	35	(100)	24	2	5	10	25
Base: Households (weighted)	778	114	85	699	154	864	39	154	324	656	201	460	42	518	101	1582	115	496
(unweighted)	389	114	85	699	154	864	27	97	203	415	133	314	28	360	71	1041	77	318

Household size and structure: comparison of 1974 and 1982 surveys

Note: 1982 figures are for areas of the type included in the 1974 survey; they are not nationally representative.

	West Indian		Asian	
	1974	1982	1974	1982
Average household size	4.3	3.4	5.2	4.8
Average number of adults	2.2	2.4	3.0	2.8
Average number of children	2.2	1.0	2.2	2.0
Per cent of households with any children	76	54	79	74
Horizontally extended, male only households, as per cent of all households	n.a.	1	4	1
Other horizontally extended households, as per cent of all households	n.a.	7	17	18
Percentages of all households which contain people in all three age groups 0-15, 16-54, 55+	2	4	7	10
Lone parent households as a percentage of all households with children	13	36	1	5

53

IV Area of Residence

In Chapter II we briefly discussed the geographical distribution of black people in this country. In the following paragraphs we give a more detailed picture of the current distribution, and then discuss how the pattern has changed over the past decade.

Major areas of residence

We saw in Chapter II that there are substantial differences between the regional distributions of the white population and the populations of Asian and West Indian origin, the most important of these being the greater concentration of the black population in Greater London and in the West Midlands. If we employ a geographical breakdown that is more sensitive to the actual residence patterns of the black population we can see differences that are even greater. Table 22 divides the country into eight areas: inner and outer London, five counties or groups of counties having relatively high concentrations of black people, and the rest. The specified counties cover a wide area (the metropolitan counties of Manchester and the West Midlands, together with Leicestershire, Nottinghamshire, Derbyshire, West and South Yorkshire, Lancashire, Berkshire, Bedfordshire and Hertfordshire). Only 37 per cent of the white population live in these compared with nearly 80 per cent of the population of Asian and West Indian origin.

From this table we can see that even within London the distributions of black and white residents are very different. Sixty per cent of white Londoners live in the outer boroughs, compared with 37 per cent of West Indian Londoners and 52 per cent of Asian Londoners. Although the Asian group as a whole is less concentrated in the inner boroughs than the West Indian group, the distributions of the different Asian ethnic groups are not all the same, and the Bangladeshi group is very heavily concentrated in inner London. Pakistanis, on the other hand, have the same inner-outer mix as the white population while African Asians and Sikhs are concentrated in the outer boroughs.

54

Outside London and the West Midlands Metropolitan County the main residential concentrations evident from Table 22 are within the different Asian groups: there are relatively large proportions of the Pakistani group in West and South Yorkshire, in Greater Manchester and Lancashire, and in Berkshire, Bedfordshire and Hertfordshire; a large proportion of African Asians live in the East Midlands counties of Leicestershire, Nottinghamshire and Derbyshire; there is some concentration of Indians in the East Midlands and Yorkshire, but the main difference between the population of Indian origin and other Asians is the extent to which they are found outside these principal areas of black residence. Nearly a third of British Indians live outside the counties listed above, compared with a sixth of other British Asians.

London, Birmingham and Manchester
In Table 23 we show the extent to which the white, Asian and West Indian population are presently located in the inner and outer areas of the three main conurbations of London, Birmingham and Manchester(1). Only six per cent of the white population is found in these inner areas, compared with 43 per cent of West Indians and 23 per cent of Asians. The West Indian population is much more concentrated in the inner areas than the Asian population, with the exception of the Bangladeshis, two-thirds of whom are found in these areas. Just over a quarter of Asians and West Indians live in the remaining areas of the three conurbations, compared with 13 per cent of whites.

Small area analysis
In Chapter II it was also pointed out that the unevenness in the residential distribution of black households increases as smaller geographical areas are considered. Table 9 showed that if we take the analysis to the level of census enumeration districts, which cover about 165 households each, nearly half the black population lives in a group of areas in which we find only four per cent of the white population; these are all enumeration districts in which at least one in every eight households is of Asian or West Indian origin. This degree of clustering is common to both Asian and West Indian households, although, as shown by Table 24, the geographical distributions of the two groups overlap only to a limited extent. The table shows the distribution of the two groups in EDs of varying concentrations of Asian households and West Indian households separately. Two-thirds of the Asian households live in a group of areas in which we find only one third of the West indian households, and vice-versa. Much of this difference can be explained by different regional and inter-urban settlement patterns, but residential segregation of this type also exists within towns and cities. It should be noted that a greater proportion of

Asian households than of West Indian households live in EDs with concentrations of their own ethnic group above 30 per cent: this reflects the greater importance of local ethnic communities in determining the residential patterns of Asians. Pakistanis and Bangladeshis are particularly likely to be found in these more concentrated EDs. The position of African Asians is interesting in that they too are more likely than Indians to be found in these EDs with high concentrations, but they are also more likely to be found in the EDs that contain very few Asians: it is in the medium-density areas that there are proportionately few African Asians.

Even though black people tend to be grouped together, most of them live in EDs where a majority of the households are white, nearly all live in electoral wards where the majority are white, and all live in local authority areas where white people are over-whelmingly in the majority. When we talk of 'areas of black residence', therefore, it is in reference to the way the small British black population is unevenly distributed between these predominantly white areas, and should not be read as meaning areas where black people form the majority of residents.

House movement and changes in geographical distribution

Informants were asked how many times they had moved house since the beginning of 1977. Taking the first selected informant as representative of the whole household, we see that over the five year period 44 per cent of West Indian households, 47 per cent of Asian households and 32 per cent of white households have moved at least once. The higher rate of geographical movement among the ethnic minority households is particularly marked in the case of the Bangladeshis (Table 25).

The age of the head of household is very strongly related to the likelihood of moving house. Detailed analysis shows that within age groups the rate of movement of black households has not been higher than that of the white households, and therefore the overall difference can be largely ascribed to the different age structures of the white and black population. In fact it is interesting to note that movement has been much more common among whites than among Asians and West Indians for heads of household aged 16-25. Even after taking into account the age structures, however, the Bangladeshis have had much higher rates of movement than whites.

The analysis presented in Tables 26 to 28 show the effect of this movement on the geographical distribution of the households in the survey. Table 26 shows the spread of Asian and West Indian immigrants in 1971 over areas of varying immigrant density alongside the spread of immigrants and people of immigrant origin found in a sample of the same areas in 1982. The table splits 1971 local authority areas into two groups: those with immigrants from the West Indies and the Indian sub-continent making up 0.5 per cent or more of their population, and those with fewer than this. Within the local authority areas with at least 0.5 per cent immigrants, census enumeration districts are divided into groups according to their own concentration of immigrants. It should be remembered that these concentrations were found in the 1971 Census, and are not now substantively valid except as aids to defining areas of immigrant settlement; the actual local densities of immigrant and ethnic minority residence in most of these districts will have changed since 1971.

One feature of the distribution found in the 1982 survey is the lack of immigrants and black people found in the low concentration local authority areas: according to the Census, seven per cent of people born in the West Indies or Indian sub-continent lived in these areas in 1971, while only four per cent were found in the survey. There can be three explanations for this. First, we have to consider the possibility of under-enumeration of black people within the survey in these areas. Different methods of finding black households were used in areas of different immigrant concentration, and although weighting factors were applied in the analysis to account for expected variations in the success of these methods, the survey findings could be misleading if the methods used in the low concentration areas were very much less successful than those used in other areas. To account for this difference of between four per cent and seven per cent, however, the efficiency of the field methods used would have to have been very different from that expected, and tests carried out to validate the enumeration procedures in low concentration areas do not support this explanation. The second possible reason for the apparently lower proportion of black people found in the low-concentration local authority areas is the inclusion of white people born in the West Indies, India or Pakistan in the figures from the census: it is impossible to estimate accurately how many people fall into this category, but we know that about eight per cent of Asian and West Indian-born people had both parents born outside the New Commonwealth at the time of the 1971 Census(2). It is certain that these people would have been more dispersed than black immigrants: if their residence patterns were the same as the general population, which is likely, then nearly four of the seven per cent of immigrants living in the low concentration local authorities in 1971 would have been made up of these white people. The third possible explanation for the difference between the census and survey figures is the existence of a genuine trend towards greater concentration at this level of geographical analysis over the period from 1971 to 1982. The black population of this country grew by about 60 per cent in that period, by immigration and natural increase in approximately equal proportions. We know that this growth has taken place to a greater extent among the Pakistani and Bangladeshi groups than among others, and that these groups are the most likely to be found in areas of high immigrant population. It follows that there would have been a trend in the overall distribution of the population towards the areas of high concentration unless a process of residential dispersal by actual house-moves were taking place. Thus, in the absence of any residential movement into the low-concentration local authorities (and we have not detected any net movements of this sort), we can explain the difference between the proportions of the black immigrant populations living in these areas in the 1971 census and the 1982 survey by a combination of the inclusion of white immigrants in the census figures and a real trend over time caused by the slower growth of the black population in these areas than in others.

The other apparent trend shown by Table 26 is in the opposite direction. In the local authority areas that had 0.5 per cent or more immigrants, we now see some five per cent of the black population living in enumeration districts (EDs) that contained no Asian or West Indian immigrants in the 1971 Census, and a smaller proportion of the black population living in areas of high immigrant density. This shows that there has been a small amount of dispersal to previously all-white EDs in these local authority areas, and a movement from the EDs of previously highest immigrant density towards those with medium density.

Because the analysis of residential concentration is so sensitive to the geographical units selected - as we have seen by observing opposite trends at a local authority and at an ED level - it is worth looking at the degree of concentration in another way - in terms of electoral wards, units which are larger than EDs but smaller than local authorities. In Table 27 it appears that there has been no growth in the proportion of the black population living in electoral wards that had zero or very low immigrant densities in 1971. If we take into account the inclusion in the 1971 figures of the white immigrants, mentioned above, it is possible to argue that there has been a tiny increase in the proportion of the black population in these low density wards, but even so this represents a very small change in such a highly clustered distribution.

We therefore now have a good indication of how the distribution of the black population has changed between 1971 and 1982. Although the size of the population concerned has grown considerably, in terms of numbers of households as well as numbers of people, the clustering of nearly all that population in a set of pre-1974 local authority areas which contain about half the general population has been preserved, as has the clustering of the black population within the electoral wards originally settled by black people within these local authorities; these wards account for about two-thirds of the general population in this group of local authorites. However, within this group of wards there has been a

58

degree of dispersal from EDs of high concentration to EDs of lower concentration, and to EDs which previously contained no black people.

It is important to note that the combination of the overall stability of the geographical distribution of the black population and the growth in size of that population means that in many areas the actual local concentration of black people has risen over the past decade. In other words, despite a limited movement towards dispersal, more black people - and a higher percentage of black people - are now living in areas of high ethnic minority concentration. The figures used in this report for the different analyses of racial disadvantage by local ethnic minority concentration are therefore those derived from the 1982 fieldwork, rather than the 1971 Census. Because of the different rates of growth of the Asian and West Indian populations over the last ten years, it is hard to tell whether one group has dispersed more than the other. Indeed, it is difficult to understand precisely what is meant by such a comparison: for instance, it would be perfectly possible for the group with the greater rate of geographical movement out of the traditional immigrant areas to become the more geographically concentrated if there were a higher birth rate and immigration rate in those areas. A preliminary comparison of the distribution changes between the 1974 and 1982 surveys, in the restricted geographical area of the 1974 survey, suggests that the overall changes in distribution have affected Asians and West Indians to a similar extent. This finding is different from those of a study of movements between the 1961 and 1971 Censuses, which showed that indices of residential segregation from white people were, in that period, increasing for Asians but decreasing for West Indians(3); putting it crudely, between 1961 and 1971 Asian households were becoming more geographically concentrated while West Indian households were dispersing. If we look at the present locations of the survey respondents who have over the past five years moved house, we can see that, in terms of movement out of the principal areas of immigrant residence, the Asian and West Indian groups followed very similar patterns (Table 28), with 66 per cent of movers from each group remaining in the areas covered by the 1974 PEP survey. There is some indication, however, that the West Indian households who have moved out of these areas have been more likely to move to areas that were previously exclusively white: 12 per cent of West Indian movers, compared to eight per cent of Asian movers, are now in wards that in 1971 had concentrations of immigrants of 0.5 per cent or lower.

Notes
(1)   See Appendix 1 for the definitions of inner and outer areas.

(2) This is calculated on a base of all resident persons born in New Commonwealth-America, India or Pakistan for whom information was available about both parents' birthplaces, using 1971 Census.

(3) G. Peach, S. Winchester and R. Woods, 'The Distribution of coloured immigrants in Britain'. In G. Gappert and H. Rose (eds) The Social Economy of Cities, 1975.

Column percentages

	White	All Asian & West Indian	West Indian	Asian	Indian	Paki-stani	Bangla-deshi	Afri-can Asian
Inner London	5	22	31	16	13	7	60	13
Outer London	7	18	18	18	16	11	3	34
West Midlands Metropolitan County	5	14	15	13	14	16	14	9
Leicestershire, Nottinghamshire and Derbyshire	4	6	2	9	9	2	7	18
West and South Yorkshire	6	9	2	13	10	30	4	3
Great Manchester and Lancashire	6	6	7	5	4	11	7	1
Berkshire, Bedfordshire, and Hertfordshire	5	4	3	5	3	10	1	4
Rest of England and Wales	63	21	20	21	31	15	6	18
Base: Households								
(weighted)	2694	4686	1834	2851	1150	751	277	604
(unweighted)	2305	3083	1189	1893	726	518	197	411

61

Table 23: Distribution of white, Asian and West Indian households in inner and outer areas of main conurbations

	White	West Indian	Asian	Indian	Pakistani	Bangla-deshi	African Asian
Inner London, Inner Birmingham, Inner Manchester	6	43	23	17	19	66	20
Rest of London, rest of West Midlands Metropolitan County, rest of Greater Manchester Metropolitan county	13	27	28	29	24	17	37
Rest of England and Wales	81	30	49	54	57	17	43
Base: Households							
(weighted)	2694	1834	2851	1150	751	277	604
(unweighted)	2305	1189	1893	726	518	197	411

Note: See Appendix 1 for definitions of inner areas.

Table 24:   Distribution of households in areas of different concentrations of Asian and West Indian residence by ethnic origin

Cumulative column percentages

Percentage of households in Enumeration District found to contain people of...	West Indian Households	Asian Households
...Asian origin:		
Over 30 per cent	2	15
Over 12 per cent	9	37
Over 4 per cent	36	65
All areas	100	100
...West Indian Origin:		
Over 30 per cent	7	1
Over 12 per cent	37	10
Over 4 per cent	61	30
All areas	100	100
...West Indian or Asian Origin:		
Over 30 per cent	18	21
Over 12 per cent	48	49
Over 4 per cent	76	75
All areas	100	100

Note: Local concentration of Asian and West Indian households are derived from the survey fieldwork.

Table 25:   House moves between 1977 and 1982

	White	West Indian	Asian	Indian	Paki- stani	Bangl- adeshi	African Asian
Number of times changed address:							
No change	68	56	53	57	51	33	57
Once	22	32	36	34	42	44	30
Twice	6	7	6	6	4	13	6
More than twice	4	5	5	3	3	11	7
Base: All Households							
(weighted)	2694	1834	2851	1150	751	277	604
(unweighted)	2305	1189	1893	726	518	197	411

and 1982: Local Authorities and EDs

	1971 Census:		PSI Survey 1982:		
Local Density of Asian and West Indian Immigrants as Measured in 1971 Census	Persons born in West Indies and Indian Sub-continent	General Population	Persons born in West Indies and Indian Sub-continent	Whites	Persons of West Indian and Asian Origin
Local Authorities with 0.5% immigrants or more:					
Enumeration Districts with 30%	10	*	8	*	7
Enumeration Districts with 20%	23	1	17	1	16
Enumeration Districts with 10%	48	4	37	2	36
Enumeration Districts with 5%	64	7	61	6	60
Enumeration Districts with 3%	74	11	72	9	70
Enumeration Districts with 1%	86	22	83	19	83
Enumeration Districts with 0.5%	91	31	88	29	87
Enumeration Districts with more than 0%	93	42	93	38	93
All Enumeration Districts	93	54	96	49	96
All Local Authorities: All Enumeration Districts	100	100	100	100	100
Base: All persons (weighted)			10751	6962	18815
(unweighted)			7284	6418	12619

Note: An Enumeration District contains on average about 165 households.

Table 27: Distribution of Asians and West Indians in areas of different immigrant densities in 1971 and 1982: electoral wards and EDs

Cumulative column percentages

Local Density of Asian and West Indian Immigrants as Measured in 1971 Census	Persons born in West Indies and Indian Sub-continent	
	1971 Census	1982 Survey
EDs above 10 per cent in wards above 0.5 per cent	45	37
All wards above 0.5 per cent	94	95
All wards	100	100

Table 28:   Present location of movers and non-movers: Asians and West Indians compared

Column percentages

Present Location (immigrant concentrations measured in 1971 census)	West Indian		Asian	
	Movers	Non-movers	Movers	Non-movers
(a) An ED with over 10% immigrants	28	37	32	38
(b) An ED with between 2.4% and 10% immigrants	38	41	34	36
(c) An ED with up to 2.4% immigrants in an electoral ward with over 0.5% immigrants	21	17	25	21
(d) An electoral ward with up to 0.5% immigrants	12	5	8	5
Base: All Households, excluding immigrants since 1976 (weighted)	755	994	1145	1407

Note: 'Movers' are those households in which the first respondent reported a house move in the last 5 years

V Housing

Housing tenure

The housing circumstances of black people in Britain are in many ways unusual and inferior to those of white people. In this chapter we describe the differences between the housing tenure and housing conditions of white, West Indian and Asian households, and consider their relationship with other factors such as geographical location, household type and social class. We also analyse recent trends and show how the differences between the ethnic groups are in some respects remaining very strong, while in other respects there has been some convergence. Overall, tenure distributions have remained distinct while there has been a change for the better in housing conditions.

Overall pattern

Nearly 60 per cent of white households own or are buying their house or flat, while 30 per cent live in houses or flats rented from the council; nine out of ten dwellings are therefore within these two sectors of the housing market (Table 29). Most of the remainder are privately rented: seven per cent of white households rent unfurnished swellings and two per cent rent furnished dwellings. Two per cent of white households live in properties that are provided by housing associations, either renting or on a co-ownership basis.

The two main tenure sectors also account for nine out of ten households of West Indian and Asian origin, but for each of these groups the balance between owner-occupiers and council tenants is very different to that found among white households. White owners outnumber council tenants by a ratio of two to one, while among West Indians there are more council tenants (46 per cent) than owners (41 per cent). By contrast, the proportion of Asian households that own or are buying their houses is very high (72 per cent) while the proportion of council tenants is relatively low (19 per cent). The tenure distribution of the remainder of black households is also different to that of white households. The main difference in tenure distribution outside the two main sectors is in the relatively large proportion of West Indian households in housing association dwellings: eight per cent of West Indian households are in this tenure sector, compared with two per cent of white and Asian households.   Also, the proportion in privately rented furnished accommodation is higher among blacks than among whites, while the proportion renting unfurnished accommodation is lower.

The overall figures given for households of Asian origin hide further variations between different Asian groups.   The level of owner-occupation is low (30 per cent) among Bangladeshis, and the levels of council tenancy and private tenancy among them are correspondingly high (53 and 11 per cent respectively).   A very large proportion of Sikhs are owner-occupiers (91 per cent) and few are council tenants (six per cent).

Tenure patterns among new households

Indications of the way these patterns may change in the near future can be obtained by looking at the housing circumstances of new households.   In the PSI survey we asked questions about house movement from beginning of 1977 up to the first half of 1982 (when the survey was conducted); in the previous chapter we discussed the effects of these moves on the geographical distribution of black households, and later in this chapter we consider the effects on tenure distribution.   For the sake of consistency, therefore, we have taken 'new household' to mean a household formed during this period, that is to say in the five years leading up to the survey(1).   Table 30 shows that black new households have tenure patterns which are strongly characteristic of their own ethnic group: half of the new households of West Indian origin are council tenants, 13 per cent live in housing association dwellings, and only 28 per cent are owner-occupiers; nearly four-fifths of new households of Asian origin are owner-occupiers, and only 14 per cent are council tenants. Among white new households the level of owner-occupation is the same as for all white households, but there are proportionately fewer council tenants (21 per cent) and more private tenants (17 per cent); this is likely to be a result of young households spending some time in privately rented housing before qualifying for council property or being able to afford owner-occupied property(2).   There is no evidence that young Asian households are following this pattern of tenure movement (only five per cent are private tenants), and the relatively low proportion of private tenants among West Indian new households (eight per cent) suggests that this movement is less common among West Indians than it is among whites.   In all, this analysis shows that tenure patterns are tending to become even more ethnically polarised than they are already.

Housing tenure and area of residence

There are geographical variations in the pattern of housing tenure and these have some effect on the differences between the housing tenure of whites, Asians and West Indians. However, the differences in tenure pattern between ethnic groups persist when regions, cities and smaller areas are considered separately.

Table 31 gives the tenure distributions in the major areas of black residence: in every area the level of owner-occupation among Asians is higher than that among whites and West Indians, and for every area where we have more than 50 households in the sample the level of council tenancy among West Indians is higher than among whites or Asians. There are indications in this table, however, that in some types of area the ethnic differences are not of the same character as those evident in the national figures, and this is demonstrated further in Table 32, which gives the tenure distributions in the inner and outer areas of the main conurbations. In the conurbations the characteristic tenure pattern of West Indian households is very marked: the proportions of council tenants and households in housing association dwellings are much higher than those among white households. But in the rest of the country the levels of council tenancy among whites and West Indians are identical, at 30 per cent, although there is still a large proportion of West Indians in housing associations. The proportion of Asians in council tenancies is very low nationally, but it is about the same as for whites in the inner areas. There is, however, a high level of owner-occupation among Asians in all areas.

One of the most startling differences evident in the inner areas is between the proportion of whites and blacks in privately rented dwellings: nearly a quarter of white households in the inner areas are private tenants, compared with seven per cent of Asian households and three per cent of West Indian households. This is as much a demonstration of how the white population differs between the inner cities and elsewhere as it is of the difference between whites and blacks in the inner cities. We have already mentioned that there are more pensioner-only households and fewer families with children in the inner cities; we shall see later that the unemployment rates in these areas are also higher.

Housing tenure and job levels

Table 33 shows the relationship between the job level of the household head and tenure. Among white people, there is a straightforward pattern: the higher the job level, the more likely the household is to be in owner-occupied property, and less likely to be in council property. Asian and West Indian households do not fit into this pattern, at least not in any straightforward way. It is the case that the proportion of council tenants among Asians grows as lower SEG groups are considered; it is also true that in the top

SEG grouping the proportion of owner occupiers among West Indians is very much larger, and the proportion of council tenants very much smaller, than for other West Indians. Otherwise, however, there is no straightforward relationship visible between job level and tenure of black households. It should also be noted that the tenure pattern of unemployed and retired people differs between the three ethnic groups: unemployed Asian heads of household are far more likely to own their homes than white or West Indians, and retired West Indian heads of household are more likely to be council tenants than whites or Asians.

Housing tenure and household type
Table 34 shows that whilst some of the ethnic variation in tenure patterns is related to the different mix of household types in the different ethnic groups, the essential tenure characteristics of the Asian, West Indian and white samples are reproduced even after separating the different household types. For almost every comparison, owner-occupation is most common among Asians, and least common among West Indians, while council tenancy is most common among West Indians and least common among Asians, with the whites constantly in between them. For all household types, West Indians are also more commonly found in housing associations than Asians or whites. White households nearly always have a larger proportion in privately rented dwellings than Asian or West Indian households.

Housing conditions
In this section we shall look at other characteristics of the dwellings occupied by survey informants: the type and the age of the property, the number of rooms, the amenities, and whether other households share the dwelling. In the paragraphs below we consider in turn each of the indicators of housing quality. Table 35, however, gives a summary of these indicators for white, West Indian and Asian households. Overall, Asian and West Indian people occupy property which is less desirable than that occupied by white people, and the position of black people only worsens when the different tenure distributions are taken into account.

Among owner-occupiers and council tenants the black households are more often found in older property than the white households, and are less often found in detached and semi-detached houses; in the council sector blacks are twice as likely as whites to be in flats. Black households have higher densities of residence (persons per room) than whites in both the main tenure sectors, and the Asian densities are particularly high. The proportions of owners and council tenants lacking or sharing basic facilities are small, but they are larger for Asians than for whites or West Indians. In the privately rented sector, however, the differences

71

between the property of black and white tenants are not as uniform: with regard to the use of basic facilities, the proportion in detached and semi-detached houses, and (especially) density of occupation, the black tenants fare worse than the white tenants in our sample, but the black tenants are more often in younger property and less often in flats.

Taking an overall view, without breaking down the samples by tenure group, we see that different disadvantages are suffered by Asians and West Indians: while both ethnic groups have a relatively small proportion of households living in detached and semi-detached houses and have older and more densely occupied property, the housing circumstances of West Indians are particularly characterised by a large proportion living in flats, while particularly large proportions of Asian households have pre-war properties and have high densities of occupation.

Type of property

Table 36 shows the types of property occupied by the different ethnic groups in the survey. It is clear that white households are found in detached and semi-detached houses twice as frequently as Asian and West Indian people. Among Asians, however, there is a sufficiently large proportion living in terraced houses to make the total proportion in houses or bungalows the same as for white people; the proportions of Asian and white households living in flats are therefore the same. The total proportion of West Indians living in houses is smaller than for Asians and whites (67 per cent, compared with 85 per cent), and the proportion living in flats is correspondingly higher (17 per cent, compared with 12 per cent). A further four to five per cent of white and black households are found in types of dwelling not classified as houses, bungalows, or flats: although some of these properties are maisonettes, the category also includes miscellaneous shared dwellings, including bedsitters and 'rooms'; it can for most purposes be regarded as part of the 'flats' category. It should be noted that there are large variations of property type between the different sections of the Asian sample: all except the Bangladeshis have larger proportions of houses than West Indians, but the ratio of terraced to other houses is much higher for Pakistanis than others. The Bangladeshi pattern is distinctive: there are 43 per cent in flats and a further eight per cent in 'other' types of property.

Table 37 breaks down the samples by tenure, and shows that there are even greater differences of property type between the black and white households within tenure sectors. The ratio of terraced houses to other houses is over two to one among Asian and West Indian owner-occupiers; among white owners, this ratio is reversed. Seventy-three per cent of white council tenants have houses, compared with only 40 per cent of black council tenants,

72

and again there is a large difference in the proportions that are detached or semi-detached. Six per cent of white council tenants are in blocks of flats with more than four floors, compared with 22 per cent of black tenants. In the private rented sector, Asian and West Indian households are more likely than white households to be found in houses, but again, a greater proportion of detached and semi-detatched properties are occupied by white households. The housing association sector is an exception to the general pattern: black households are more likely to be found in houses (and in detached houses) than white households. However, we need to be cautious about this comparison because so few of the white people in the survey are in this type of housing: the base for the housing association figures is only 37 white households, compared with 117 black households.

Table 38 shows the floor level of the council flats occupied by white and black households. It can be seen that black tenants in flats are generally further from the ground than white tenants. This table understates the real scale of the difference, because it excludes all tenants in houses. As a proportion of all council tenants, the number in flats above the third floor is over ten per cent for black households and three per cent for white housesholds; the corresponding figures for council dwellings with entrances above ground level are about 16 per cent for whites and over 35 per cent for blacks.

Age of property
In Table 39 we show the age of the building as assessed by the informant or, where the informant was unable to do this, by interviewer. Asian and West Indian people are more commonly living in property built before 1945 than white people; only 26 per cent of Asian households, and 40 per cent of West Indian households, live in post-war property, compared with 50 per cent of white households. Equivalent proportions of white and West Indian households live in properties built before 1919, but the proportion of Asian households is higher. Table 40 shows that for each tenure group the Asian and West Indian households taken together occupy property that is older than that occupied by white people, with the exception of the privately rented properties. It should be remembered that there are considerable differences between the way in which the private sector is used by white and black households: white tenants in the private sector are often older people who are long-standing tenants of unfurnished property, or people from lower SEG groups, while black tenants are more likely to be younger people from higher SEG groups in furnished property.

Available space
Table 41 shows a number of indicators of available space in the properties occupied by different ethnic groups. On all of these

measures, the Asian and West Indian households fare worse than the white households. The first indicator is the proportion sharing part of their dwelling - any room, including bathroom, kitchen and WC - with another household. One per cent of white households, but over four per cent of Asian and West Indian households, share their dwellings. The second indicator is the number of rooms, excluding bathrooms, WCs and small kitchens, available for the household's use, excluding rooms shared with other households. The average number is lower for black households than white households, despite the fact that black households are larger and therefore need more space. The third indicator takes household size into account, by showing how many persons there are in the household per room in the dwelling. It can be seen that in these terms white households have, on average, twice the amount of space available to Asian households, and over one-and-a-half times that available to West Indian households. The fourth indicator is the proportion of households with more than a given number of persons per room. Only three per cent of white households have more than one person per room, compared with 16 per cent of West Indian households and 35 per cent of Asian households. The corresponding figures for those with more than 1.5 persons per room are 1, 3 and 12 per cent.

Among the Asians, the Bangladeshis stand out as having very small accommodation in relation to their needs, and as sharing their dwellings most frequently. Sixty per cent of Bangladeshi families have more than one person per room; this is twenty times more than for the white households. Although the Pakistanis are not more likely to be found in shared dwellings than other Asian groups, and, on average have the larger properties among Asians, they have a high ratio of persons per room because, like the Bangladeshis, they have large households.

Table 42 shows the indicators of available space for different tenure groups. Among both white and black households, the proportion of households sharing a dwelling is strongly related to tenure : sharing is very much more common in privately rented dwellings than in other tenures, although within the private rented sector the extent of sharing is much greater for black people than white people. In every tenure sector the black households have fewer rooms than white people, with the result that there is a much higher percentage of black people in every tenure with more than one person per room. It is worth noting that 29 per cent of black households in the council sector have more than one person per room, compared with five per cent of white council tenants; the difference is almost as large as that between black and white owner-occupiers, and is larger than the difference in other sectors.

74

Amenities

The amenities available to households as part of their dwelling structure, or as durable additions, are shown in Table 43. As far as the basic amenities are concerned - that is, the availability of a bath, plumbed hot water and an inside WC, without having to share with another household - West Indians and whites are equally well housed, with 95 per cent of households having these amenities to themselves. Slightly fewer Asian households have all basic amenities without having to share, though this hides a considerable variation among Asian ethnic groups. Indians and African Asians have all basic amenities as often as whites and West Indians, while Pakistanis are slightly less often in this position (93 per cent), but Bangladeshis are very poorly housed in this respect: only 82 per cent have all basic amenities to themselves. The 18 per cent of Bangladeshis who fall outside this group are not only those who share a dwelling; over a third of them actually lack one or more of these facilities. Fewer Asian and West Indian households have access to a garden than white households, and this, again, is particularly acute for Bangladeshis, among whom fewer than half have a garden. Central heating is, overall, installed in the dwellings of white and black people to a similar extent. In fact, West Indian, Indian and African Asian households more often have central heating than white households, although it is much less common among Pakistanis and Bangladeshis. Possession of a refrigerator and a telephone are both related to ethnic group in a similar way, with West Indians, Indians and African Asians having either a similar or better position than whites, but Pakistanis and Bangladeshis being far worse off. Ownership of a washing machine, however, is less common among all groups of black households than white households, with the exception of African Asians.

The distribution of amenities is strongly related to tenure. Table 44 shows that the proportion of private tenants making sole use of all basic amenities is much higher, for white and black households, than in other tenure sectors. Even so, the proportions for blacks are higher than for whites in all except the housing association sector. The proportions lacking a garden are also larger for black people in each sector, and the largest difference is for council tenants, among whom 54 per cent of black households lack a garden, compared with 17 per cent of white households. Black owner-occupiers and housing association tenants are without central heating more commonly than the same tenure groups among whites, but the opposite is true for council and private tenants. These findings for council tenants fit in well with what else we know of the ethnic differences in this sector: black people tend to be housed more often than white people in blocks of purpose-built flats, therefore it is not surprising to find that fewer of the properties occupied by black people have gardens, and that more of them have central heating.

75

Housing satisfaction

We asked informants whether they were satisfied or dissatisfied with their house or flat, then asked how strongly they held that view, that is whether they were 'just satisfied' or 'very satisfied', and the same for those who were dissatisfied. The results are shown in Table 45. About the same proportions of white and Asian informants say they are dissatisfied with their housing (10 per cent and 12 per cent respectively) but the proportion is much larger among West Indian informants (23 per cent). Asians are, however, less likely than whites to say they are 'very satisfied' with their dwelling (41 per cent as opposed to 56 per cent); and, within the Asian group the Bangladeshis stand out as much less happy with their housing, for 27 per cent say they are dissatisfied. These overall differences hide very large differences between the tenure groups, as shown by Table 46. Owner-occupiers report much higher levels of satisfaction than council tenants or private tenants, and this is true for both blacks and whites, but even within the tenure groups the black informants are less likely to say they are satisfied and more likely to say they are dissatisfied. This is particularly the case among council tenants, of whom 34 per cent of blacks say they are dissatisfied compared with 17 per cent of whites. These differences are broadly in line with the differences between the quality of the dwellings of black and white people within the various tenure groups. The gap between the types of property occupied by black and white households is greatest in the council sector, where the proportions living in flats are 54 per cent and 27 per cent respectively, and it is therefore not surprising that it is among council tenants that we find the largest ethnic differences in satisfaction with housing.

Table 45 also shows the responses to a question about satisfaction with the neighbourhood. There is here less difference between the ethnic groups, and this is perhaps surprising, given the very different areas in which the majority of black people and the majority of white people live. We shall see later that reported satisfaction with neighbourhood is strongly related to whether the area is in the inner cities or not, but that this relationship is very much weaker among blacks than it is among whites.

Housing quality and area of residence

Table 47 shows summary indicators of housing quality for the white, West Indian and Asian samples in the inner and outer areas of the three main conurbations and in the rest of the country. It can be seen that the less desirable property tends to be located in the conurbations, and particularly in the inner areas; because these are the areas in which a large part of the black population is found, these geographical differences have an important effect on the comparisons of housing quality at a national level. In other words,

76

because the areas in which black people live are characterised by poor housing, the differences of housing quality are much sharper when making national comparisons between whites and blacks than when making comparisons at a local level.

The difference between the housing conditions of those in the inner cities and those elsewhere is much stronger among white people than among black people. As we saw earlier, the white population in the inner cities differs from the rest of the white population in that it contains higher proportions of pensioner households, of council tenants and of private tenants, while the black population in these areas is less clearly differentiated from the black population in other areas: there is a larger proportion of council tenants in the inner cities, but there are very few pensioners, and the proportion of private tenants is very low (five per cent, compared with 23 per cent among whites). Over half the white inner-city population lives in flats, compared with less than a fifth of the white population elsewhere; their properties tend to be older than those elsewhere; and 20 per cent of white households in the inner-cities lack or share basic amenities, compared with only about five per cent elsewhere. Asian and West Indian households in the inner cities are also more likely than those elsewhere to be in flats, but the difference is not so dramatic as it is among whites, and as regards age and amenities there is no consistent relationship: in fact a larger proportion of their dwellings in the inner cities were built after the war than those elsewhere. In terms of property age, property type and amenities, white households in the inner-city areas are, overall, in less desirable dwellings than are Asians and West Indians. Although some of this difference remains when tenure is taken into account, the pattern of tenures accounts for most of it: privately rented properties, as we saw earlier, are of markedly inferior quality than owner-occupied and council properties.

In the outer conurbation areas and in the rest of the country the picture is different: black people are more often than white people in older property and are less often in detached or semi-detached houses; West Indians are more often found in flats than are whites or Asians. In these areas there are few households lacking or sharing amenities, but the overall proportion is slightly larger among blacks than among whites.

One indicator of housing conditions is considerably worse for black households than for white households in the inner areas as well as elsewhere: the proportion with more than one person per room in their dwelling. Seventeen per cent of West Indian households and 44 per cent of Asian households have densities of occupation above this level in the inner cities, compared with only one per cent of the white population. This is related to the differences between the types of black and white household living

77

in the inner cities: 37 per cent of the white households in these areas in our sample comprise just one person, compared with seven per cent of Asian households and 13 per cent of West Indian households. It should be noted that densities of occupation among whites are lower in the inner city than elsewhere, while among Asians they are higher; among West Indians densities are higher in the conurbation areas but the relationship is not very strong.

The differences of tenure and housing quality between the inner-urban areas, the outer areas and the rest of the country are reflected in the levels of housing satisfaction reported by informants. Table 48 shows the proportions of white, West Indian and Asians who say they are dissatisfied with their housing, and in all three cases this response is given most often in the inner areas and least often in the areas outside the conurbations. The table also shows the proportion who report dissatisfaction with their neighbourhood, and it is interesting to note that here the relationship between area type and satisfaction becomes less clear for Asians and West Indians but becomes stronger for whites. In other words, although black people tend, with white people, to be critical of the poor housing in the inner city areas, they tend to be less critical than whites of the areas themselves. The most likely explanation of this is the availability in the informants' own areas of shops and facilities for their ethnic group, and support from relations and friends: the absence of these may weigh against the advantages that other areas have.

Later in this chapter, in the paragraphs on council housing, we give further consideration of the ethnic variations in housing quality.

Financing of Owner-Occupation

Further details of the tenure of owner-occupiers are given in Table 49. It can be seen that the ratios of freehold to leasehold properties owned by white, West Indian and Asian people are very similar. Very few have leases that have less than 20 years to run, although these are a little more common among Asian households (three per cent) than others.

The proportion of properties owned outright is twice as large for white households as for Asian and West Indian households. The explanation for this is that black owner-occupiers are predominantly young and are comparatively recent entrants to the British housing market. Although when compared to whites the Asians and West Indians are very similar in this respect, the difference between the Asians and West Indians is the opposite to what might be expected from the average length of time that people from the two groups have been in Britain. West Indian people have, on average, been here longer, and one might expect a higher percentage to have bought their homes outright, but this is not the case.

In fact, as time passes, it is the West indian households who are 'catching up' with the Asian households. The reason for this paradoxical trend is the special history of owner-occupation among Asian people. The high level of Asian owner-occupation was in part a response to the limited opportunity to find rented accommodation in the public or private sector, and was often characterised by the outright purchase of relatively cheap, poor quality houses. Over the years the nature of owner-occupation among Asians has become more like that within the rest of the population, and the proportion of loans and mortgages being paid off has been balanced by a decline in the proportion of these poor quality outright-owned properties. Thus the proportion of outright owners among Asians has remained static whilst among West Indians it has grown as loans and mortgages have been paid off.

The proportion of owner-occupied properties that have joint ownership is different for the three ethnic groups. Sixty-three per cent of West Indian owners are joint owners, compared with 58 per cent of white owners, and a much lower 40 per cent of Asian owners. For all three groups the joint owners are nearly always husband and wife, but it is slightly more common among Asian households for properties to be owned jointly by members of the same family related in other ways.

The main source of finance for those buying with a loan or mortgage is shown in Table 50. A majority of whites, Asians and West Indians are buying with money borrowed from a building society, although other sources of finance are used more commonly by Asians and West Indians than by whites. West indian mortgagors are twice as likely to have borrowed from a local authority as whites. The percentage of Asians borrowing from banks is higher, at 12 per cent, than for whites or West Indians, at four per cent and one per cent respectively. Few owner-occupiers have finance from any other source. The relatively large proportion of Asians who have loans from banks is a reflection of the difficulty with which Asians have been confronted when seeking to buy property that they can afford and that is large enough for their households: the property is often in an area not popular with building societies, and sometimes is rejected as not suitable for an advance because of its poor quality. Potential buyers have found banks (in particular the Asian banks) an easier source of funds, although the loans arranged in this way have often attracted higher interest rates.

The source of the deposit needed for purchase of property with a loan or mortgage is also shown on Table 50. Thirty-nine per cent of white mortgagors had their deposit as a result of the sale of another property, but this figure was much lower among Asians and West Indians, at 12 per cent. Three-quarters of black mortgagors used savings for the deposit, compared with 44 per cent of whites. The other major difference is the relatively large

79

proportion of Asians who received the money as a loan or a gift from relatives (13 per cent, compared to two per cent and four per cent among whites and West Indians).

Taken together, these findings show that establishing the funding for house purchase is more of a problem for black people than for white people. This is certainly due to a combination of factors: black people have lower earnings, they have less capital already invested in property, the areas in which they live are often regarded as presenting problems for lending, and there may be other elements of racial disadvantage and outright discrimination.

The final table showing owner-occupiers separately gives the proportions who have approached the council for an improvement grant for their home (Table 51). As we might expect from the differences in housing conditions, more Asians and West Indians have approached the council than whites. The proportion of West Indian owners who have made an approach is the largest, although it is worth noting that fewer of them actually received a grant than white or Asian applicants. Forty-five per cent of West Indian applicants received a grant, compared with 64 per cent of white and Asian applicants. This means that on a base of all owner-occupiers, the percentages in receipt of an improvement grant are quite similar for the three groups; for whites, West Indians and Asians they are 14 per cent, 15 per cent and 17 per cent respectively. We might have expected these figures to be further apart: the property occupied by black and white households is substantially different, and although we have no measure of how much work of the type eligible for improvement grants is needed on each property, it would have been no surprise to find the numbers of applications and grants to be much higher among blacks. The refusal rate is rather higher among West Indians than others (most refusals were due to non-eligibility) but there is a larger difference between the proportions of black and white applicants who did not eventually receive a grant for other reasons. This may indicate that there are more complex reasons for the final take-up rate being lower than might be expected; if we also look at the reasons given for making no approach to the council, we see that the Asians and West Indians tend to indicate that the workings of the scheme are not well enough publicised, and this may be part of the same problem. Although we have no further evidence of this, we can see that the scheme is not being used by some of those who need it most, and the explanation could be that the information on the terms of eligibility, the application procedures, and the types of work covered is inadequately targeted towards ethnic minorities.

Council Housing
Allocation

We asked all council tenants how they had originally been allocated a property. Table 52 shows that the patterns for white, Asian and West Indian tenants are all different. Half of white and West Indian tenants were housed from the waiting list, but only 38 per cent of Asian tenants were allocated a dwelling in this way. Many more Asians and West Indian tenants than white tenants were housed because they were homeless, and more white tenants were allocated property for 'other' reasons (these include 'key worker' schemes and other ways in which accommodation and employment are offered together). The gap between the proportions of Asians and West Indians housed from the waiting list is partly made up by Asians housed because of demolition of their previous property.

As we saw earlier, the properties occupied by black people are, overall, markedly inferior to those occupied by white people : they are smaller, and certainly more crowded; they are more often flats, and those flats allocated tend to be on higher floors; they rarely have access to a garden; even the indicator of housing quality that shows up as better for black tenants, the installation of central heating, is only a feature of the allocation of so many flats. It is therefore not surprising that a quarter of all black council tenants have applied for and are still waiting for a transfer to another property. The proportion among white tenants is less than half of this.

Table 53 shows how many of the households not in council dwellings have applied for council housing and are still on the waiting list. The proportion is quite small for all groups, but it is higher for West Indians and Asians than for whites : of those outside the council sector, eight per cent of West Indians, six per cent of Asians and three per cent of whites are on the waiting list. Examination of the length of time these applications have been waiting shows little difference between blacks and whites.

Housing conditions of black and white tenants: controlled comparisons

The housing conditions of council tenants are related strongly to their recency of entry into local authority housing, to their household type and to the area in which they live. Because there are differences between the black and white tenants in terms of these variables, there is an extent to which these relationships contribute to the general inferiority of the property allocated to black tenants. However, when comparisons are made within separate categories of household type, allocation date and area of residence, there remain considerable differences between the circumstances of black and white tenants. Table 54 shows selected indicators of property type and density of occupation for white, Asian and West Indian tenants in the different categories.

81

The first comparisons are for tenants who are living in their first council dwelling and for those who are living in second or subsequent dwellings. For all ethnic groups the first-dwelling tenants have a higher percentage of flats and lower percentage of detached and semi-detached houses than tenants in second and subsequent dwellings, but it can be seen that in both categories the Asian and West Indian tenants' properties are, when compared with those of white tenants, more likely to be flats and less likely to be detached or semi-detached houses. There is no consistent difference between the densities of occupation of first-dwelling tenants and others, and in both categories the densities for Asians and West Indians are higher than for whites.

The second set of comparisons is for tenants who were first allocated council dwellings at different times. Among whites and West Indians the tenants first housed after 1975 are more likely to be found in flats and less likely to be in detached or semi-detached houses than those housed earlier. Asians housed after 1975 are also less likely to be in detached and semi-detached houses than those housed earlier, but the proportion of new tenants (those housed after 1980) in flats is lower than for those housed before 1975. Despite the fact that the more recent tenants tend to be in property that we would expect to be smaller (flats and terraced houses), their densities of residence in all three ethnic groups are lower than those who became tenants earlier; this is likely to be the result of tenants having children after they have been allocated a property, and household sizes consequently growing sufficiently to outweigh any advantage that the longer-established tenants may have in terms of property size. Among the tenants who were first allocated property in each of the periods considered, blacks have generally inferior types of property and higher densities of occupation. There is also a higher proportion of more recent tenants among the Asians and West Indians than among the whites, and this further depresses the relative quality of the property occupied by the black tenants by raising the overall proportion of flats and lowering the overall proportion of detached and semi-detached houses.

The third set of comparisons is for different household types. In the table we show separate figures for pensioner-only households, nuclear families, lone parents and lone adults. For each of these household types the Asian and West Indian tenants have higher proportions of flats, and lower proportions of detached and semi-detached houses, than the white tenants. There are within each ethnic group large variations between the housing circumstances of the different household types, and, knowing that the three ethnic groups have different mixes of household types, we might expect these variations to contribute substantially to the overall differences between the housing circumstances of black and white council tenants. In fact, this is not the case. Only the relatively large proportions of lone parents and lone adults in the West Indian sample produce any effect of this kind, and it is very limited: lone parents and lone adults tend to be found in flats more often than nuclear families, and this means that the overall proportion of West Indian council tenants in flats is higher than it might otherwise be. But there is no effect of this sort among Asians, the vast majority of whom live in nuclear and extended families with children, both of which are household types normally found less frequently than others in flats. Also, there are very few pensioner-only households among blacks, and these households are also more commonly found in flats than other households, and we would therefore expect this to counterbalance the effect of the relatively large proportions of lone parents and lone adults among the West Indians. It is the case, however, that the larger proportion of households with children among the black population contributes to the very large differences between the overall densities of occupation of blacks and whites, but even this is not an 'explanation' of the differences, for the actual properties allocated to black households have fewer rooms on average than those allocated to whites (Table 38) and this results in blacks having higher densities even when the comparison is restricted to families with children.

The final comparisons presented in Table 54 take account of the different residential distributions of black and white tenants. Here we can see that among council tenants the type of property occupied is strongly related to the area in which it is found, as we saw to be the case for all tenures taken together in Table 43. In the conurbations, and particularly in the inner areas, the proportion of flats is higher than elsewhere, and the proportion of detached and semi-detached houses is lower. This does contribute to the overall differences between the properties occupied by white and black tenants, but, again, it does not explain away the differences, because in the outer areas and in the areas outside the conurbations the properties of black tenants are still more frequently flats, and less frequently detached semi-detached houses, than the properties of white tenants.

In the inner areas we can see that the proportions of flats allocated to the white and black tenants in the survey are about the same, and a few black tenants have detached or semi-detached houses whereas there are none among the white tenants. We therefore have no evidence to suggest that within these areas the type of property allocated to black tenants is worse than that allocated whites, although perhaps we should put this in perspective by pointing out that only eight per cent of the white tenants in the survey (54 households) are in these areas, compared with 52 per cent of the black tenants (733 households). As with all the other comparisons, densities of occupation are consistently higher for black tenants than for white tenants.

Thus we see that the type of property allocated to tenants is related to household structure, to the period in which the first allocation was made, and to geographical area, but that only the last of these factors makes an important contribution to the overall differences between the housing conditions of black and white tenants.

Racial discrimination - reported experience and beliefs

Although the private rented sector is now very small in relation to other tenures, it is still the only tenure that is not governed by elaborate formal allocation procedures, and for a minority of white and black households it is the only type of housing feasibly available in the short or medium term. Racial discrimination by landlords can therefore be a major source of disadvantage to a section of the black population. Research has in the past been carried out to obtain a minimum assessment of the extent of discrimination; this has been done by black and white actors making test applications for rented property. In the set of tests conducted as part of the 1974 PEP study, black applicants met with racial discrimination in over a quarter of the cases. Objective data of this kind is not available from interview surveys, but in 1974 it was demonstrated that, when asked about their views and experiences, black survey informants tended to understate the problem rather than exaggerate it(3).

In the 1982 survey Asian and West Indian informants were asked whether they had ever been refused accommodation by a private landlord for reasons to do with race or colour. We show the results in Table 55; only those who are outside the two main tenures (owner-occupation and council renting) and who have at some time approached a white landlord seeking accommodation are included in the table. About half of the West Indians and over a third of the Asians say they have personally experienced racial discrimination. Sixty per cent of these incidents were in the period between 1976 and the survey. In a third of the cases the informants had evidence of discrimination in addition to the attitude of the landlord: they were told the property had already been let, but later discovered that it was still available.

We also asked all informants whether they thought there were landlords who would refuse a person accommodation because of their race or colour. Over 80 per cent of white informants and 72 per cent of West Indian informants said they believed there were landlords who would do this, but the proportion of Asians who said this was much smaller, at 34 per cent (Table 56). This pattern changes radically if we consider only those who have been exposed to potential discrimination of this kind, for we find that three-quarters of Asians in this group, and 90 per cent of West Indians, believe that at least some landlords discriminate.

The small size of the private rented sector does mean, however, that the existence of direct or indirect racial discrimination in the allocation of council housing and in the owner-occupied housing market has an even greater effect on the position of black people. The same questions were not repeated for the council and owner-occupied sectors, but informants' views were obtained on the general racial bias of the institutions governing access to housing and housing finance in these sectors. The results are presented in Table 57. We asked about the treatment of Asian and West Indian people by building societies, banks, estate agents and council housing departments; it should be noted that we asked the ethnic minority respondents about the treatment of their own ethnic group, rather than all black people. Looking first at the figures for building societies, we see that Asian and white people give very similar responses : over a third decline to express a view, but half say that they think people are treated the same. Of the remainder, most of the white people (nine per cent) say that black people are treated worse, and a similar pattern is seen among the Asians. A higher percentage of West Indian informants say that their group is treated worse than white people by building societies, but there are still 40 per cent who say that they are treated the same, and 45 per cent who give no view.

The pattern of the informants' views on the way banks treat Asian and West Indian people follows almost the same pattern, except that a larger proportion of West Indian people were critical of the banks than of the building societies. The banks were not mentioned specifically in the context of housing finance, so this has to be interpreted as part of a general view of their services. The pattern changes a little more when we look at the results for estate agents. Half of whites and Asians say that the estate agents give equal service, but twice as many whites (20 per cent) as Asians say that black people are given worse treatment. The proportion of West Indians who declined to give a response to this question is higher than for others, but of those the proportion who said that West Indians were given worse treatment was the same as for whites. Thus we see that for these organisations that manage the sale of properties and allocation of funds in the owner-occupied market, a minority of Asian and West Indian people are critical of the way their own group are treated. White people claim that the racial bias is in favour of whites more commonly than in favour of blacks, and they are equally critical as Asians (more so, over estate agents). West Indian informants are rather more critical than Asians, but they are also less likely to express a view, presumably because fewer have had personal experience in the owner-occupied sector themselves.

85

The views expressed over the treatment by council housing deparments are different. To begin with, more Asians than West Indians decline to express a firm views, and again this can be explained by the levels of experience of dealing with the institution concerned. About a third of Asians and West Indians say that council house departments deal equally with whites and their own ethnic group, compared with about a half of white informants. Of the remainder of Asians and West Indians, nearly all say that whites are treated better, but the remainder of the white informants are split between those saying they are treated better and those saying they are treated worse. This is disturbing, because on all the other subjective measures of this kind covering housing (and employment) in this and our previous surveys, white people have been as likely as black people to claim that Asian and West Indian people face racial discrimination. In reality, the position is quite clear: the overall proportion of black households living in council accommodation is identical to the proportion among white households; the property occupied by black tenants is inferior to that occupied by white tenants, and blacks are therefore more often found waiting for a transfer than whites; there are proportionately more Asians and West Indians than whites having to wait for a council property; overall, the proportion of manual worker heads of household in council property is 31 per cent among blacks and 43 per cent among whites, so it cannot even be claimed that working class blacks are, because of their disadvantaged position, more commonly found in council tenancies. Research studies of the workings of the council housing allocation procedures in specific local authorities have shown directly that Asian and West Indian people have been disadvantaged by a number of factors: black people in acute housing need can be denied eligibility or allocation by rules originally drawn up for very different reasons (for example, the exclusion of owner-occupiers from a waiting list means that families in cheap, poor quality houses, who have little hope of moving to other owner-occupied property, are completely trapped); the actual council properties that become available for letting are often smaller than would be necessary for black households, which are on average larger than white households, and in these cases black families who qualify for a letting are passed in the queue by white families; and, perhaps now most important, the property let to black households is very inferior to that let to white households(4). Why, therefore, is there a significant minority of whites who say that black people get better treatment than white people?

Although black people when considered as a single group have the same level of council tenancy as the white population, this is the result of a lower level among Asians and a higher level among West Indians; as a consequence, in areas of relatively concentrated

West Indian residence - particularly in the major conurbations - the proportion of West Indians in council housing is higher than the proportion of white people in council housing. This alone may be perceived by white residents as better treatment, despite the poorer quality of properties given to West Indian tanants. In fact it has come about simply because a large proportion of West Indians fall into the categories of the general population for which council accommodation has been reserved: urban working-class families with children and those in special housing need. The eligibility of West Indians has been limited by the problems mentioned above to a lesser extent than the eligibility of Asians, and they have therefore been relatively successful in obtaining tenancies. Although this is not 'better treatment' than that given to whites, the existence of a relatively large proportion of West Indian council tenants in a locality could, for some white people, in the absence of a good understanding of the complexities of the council allocation system, look like evidence of a bias in favour of blacks. This is made more likely by the practice of allocating black people to accommodation on specific estates and thereby creating high local densities of black tenants: on these estates the balance of white and black people is very different from that within surrounding areas, and white residents may get the impression that council allocations to white and black people are generally made in these proportions. In areas of relatively dense black residence the proportion of whites saying blacks are treated better rises to a quarter.

Having suggested reasons for the minority view among whites that council housing departments have a bias in favour of Asians and West Indians, we should perhaps keep the matter in perspective by noting that only one in seven of white informants give this view. Although the challenge of countering these views (and the political movements that can take advantage of them) should be taken seriously, it can be taken up with the confidence that they are not the views of the white majority.

Patterns of change
Tenure
Changes in the tenure distributions of the different ethnic groups in the survey can be examined using information on individual house movements over the period between 1977 and 1982. Additionally, the present tenure distributions can be compared with those from earlier surveys. These analyses are fairly complex and present some difficulties of comparison between the different surveys, but we can be confident about the overall trends described here. There have been changes in the tenure patterns of whites, Asians and West Indians, resulting from both the establishment of new households and movement among already existing households,

87

but there is little sign of the three patterns converging, with the exception of the rapid growth of the presently small proportion of Asian council tenants. The patterns have therefore remained ethnically distinct. Among West Indians the relatively large proportion of council tenants has grown, and is largest among new households. Among Asians the proportion of owner-occupiers has remained large and may have grown; new Asian households have the highest levels of owner-occupation. The housing association sector has grown in importance for West Indians. The proportion of black households in the privately rented sector was once much larger than among white households, but now there are proportionally fewer private tenants among blacks than among whites.

It is best to start our analysis of tenure change by showing how the survey informants themselves have moved over this period. We asked respondents for details of their accommodation at the beginning of 1977, and by combining this with the information on present accommodation we are able to get a picture of their movements over the period to 1982 (Table 58). The tenure movements analysed are those of the first person selected for interview in the household, and these are used as a proxy for the moves of the whole household. Although the first selected person is frequently the head of household (and this is always the case when there are only one or two adults in the household), there is bound to be within the analysis a number of moves reported by individuals that are different from those of the rest of their households. It is unlikely that these produce a net effect of any size on the results: where the first informant is not the head of household, he or she is most likely to be the spouse or an adult son or daughter, and will have moved at the same time as the head of household. A number of Asian and West Indian informants came to Britain after the beginning of 1977, and in the context of the analysis here it would not be possible to make any sense of a tenure move that started overseas, therefore these informants have been omitted from the 'moved tenure' category. Because the patterns and extent of moves of households that have formed since 1977 are for obvious reasons very different to other households, we present the tenure move data separately for the group we can identify as new households; in nearly every case the tenure move shown for new households is the move made by the head of household.

Sixty-eight per cent of both Asian and West Indian new household heads have switched tenure in setting up their household, although the direction of movement has differed between the two groups. The Asian new households have primarily moved into owner-occupation, from private renting, with a much smaller group moving to council property, while West Indian new households moved in a far more diffuse manner: 21 per cent have moved into owner occupied property, 28 per cent into council tenancy, 11 per cent into housing associations and even seven per cent into the private rented sector. Tenure movement among established households has been far less common. According to the table, about 15 per cent of Asian and West Indian established households have changed tenure but it must be remembered that within this group are some hidden new households, and this figure is therefore likely to be an overestimate. The directions of tenure moves among established West Indian households have been similar to those of established Asian households, with the move out of the private rented sector splitting between destinations in the council and owner-occupied sectors in a ratio of about two to one. It is noticeable, however, that more West Indians than Asians have moved into housing association property and private rented property.

Among whites, 59 per cent of new household heads have changed tenure in setting up their household, and their moves have been different to those of their Asian and West Indian counterparts: only six per cent of new households moved into council accommodation from another tenure, while 14 per cent moved into the private rented sector. Tenure movement among established white households has been a little less common than among established black households, but has been of a similar character.

The overall tenure distributions for 1977 can be worked out from these data, and are shown in comparison with the 1982 distributions in Table 59. This table suggests the net results of the tenure moves by new and established households has been as follows. The overall level of owner-occupation has remained fairly stable among all ethnic groups: it has risen a little among whites and Asians and fallen a little among West Indians. The level of council tenancy has risen substantially among West Indians (from 37 to 46 per cent) and among Asians (from 14 to 19 per cent). The levels of private tenancy among all three groups have fallen, but more steeply among blacks than among whites. The proportion in 'other' tenures - nearly all of them housing association tenants - have risen steeply among West Indians, but only a little among whites and not at all among Asians.

Some difficulties arise when similar comparisons are made with other surveys, rather than with the previous tenure of the same informants. In Table 60, the 1982 distributions are compared with those found by the 1977 National Dwelling and Household Survey. The trends evident among whites and Asians are broadly similar to those described above, although the actual 1977 figures are rather different from our own. In the case of the West Indians, however, both the 1977 distribution and the trend shown between 1977 and 1982 are different. According to the NDHS the level of council tenancy among West Indian households in 1977 was already 45 per cent, and the present level of 46 per cent therefore indicates no increase in council tenancy during the intervening period; also the NDHS figure for owner occupation was 36 per cent, so the present 41 per cent indicates an increase in the proportion of owners. Because the PSI survey finds that there has been a net individual movement into the council sector during this period, and no such net movement into owner-occupation, it must be inferred that either the PSI survey seriously underestimates the 1982 level of council renting among West Indians, or the 1977 NDHS figure is an overestimate. There are three other sources of data to which we can look for help with this puzzle: the 1981 census, the 1981 Labour Force Survey (LFS) and the 1974 PEP survey. The census and the LFS give the proportion of council tenants among West Indian households as 45 per cent and 46 per cent respectively; as these are the same as the level found in the PSI survey, it is unlikely that the latter is an underestimate (Table 61). The 1974 PEP survey gives a level of council tenancy which is much lower than would be expected working back from the 1977 NDHS figure: the 1974 figure is 26 per cent, and it seems unlikely that the level would rise to 45 per cent in just three years (Table 62). These three independent checks therefore support the finding that the present level of council tenancy among West Indians is around 45 per cent and that this has grown from a rather lower level in 1975, while the level of owner-occupation has remained static.

Table 62 also makes a comparison of the tenure distributions of black households in 1974 and 1982 in the types of area covered by the 1974 survey (that is to say in EDs that had a local concentration of black immigrants of at least 2.4 per cent in the 1971 Census). The trends towards council tenancy and away from private tenancy are repeated in this table, but the level of owner-occupation appears to have fallen, particularly among West Indian households. It is possible that among Asians the fall from 76 per cent in 1974 to 74 per cent in 1982 is an artificial product of the different survey techniques and definitions used for the two surveys, for the 1974 survey may have tended to overestimate the level of owner-occupation among large extended households. But the apparent fall in the level of owner-occupation among West Indians in these areas is unlikely to be the product of methodological differences (because of the smaller proportion of households with complex structures), and therefore indicates that the growth of the council and housing association sectors has not been at the expense of the privately rented sector alone, but in these areas has also lowered the proportion of owners.

It should be noted that the proportion of Asian council tenants found in the PSI survey is rather higher than found in the Census and in the LFS (19 per cent compared with 14 per cent). Although this difference is partly located among the Indian and Pakistani groups, for which the levels of council tenancy in the PSI survey are 16 per cent and 13 per cent respectively, as opposed to 13 per cent and 11 per cent in the Census, it is over the Bangladeshi group that there is the greatest discrepancy: the PSI figure is 53 per cent while the Census figure is 32 per cent. It is very difficult to assess whether this represents a real trend between 1981 and 1982 or a product of the differences between the survey and Census methodology, because on the one hand the Bangladeshi group are known to have been highly mobile within their localities in recent years and, because they are often particularly disadvantaged and are resident in local authorities with a large council stock, have gained access to council accommodation, while on the other hand they are a small, highly clustered population and this may have resulted in the Bangladeshi sample in the PSI survey being unrepresentative. Whatever its cause, this difference between the figures for Bangladeshis is responsible for most of the gap between the overall Asian figures from the two sources.

Other aspects of housing tenure have changed in the period between the 1974 PEP survey and the present survey. The most important of these has been a shift in the patterns of finance for house purchase among Asian and West Indian owner-occupiers. Table 63 shows that, for both groups, building societies have become more important as sources of funds as local authorities and private loans (from friends or relatives) have become less important. Although these changes are towards the pattern of borrowing in the general population, there are still considerable differences between the patterns among whites and blacks, as we saw earlier (Table 50). There has been little decline in the importance of banks as sources of finance for Asian owner-occupiers.

During the same period the proportion of Asian owner-occupiers in leasehold property, and especially in short-lease property, has fallen considerably: in 1974 over a third were in leasehold dwellings, and over ten per cent had leases shorter than 16 years. Now only 13 per cent have leasehold property, and only three per cent have leases shorter than 20 years. The proportion of Asians owning their homes outright has remained at about the same level, while it has grown among West Indians from ten per cent to 26 per cent. The reasons for these different trends were mentioned earlier in this chapter. Joint ownership has become more common among all ethnic groups, but the growth has been particularly noticeable among Asians. Within the areas covered by the 1974 survey, the percentage of joint owners has risen from 15 to 36 per cent for Asians, from 42 to 60 per cent for West Indians and from 54 to 58 per cent for whites.

There have also been changes in the routes by which black council tenants come to be housed by the local authorities. We saw earlier that black tenants were more likely than white tenants to have been housed because they were homeless, and that Asian tenants were less likely than whites or West Indians to have been housed from the waiting list. Between the two surveys the proportions housed because of homelessness or on medical or social services advice have hardly changed for any of the groups: in other words, this figure was higher for black people in 1974 as well. But the proportions of black households who were allocated property because of demolition and clearance was twice as large in 1974, and the proportions housed from the waiting list were smaller. The growth in waiting list allocations among Asians is particularly large: in 1974, only 14 per cent of Asian tenants had obtained their house or flat in this way, while by 1982, in the equivalent areas, this figure has risen to 42 per cent.

Tenure, area of residence and job levels

In the 1974 survey, tenure was analysed by the local concentration of immigrants, and strong relationships were revealed. Now those relationships are breaking up, and some have vanished altogether. At that time owner-occupation levels were substantially higher in the higher density areas for Asians and West Indians (there is a much weaker association now), council housing was much less common in higher density areas (this is now only the case for Asians, and the relationship is much weaker), private renting was less common among Asians, and more common among West Indians, in high density areas (the Asian figure remains fairly stable in the different areas now, and the West Indian pattern has reversed). If the comparisons are made on the basis of the local concentrations of the informant's own ethnic group, the contrast with the 1974 survey becomes even greater. For example, the 1974 survey showed that only six per cent of West Indians in EDs with over 12 per cent West Indian immigrants were council tenants, while in the 1982 survey, in EDs with over 12 per cent West Indian households, 50 per cent of West Indians are in council property.

One of the major findings of the 1974 PEP survey was that the traditional relationship between occupational class and housing tenure did not hold among Asian and West Indian households. In 1982 we still find that the housing of black people does not fit into the same patterns as that of white people with respect to job levels. Changes have occurred, however, with the effect of moving the Asian pattern towards the white pattern, and moving the West Indian pattern away from the white pattern. At the bottom of Table 33 we show for Asians the proportion of each occupational group who were owner-occupiers in 1974, along with the 1982 figures for the corresponding geographical areas. In 1974, owner-occupation was more common in the lower SEG groups than in the higher SEG groups; in other words, the relationship between class and tenure was the opposite to that among white people. Although it is still the case that owner-occupation is more common among skilled manual workers than any other Asian group, the overall pattern has now disappeared: the level of owner-occupation has risen in the upper SEG groups, and fallen in the lower SEG groups. In 1974, the proportion of Asian council tenants was very small and there was no association with SEG: now we see a clear, traditional pattern emerging, although the proportions are still much smaller than among whites or West Indians in all but the top SEG group. Thus the trend is towards a relationship between job level and housing tenure that resembles that of white people. Among West Indians, the major features of the tenure-class pattern were a high level of owner-occupation among skilled manual workers, a low level among non-manual workers, and a relatively stable level of council tenancy in the different SEG groups, with the lowest level among skilled workers. Within each of the manual categories, the West Indians had a higher level of owner-occupation, and a lower level of council tenancy, than whites. Now we find that within the West Indian group the distinctive features of the tenure-class pattern have been maintained, while owner-occupation has become less common throughout, and council tenancy more common. Only among unskilled workers is council housing now more common among white people than among West Indian people.

One important feature of the original pattern discovered by the 1974 survey persists for both Asians and West Indians. Heads of households with non-manual occupations are far more likely to be in privately rented property than those with manual occupations. The opposite is true for white heads of households. Clearly, as the private rented sector has become much less important for all ethnic groups since 1974, this is of less significance today. It is, however, a further reminder that although the tenure patterns have changed considerably since 1974, a large element of the special nature of Asian and West Indian housing is still evident.

Housing conditions
Although there are still very large inequalities between white and black housing conditions, it is true to say that there has been a considerable improvement in the housing of black people between 1974 and 1982. In Table 64 we can see that there have been a number of changes that have accompanied the moves that have taken place between the two surveys, particularly the moves away from the private rented sector and into the council sector, and moves to better owner-occupied property. The biggest changes are in the proportions of households sharing a dwelling and lacking exclusive use of basic amenities (it should be remembered that these measures are not independent of each other, for most households who share also fall into the 'lacking exclusive use of facilities' category because the bathroom and/or WC are the rooms

93

they are most likely to share). The proportion of sharing house-holds has fallen among whites from four per cent to one per cent, but has fallen more steeply among blacks from 26 per cent to five per cent; an equal contrast is seen in the fall in the proportion of white households without sole use of basic amenities from 18 per cent to five per cent compared with the fall among blacks from 37 per cent to seven per cent (in fact, all of the overall gap between whites and blacks is now located in the Asian sample: the propor-tion of West Indians lacking or sharing facilities in these areas is the same as for whites). Changes can also be seen in the age of the property occupied by black people: while 46 per cent was pre-1919 in the 1974 survey, this has fallen to 35 per cent now, and the proportion of post-war property has risen from 12 per cent to 24 per cent.

Some of this apparent improvement is, however, deceptive. In particular, the move into younger property does not necessarily mean a move to better property: many of the newer dwellings allocated to black council tenants in blocks of flats are much less desirable than the older properties on cottage estates, or than many older owner-occupied houses. This point is underlined by the difference between white and black households with regard to the type of dwelling they occupy. In 1974, the proportion of white people in detached and semi-detached houses was 57 per cent, compared with 16 per cent of black people, and now the figures are 54 per cent and 18 per cent respectively. This very slight convergence is more than balanced by the faster rise in the proportion of black people in flats from 15 per cent to 22 per cent; among whites this rise has only been from 12 per cent to 15 per cent.

Notes
(1)   Over a quarter of the households in the Asian and West Indian survey did not exist as separate entities in this country at the beginning of 1977. We have identified over three-quarters of these new households, using the following definition: (a) all households with heads aged under 25, plus (b) all households that reported that their last house move was to set up their own house, plus (c) all households where the first informant came to Britain after the beginning of 1977. Twenty-one per cent of the households of Asian and West Indian origin in the survey fall within this definition.
(2)   Our own research has shown that this pattern of tenure movement was common among young newly-formed house-holds between 1975 and 1978. Of a sample of young married couples over a third were private tenants when they first established their own household, but most moved within two and a half years to owner-occupied or council property, in a

ratio of three to two respectively. See 'First Homes: A Survey of the Housing Circumstances of Young Married Couples', PSI Report 600, J. Madge and C. Brown, December 1981.

(3)   See The Extent of Racial Discrimination, N. McIntosh and D.J. Smith, PEP Report 547, 1974. Field tests showed that at least one in four applications to private landlords and accommodation agencies met with racial discrimination; the 1974 PEP survey showed that at the time about three-quarters of West Indian adults, and less than half of Asian adults, believed that there were landlords who discriminated.

(4)   See Racial Minorities and Public Housing, D.J. Smith and A. Whalley, PEP Report 556, 1975, and Stacking the Decks, a Study of Race, Inequality and Council Housing in Nottingham, Alan Simpson, NDCRC; Race and Council Housing in Hackney. Report of a Formal Investigation, Commission for Racial Equality, January 1984.

Table 29:   Tenure patterns

Column percentages

	White	West Indian	Asian	Indian	Paki-stani	Bangl-adeshi	Afri-can Asian	Muslim	Hindu	Sikh
Owner-Occupied	59	41	72	77	80	30	73	67	73	91
Rented from Council	30	46	19	16	13	53	19	24	16	6
Privately Rented	9	6	6	5	5	11	5	6	8	3
(Furnished)	2	3	4	4	4	8	4	5	6	1
(Unfurnished)	7	3	1	1	1	2	1	1	1	1
Housing Association	2	8	2	2	1	4	2	2	3	*
Other	*	-	*	*	-	*	1	*	1	*
Base: Households										
(weighted)	2694	1834	2851	1150	751	277	604	1339	748	520
(unweighted)	2305	1189	1893	726	518	197	411	937	481	349

Table 30:   Tenure pattern of new households

Column percentages

	White		West Indian		Asian	
	Known new house- holds	Others	Known new house- holds	Others	Known new house- holds	Others
Owner-occupied	58	59	28	43	78	71
Rented from Council	21	31	49	45	14	20
Privately rented furnished	11	2	6	2	4	5
Privately rented unfurnished	6	7	2	3	1	1
Housing Association	2	2	13	5	1	2
Base: Households						
(weighted)	222	2472	302	1532	419	2432
(unweighted)	220	2085	181	1008	286	1607

Table 31:   Tenure in major areas of black residence by ethnic group

Column percentages

	Inner London	Outer London	West Midlands Met. County	Leicester-shire, Nottingham-shire and Derbyshire	West and South York-shire	Greater Manchester and Lanca-shire	Berks, Bucks, Herts	Rest of England and Wales
White Households								
Owner-occupied	27	63	47	62	57	67	60	61
Rented from Council	43	24	41	30	35	22	35	29
Privately rented	21	9	11	7	5	9	5	9
Housing Association	8	3	2	1	2	2	1	1
West Indian Households								
Owner-occupied	27	48	34	(55)	(43)	46	(75)	50
Rented from Council	59	43	58	(25)	(25)	46	(22)	31
Privately rented	3	4	1	(16)	(18)	2	(4)	12
Housing Association	11	5	7	(5)	(14)	6	(-)	7
Asian Households								
Owner-occupied	34	75	76	84	91	80	83	78
Rented from Council	50	17	19	8	3	15	14	13
Privately rented	9	5	3	5	5	3	4	7
Housing Association	5	1	2	2	1	3	-	2

Table 32: Tenure in inner cities by ethnic group

Column percentages

	Inner London, Inner Birmingham, Inner Manchester	Outer London, Rest of W. Midlands & Greater Manchester Met. Counties	Rest of England and Wales
White Households			
Owner-occupied	29	62	61
Rented from Council	42	28	30
Privately rented	23	7	8
Housing Association	6	2	1
West Indian Households			
Owner-occupied	28	48	52
Rented from Council	59	44	30
Privately rented	3	3	11
Housing Assiciation	10	6	7
Asian Households			
Owner-occupied	44	79	82
Rented from Council	42	15	10
Privately rented	7	4	6
Housing Association	5	1	1

Table 33: Tenure and job level of household head

	Professional, Employer Manager	Other Non- Manual	Skilled Manual, Fore- man	Semi- Skilled Manual	Un- Skilled	Unemp- loyed	Re- tired
Percent who are owner Occupiers...							
White	86	64	52	40	21	25	52
Asian	73	66	78	70	72	55	59
West Indian	(78)	26	44	34	33	21	37
Percent who are Council Tenants...							
White	10	24	34	48	66	53	35
Asian	14	18	17	22	24	32	31
West Indian	10	55	44	53	53	62	56
1974 Survey Areas, Percent who are owner Occupiers...							
Asians, 1974	58	59	81	82	85		
Asians, 1982	70	66	83	71	73		

Notes: (1) The table shows the percentage of households within a given socio-economic and ethnic group who are owner-occupiers and council tenants; for example 86 per cent of white households in the professional group are owner occupiers.
(2) 1982 base = All households where head was interviewed as a sampled individual. This includes 80% of Asian and West Indian households, and 57% of white households.

Table 34:   Tenure patterns of different household types

Column percentages

	Pension-er(s) only	Extended House-holds	Lone Parent	Others with Children	Lone Adult	Adults without Children
West Indian						
Owner-Occupied	(21)	38	11	51	26	56
Rented from Council	(67)	35	74	40	46	37
Privately Rented Furnished	(3)	9	2	1	10	*
Privately Rented Unfurnished	(3)	7	3	2	6	3
Housing Assn.	(8)	10	11	7	11	5
Asian						
Owner-Occupied	(41)	79	44	75	32	74
Rented from Council	(48)	14	44	18	30	17
Privately Rented Furnished	-	5	1	3	22	5
Privately Rented Unfurnished	-	1	1	1	6	1
Housing Assn.	(7)	*	8	2	3	2
White						
Owner-Occupied	55	55	35	66	39	63
Rented from Council	31	27	55	28	36	29
Privately Rented Furnished	-	8	5	1	16	2
Privatley Rented Unfurnished	12	8	1	4	6	5
Housing Assn.	2	1	3	1	3	2

Note: For household type definitions, see Chapter II.

101

Table 35: Housing conditions of white, West Indian and Asian households: summary statistics

Row percentages

	Per cent in flats	Per cent in detached or semi-detached houses	Per cent in dwellings built before 1945	Per cent lacking exclusive use of bath, hot water or inside WC	Per cent with over 1 person per room
All Tenure Groups					
White	15	54	50	5	3
West Indian	32	23	60	5	16
Asian	16	26	74	7	35
Owner-occupiers					
White	5	67	56	3	2
West Indian	1	37	84	3	13
Asian	4	29	81	5	33
Council Tenants					
White	27	39	27	3	5
West Indian	54	9	34	3	20
Asian	54	11	35	7	43
Private Tenants					
White	32	33	87	27	2
West Indian & Asian	24	21	83	32	22

102

Table 36:   Dwelling type by ethnic group

	White	West Indian	Asian	Indian	Paki-stani	Bangla-deshi	African Asian
Detatched House/Bungalow	18	4	7	8	3	1	10
Semi Detached House/Bungalow	36	19	19	21	10	8	27
Terraced House	31	44	59	58	79	40	48
Flat in building up to 4 floors	9	16	8	7	3	31	6
Flat in building over 4 floors	2	11	4	2	2	12	5
Other	4	5	4	3	3	8	4
Base: All Households							
(weighted)	2671	1669	2768	1127	741	250	581
(unweighted)	2284	1082	1838	711	511	178	395

Note: Bases exclude households where dwelling type not adequately recorded (five per cent of Asian and West Indian households).

103

Table 37: Dwelling type by tenure and ethnic group

Column percentages

	White Households				Asian and West Indian Households			
	Owner	Council Tenant	Private Tenant	Housing Assn.	Owner	Council Tenant	Private Tenant	Housing Assn.
Detached House/Bungalow	28	2	10	-	8	1	6	4
Semi-detached House/ Bungalow	39	37	23	(4)	25	9	15	7
Terraced House	28	34	35	(30)	65	30	54	48
Flat in building up to 4 floors	2	17	19	(50)	1	31	6	27
Flat in building over 4 floors	1	6	2	-	*	22	*	2
Other	2	4	11	(15)	2	6	18	12
Base: Households (weighted)	1573	812	236	46	2730	1267	248	164
(unweighted)	1361	692	192	37	1867	761	158	117

104

Table 38:   Floor level of entrance to council flat

Column percentages

	White	Asian and West Indian
Below Street	–	1
Ground Floor	42	29
1st Floor	34	15
2nd Floor	8	18
3rd Floor	4	15
4-9th Floor	6	15
Over 9th	6	5
Base: Households in Council Flat		
(weighted)	187	581
(unweighted)	147	330

Note: Bases exclude households where floor level of entrance not adequately recorded (14 per cent of Asian and West Indian sample).

Table 39:   Dwelling age by ethnic group

Cumulative column percentages

	White	West Indian	Asian	Indian	Paki-stani	Bangla-deshi	African Asian
Dwelling Built:							
Before 1919	24	23	34	31	44	38	26
Before 1945	50	60	74	73	86	59	64
Base: Households							
(weighted)	2683	1480	2563	1053	668	214	563
(unweighted)	2296	959	1702	665	461	152	383

Note: Base excludes households where informant and interviewer were unable to assess the age of the building (14 per cent of the Asian and West Indian sample).

105

Table 40:   Dwelling age by tenure and ethnic group

Column percentages

	Owner	Council Tenant	Private Tenant	Housing Assn.
White Households:				
Before 1919	29	5	57	(29)
Before 1945	56	27	87	(44)
Asian and West Indian Households:				
Before 1919	36	12	40	34
Before 1945	82	35	83	67

Table 41:   Size of dwelling, and sharing, by ethnic group

	White	West Indian	Asian	Indian	Paki- stani	Bangla- deshi	African Asian
Per cent in dwelling shared with other household(s)	1	4	5	3	4	12	4
Mean number of rooms for own exclusive use	5.0	4.3	4.6	4.8	4.7	3.9	4.6
Mean number of persons per room	0.5	0.8	1.0	0.9	1.1	1.3	0.9
Per cent with over 1.0 persons per room	3	16	35	26	47	60	26
Per cent with over 1.5 persons per room	1	3	12	7	17	32	7
Base: Households (weighted)	2694	1834	2851	1150	751	277	604
(unweighted)	2305	1189	1893	726	518	197	411

Notes: (1) Mean persons per room calculated as mean number of persons in household divided by mean number of rooms for own exclusive use.
(2) Per cent above 1.0 and 1.5 persons per room calculated as above, but adding half a room for every shared room, as in the National Dwelling and Household Survey.

107

Table 42: Size of dwelling, and sharing, by tenure and ethnic group

Column percentages

	Owner	Council Tenant	Private Tenant	Housing Assn.
White Households:				
Per cent shared dwelling	*	1	10	-
Per cent with over 1.0 persons per room	2	5	2	(2)
Mean number of unshared rooms	5.4	4.4	4.2	(3.7)
Asian and West Indian Households:				
Per cent in shared dwelling	2	2	33	5
Per cent with over 1.0 persons per room	27	29	22	16
Mean number of unshared rooms	5.0	3.9	3.3	3.5

Note: Shared rooms each counted as half rooms in persons per room count.

Table 43:   Amenities by ethnic group

Column percentages

	White	West Indian	Asian	Indian	Paki-stani	Bangla-deshi	African Asian
Lack exclusive use of bath, hot water or inside WC	5	5	7	5	7	18	5
No garden	11	32	21	15	21	56	18
No central heating	43	38	44	37	66	56	27
No refrigerator	6	6	11	4	19	37	5
No washing machine	22	37	44	38	61	78	22
No telephone	24	24	24	18	34	44	14
Base: Households							
(weighted)	2694	1834	2851	1150	751	277	604
(unweighted)	2305	1189	1893	726	518	197	411

109

Table 44:   Amenities by tenure and ethnic group

Column percentages

	Owner	Council Tenant	Private Tenant	Housing Assn.
White Households:				
Lack exclusive use of bath, hot water, or inside WC	3	3	27	(8)
No garden	5	17	22	(21)
No central heating	32	54	83	(27)
Asian and West Indian Households:				
Lack exclusive use of bath, hot water, or inside WC	4	5	32	3
No garden	10	54	30	34
No central heating	42	35	59	53

Table 45: Housing and neighbourhood satisfaction by ethnic group

Column percentages

	White	West Indian	Asian	Indian	Paki-stani	Bangla-deshi	African Asian
Satisfaction with house or flat							
Very satisfied	56	30	41	41	40	26	45
Just satisfied	33	47	46	49	47	43	43
Just dis-satisfied	5	11	6	6	7	9	5
Very dis-satisfied	5	12	6	4	5	18	6
Satisfaction with neighbourhood							
Very satisfied	58	34	48	49	49	41	48
Just satisfied	31	52	44	44	45	48	43
Just dis-satisfied	6	7	3	3	2	4	3
Very dis-satisfied	4	6	3	3	3	4	5
Base: Adults							
(weighted)	5375	3465	6894	2672	1840	617	1634
(unweighted)	2265	1678	3323	1241	935	336	743

Table 46: Housing satisfaction by tenure

Column percentages

	Owner	Council Tenant	Private Tenant	Housing Assn.
White Adults				
Very satisfied	64	47	34	(62)
Just satisfied	30	37	44	(32)
Just dissatisfied	4	8	7	(5)
Very dissatisfied	1	9	15	(1)
Asian and West Indian Adults				
Very satisfied	44	23	24	25
Just satisfied	48	43	51	51
Just dissatisfied	5	14	10	13
Very dissatisfied	3	20	15	9

Housing conditions of white, West Indian and Asian households in the inner cities and elsewhere

Row percentages

	Per cent in flats	Per cent in detached or semi-detached houses	Per cent in dwellings built before 1945	Per cent lacking exclusive use of bath, hot water or inside WC	Per cent with over 1 person per room
Inner London, Inner Birmingham, Inner Manchester					
White	55	7	73	20	1
West Indian	39	11	57	4	17
Asian	34	13	63	11	44
Rest of London, West Midlands Metropolitan County and Greater Manchester					
White	18	53	63	5	4
West Indian	31	25	69	4	16
Asian	15	31	78	7	35
Rest of the Country					
White	11	58	46	4	3
West Indian	15	33	60	8	14
Asian	5	29	74	5	30

Table 48:   Housing and neighbourhood satisfaction in the inner cities and elsewhere

Row percentages

	Per cent dissatisified with their housing	Per cent dissatisfied with their neighbourhood
Inner London, Inner Birmingham, Inner Manchester		
White	22	26
West Indian	27	16
Asian	19	8
Rest of London, West Midlands Metropolitan County and Greater Manchester		
White	10	14
West Indian	22	12
Asian	11	6
Rest of England and Wales		
White	9	8
West Indian	18	13
Asian	9	6

Table 49: Owner-occupiers: details of ownership

Column percentages

	White	West Indian	Asian
Freehold	89	88	87
Leasehold	11	12	13
Lease under 20 years	*	1	3
Owned Outright	46	22	27
Mortgaged	54	78	73
Single Owner	42	36	60
Joint Owners (married or cohabiting couple)	56	61	36
Joint Owners (other)	2	2	4
Base: All owner-occupiers			
(weighted)	1587	745	2065
(unweighted)	1373	532	1390

Table 50:   Owner-occupiers: sources of finance for purchase

Column percentages

	White	West Indian	Asian
Main source of Loan/ Mortgage:			
Building Society	77	65	68
Local Authority	12	28	17
Bank	4	1	12
Insurance or Finance Co.	3	2	1
Own Employer	1	1	*
Relatives or other individual	1	1	1
Main source of Deposit:			
No deposit - 100% loan/ mortgage	6	4	2
Sale of previous dwelling	39	12	12
Bank Loan	*	1	2
Savings	44	74	76
Relatives	2	4	13
Inheritance	1	-	1
Other	3	2	1
DK/No Answer	4	7	4
Base: All owner-occupiers with mortgage or loan			
(weighted)	850	576	1488
(unweighted)	838	399	964

Table 51: Owner-occupiers: applications for improvement grants

Column Percentages

	White	West Indian	Asian
Approached Council	22	35	28
Not Approached Council	78	63	71
Result of Approach:			
Received Grant	14	15	17
Application Turned Down	4	8	3
Did not Receive Grant, for Other Reason	4	11	7
Reason for Not Approaching Council:			
No need/Nothing needs fixing	37	19	35
Know not eligible	19	10	9
Difficulty with forms/dislike forms	1	2	3
Don't know about grants	7	12	15
Other	11	10	5
DK/No reason given	2	10	4
Base: All owner-occupiers			
(weighted)	1587	745	2065
(unweighted)	1373	532	1390

Table 52: Council tenants: details of allocation and whether on transfer list

Column percentages

	White	West Indian	Asian
Category of Original Allocation of Council Accommodation:			
Waiting List	50	52	38
Demolition/Clearance	15	11	18
Homeless	6	23	23
Medical or Social Services Advice	6	5	6
Other	10	1	3
Don't know/No answer	14	9	12
Whether now on Transfer Waiting List:			
Yes	10	25	24
Base: All Council Tenants			
(weighted)	776	844	544
(unweighted)	660	496	338

Table 53:   Households waiting for council accommodation

Column percentages

	White	West Indian	Asian
Council Tenant	29	46	19
Others not on Waiting List	69	50	76
On Waiting List	2	4	5
Base: All Households			
(weighted)	2694	1834	2851
(unweighted)	2305	1189	1893
Those on list:			
Joined List			
before 1977	(32)	(28)	23
1977-1978	(10)	(11)	16
1979-1980	(24)	(34)	23
1981	(18)	(17)	29
1982	(16)	(5)	7
Base: All on waiting list			
(weighted)	50	76	128

Table 54: Council tenants: type of property and density of occupation by ethnic group; various breakdowns

Percentages

	Per cent in flats			Per cent in detached or semi-detached houses			Per cent with over 1 person per room		
	White	West Indian	Asian	White	West Indian	Asian	White	West Indian	Asian
Whether first council dwelling									
First	38	68	61	37	8	10	6	19	40
Not first	25	48	50	39	12	20	5	22	48
Date of first allocation									
before 1975	23	49	52	40	15	24	6	28	45
1975-1979	34	71	67	33	8	8	4	16	42
1980 and after	48	68	45	30	1	10	3	10	40
Household type									
Pensioner only	38	(88)	(45)	31	(-)	(10)	1	(-)	(-)
Nuclear family	10	43	62	45	13	11	16	38	57
Lone parent	(20)	65	(21)	(38)	10	(34)	(4)	16	(34)
Lone adult	55	81	(68)	19	5	(-)	-	-	-
Area									
Inner London, Inner Birmingham, Inner Manchester	71		69	-		6	1		32
Rest of London, West Midlands Met. County & Greater Manchester	36		64	31		15	9		33
Rest of England and Wales	23		31	41		18	5		16

Note: The figures are the numbers in flats, detached or semi-detached houses, and with more than one person per room, expressed as percentages of council tenants in a given ethnic group in a

Table 55: Experience of racial discrimination by private landlords

Column percentages

Have you yourself ever been refused accommodation for reasons which you think were to do with race or colour?	West Indian	Asian
Yes	49	(39)
No	49	(55)
Don't know	3	(6)
Base: All adults not in council or owner-occupied property who have in the past applied to a white landlord		
(weighted)	101	75
(unweighted)	63	42

Table 56: Belief in private landlords' racial discrimination

Column percentages

Do you think there are private landlords in Britain who would refuse a person accommodation because of their race or colour?	White	West Indian	Asian
Yes	82	72	34
No	8	6	22
Don't know/Other	10	21	44
Base: All Adults			
(weighted)	5375	3465	6894
(unweighted)	2265	1678	3323

Table 57: Beliefs about treatment of ethnic minorities by building societies, banks, estate agents and council housing departments

Column percentages

Are people of Asian/West Indian origin treated the same, better or worse than white people by...	White	West Indian	Asian
Building Societies:			
Same	53	40	52
Better	2	*	4
Worse	9	14	7
DK	36	45	36
Banks:			
Same	67	48	68
Better	1	1	4
Worse	5	20	6
DK	26	3	23
Estate Agents:			
Same	52	31	48
Better	2	1	2
Worse	20	19	9
DK	26	50	42
Council Housing Depts.:			
Same	53	31	32
Better	15	2	1
Worse	13	34	22
DK	19	32	45
Base: Adults			
(weighted)	5375	1878	3486
(unweighted)	2265	913	1694

122

Table 58:   Individual tenure movements 1977-1982

Column percentages

| | West Indian | | Asian | | White | |
	Known new house-holds	Others	Known new house-holds	Others	known new house-holds	Others
Moved into owner-occupied dwelling from another tenure	21	3	56	5	35	4
...from council	10	1	8	1	17	1
...from private renting	10	2	40	3	15	2
Moved into council tenancy from another tenure	28	9	11	7	6	5
...from owner-occupation	17	1	6	2	3	1
...from private renting	10	7	3	5	2	3
Moved into housing association from another tenure	11	3	1	1	2	1
Moved into private renting from another tenure	7	2	1	1	14	2
Changed tenure at all	68	17	68	15	59	11
Base: All households where first informant was resident in UK in 1976 (weighted)	302	1515	387	2204	222	2472

Table 59: Change of tenure distribution among PSI survey informants 1977-1982

Column percentages

	West Indian		Asian		White	
	1977	1982	1977	1982	1977	1982
Owner-occupiers	42	41	71	72	57	59
Council tenants	37	46	14	19	28	30
Private tenants	14	6	13	5	12	9
Others	4	8	2	2	1	2

Note: 1977 percentages based on households already established in UK in 1977; 1982 percentages based on all households

Table 60: Comparison of tenure distribution found in 1977 National Dwelling and Housing Survey and 1982 PSI Survey

Column percentages

	West Indian		Asian		White	
	1977 NDHS	1982 PSI	1977 NDHS	1982 PSI	1977 NDHS	1982 PSI
Owner-occupiers	36	41	70	72	55	59
Council tenants	45	46	10	19	30	30
Private tenants	15	6	20	5	14	9
Others	4	8	*	2	1	1

Table 61: Comparison of tenure patterns from 1981 Census, 1981 Labour Force Survey (LFS) and 1982 PSI Survey

Column percentages

	White Households			West Indian Households			Asian Households		
	1981 Census	1981 LFS	1982 PSI	1981 Census	1981 LFS	1982 PSI	1981 Census	1981 LFS	1982 PSI
Owner-occupied	58	55	59	43	37	41	75	75	72
Rented from Council	29	32	30	45	46	46	14	14	19
Other tenants	13	13	11	12	16	14	11	11	8

Note: Ethnic origins defined as follows in Census and LFS:

Census:
White households — Head of household born in UK or Irish Republic
West Indian households — Head of household born in Caribbean New Commonwealth
Asian households — Head of household born in India, Pakistan, Bangladesh or East Africa.

Labour Force Survey:
Head of household self-assessed white
Head of household self-assessed West Indian or Guyanese
Head of household self-assessed Indian, Pakistani or Bangladeshi

125

Table 62:   Tenure: Comparison of 1974 PEP Survey and 1982 PSI Survey

Column percentages

| | Black Households in Areas included in 1974 PEP Survey | | | |
| | West Indian | | Asian | |
	1974	1982	1974	1982
Owner-Occupied	50	44	76	74
Rented From Council	26	44	4	18
Privately Rented	24	3	19	6
Housing Association		9		2

Table 63:   Owner-Occupiers; changes in borrowing pattern 1974-1982

Column percentages

| | West Indian | | Asian | |
	74	82	74	82
Main source of loan/mortgage:				
Building Society	51	61	43	63
Local Authority	39	32	33	21
Bank	2	2	15	13
Insurance Company	1	1	2	*
Private Source	6	1	6	1
Other	1	2	2	1

Note: 1982 figures based on 1974 survey areas.

Table 64: Comparison of housing conditions found in 1974 and 1982 surveys

Column percentages

	White		Asian and West Indian	
	74[2]	82	74	82[1]
Detached	21	18	1	3
Semi-detached	36	36	15	15
Terraced	30	31	66	59
Flat or 'Other'	12	15	15	22
Dwelling built...				
before 1914	24		46	
before 1919		24		35
before 1940	48		88	
before 1945		50		76
Dwelling shared with other household(s)	4	1	26	5
Lack exclusive use of bath, hot water or inside WC	18	5	37	7

Notes: (1) 1982 figures for Asian and West Indian sample based on 1974 survey areas.
(2) White figures for sharing and use of facilities based on 1971 census.

VI Language, Education and Qualifications

Fluency in English

In the 1974 PEP survey it was shown that for people of Asian origin a lack of fluency in English was, as well as being a disadvantage in itself, often a contributory factor to other aspects of racial disadvantage. In the 1982 survey, interviewers were asked to assess the level of fluency of informants during the interview, or, where the interview was mainly conducted in an Asian language (as was the case for 30 per cent of Asian men and 38 per cent of Asian women), to attempt an English conversation with the informant in order to judge their fluency. The overall results are shown in Table 65, from which it can be seen that fewer than half of the Asian adults speak English 'fluently', a third speak English only 'slightly' or 'not at all', and the fluency of women is less than the fluency of men. Forty-eight per cent of Asian women speak English 'slightly or not at all', compared with 21 per cent of Asian men.

The proportion lacking fluent English differs between the Asian ethnic groups as well as between men and women, as Table 66 shows. It is higher among Bangladeshis and Pakistanis than among Indians and African Asians, and is low among the small group of Sri Lankans. The position of Bangladeshi and Pakistani women is particularly serious: over two-thirds of them speak English 'slightly or not at all'.

The table also shows a comparison with 1974, for the areas included in that survey, and we can see that there has been a net improvement in the command of English among both men and women but that the improvement has not been great. The percentage speaking English 'slightly or not at all' has fallen from 30 to 23 among men, and from 52 to 50 among women.

Table 66 also shows how fluency in English is strongly related to age and to the concentration of black households among the local population. Less than a quarter of Asian adults aged under 35 speak English 'slightly or not at all', compared with over a half of Asians aged 55 or over. Also, the proportion of Asians with poor English fluency is twice as large in areas of high density of black residence as in areas of low density (37 per cent compared with 18 per cent). It is in the high density areas that the disadvantages of limited English can best be avoided through the reliance on employers, shops and other facilities where Asian languages are spoken; but this also serves to restrict the opportunity for contacts outside the Asian community and to discourage movement to other areas, thus perpetuating the limited command of English.

Among immigrants, fluency in English is not related in a straightforward way to length of residence in Britain. In Table 67 we can see that poor English is almost as common among Asian men who came here before 1962 as it is among those who came here in the last five years, and those who came between 1962 and 1966 are more likely to have poor English than those who came here between 1967 and 1976. For those who came to Britain after 1972, fluency is associated with length of stay. This pattern is partly the result of the different English skills the immigrants brought with them in the different phases of the migration; the African Asians who came in the late 60s and early 70s were already more fluent in English than the Indians and Pakistanis who preceded them. Overlaid on this is a modest tendency for English to improve with length of stay. Among women these factors produce a slightly different pattern: although those who came to Britain before 1962 more commonly have poor English than those who came between 1962 and 1976, there is a stonger relationship between length of stay and fluency. Under 50 per cent of Asian women who came to Britain in the 60s and 70s have poor English, compared with over 60 per cent of those who came after 1978. This analysis shows that the improvement in fluency on the part of those who have lived here since 1974 is greater than is suggested by the figures given in Table 66, because a fifth of the Asian informants included in the table came to Britain after this date and their English skills are presently less developed than those of earlier migrants. Nevertheless, among these earlier migrants over 20 per cent of the men and over 40 per cent of the women still speak English 'only slightly' or 'not at all'.

Lack of fluency in English and other disadvantages
Table 68 gives examples of how lack of English fluency is assoc-iated with disadvantage in housing and employment. The propor-tion of Asian households lacking exclusive use of basic amenities is twice as high for household heads with poor English as it is for those with fluent English. Among Asian men with poor English the unemployment rate is twice that among Asian men with fluent English, and among women this relationship is almost as strong. More details of the association between disadvantage in employ-ment and poor English are given later, in the chapter on employ-ment. Of course, these associations between poor fluency and

disadvantage are not necessarily direct causal relationships; degrees of disadvantage vary between ethnic groups for reasons which may be entirely independent of language problems, while command of English also varies between these groups, so that disadvantage appears to vary with fluency. However, in many cases a lack of English fluency does work directly to limit opportunities and therefore adds to the existing disadvantages in the job market and the housing market.

Given the large proportion of Asians with poor English and the clear association between poor English and poor jobs, it is interesting that relatively few report having difficulty obtaining work, or having difficulties at work, because of language problems (Table 69). Only eight per cent of those who have had or tried to get a job say they have experienced difficulties obtaining work as a result of language problems, and only three per cent of those working or seeking work say that language has caused difficulties at work (although these figures are about doubled in the case of Bangladeshis). Part of the explanation for this is likely to be that those with poor English avoid the discomfort and disadvantage caused by language problems by avoiding situations where English skills are important, often by seeking employment in workplaces where Asians are already established as part of the workforce, or by seeking employment where English skills are unnecessary. But it would be wrong to suggest that this is a strategy consciously adopted by individuals; it is more likely that Asians who do not speak English well have horizons of expectation that are limited by their traditional location (both social and geographical) in the labour market. This does mean that language difficulties are minimised, but it does not mean the employment position of Asians with poor English is unaffected: in avoiding employers who have not recruited Asian people, and employers that require English skills, Asians with poor English remain at the lower end of the job market and have little chance of moving up.

We asked all Asian adults whether they had attended any classes to improve their English, excluding any classes as part of their school curriculum. Ten per cent of men and women have attended such classes; the proportion who have done so is the same among young people (under 25) and older people (Tables 70 and 71). In most cases these people have attended classes at a local school or college, but a third of the women have been to classes organised by an ethnic minority organisation or received tuition in their own home. Those who have attended classes tend to be those with poorer English, although the proportion who have attended classes is larger among those who speak English 'slightly' than among those who speak no English. When we asked informants whether they would like the opportunity to improve their English skills, 24 per cent of men and 38 per cent of women said they would. This figure is higher for older people than younger people, and higher for women than men in both age groups; among the different ethnic groups it is highest for Bangladeshis and lowest for African Asians and Sri Lankans. Desire for English classes is therefore most common among the groups with poor English, as might be expected, and it displays a strong direct relationship with English fluency (Table 71). It is interesting to note, however, that the desire for the opportunity to improve English skills is less common among those who speak no English than among those who speak English 'slightly'. This is the same as the finding for past attendance of English classes, as mentioned above, and suggests that there is a group of Asian adults who speak very little English and see no need to learn more; this is likely to be made up largely of older people who live with their families in Asian communities, and who may have have little need of English for most of their daily lives.

Attitude towards retaining the mother-tongue

Although just over half of those who speak English 'slightly or not at all' say they would welcome the opportunity to improve their English, which must be interpreted as widespread recognition that poor English is a source of disadvantage, this has to be seen in the context of a real commitment by Asians to preserving their mother-tongue. In the attitudes section of the questionnaire we included two items to test the feelings of Asian people on this issue. Table 72 shows that there is an overwhelming majority in favour of the preservation of their languages in this country. Informants were asked whether they agreed or disagreed with each of two statements. The first statement was simply 'it is a good thing to be able to speak the language of your family's area of origin' (the term 'family's area of origin' was used throughout the interview to refer to the part of the Indian sub-continent that the family came from). Over 90 per cent of all Asian groups, male and female, say they agree with this. The second statement was 'children should be taught the language of their family's country of origin.' Almost the same proportions say they agree with this statement as with the other, although a larger proportion of them say they hold this view 'strongly'. It is very important to note that there is little difference between the young and old informants or between those having fluent English and poor English in their responses to these questions. Clearly, any attempt to tackle the lack of English fluency as a problem contributing to racial disadvantage has also to recognise the importance of the Asian languages in the lives of Asians in this country, and the very positive attitudes that Asian people of all ages have towards them.

131

Education

Age on completing education

Comparison of the length of time spent in full-time education and the qualifications obtained reveals large inequalities between white, West Indian and Asian people. The differences are by no means straightforward, because the pattern varies between age groups and between men and women. In general the differences are of a very similar character to those found in the 1974 PEP survey, although some of the gap between whites and blacks has closed.

Looking first at the age of completion of full-time education (Table 73) we see that over half of white men and women left school before they were 16, compared with a third of West Indian men and women. This is a reflection of the younger average age of the West Indians: many of the white informants had their schooling a long time ago, when the normal leaving age was lower than 16. We see that similar proportions of West Indian people and white people left full-time education aged 17 or over, though within this group a larger proportion of white people stayed on until they were 20 or older.

Within the Asian community in Britain there are substantial numbers of people who are very poorly educated and substantial numbers of people who are very well educated, and the gulf between these groups is far wider than within the more homogeneous populations of West Indian and white people. Fifteen per cent of Asian men left full-time education before they were 13 years old (this includes those who had no formal education), compared with two per cent of West Indian men and less than half a per cent of white men. However, the proportion who left school before the age of 16 is smaller than for white or West Indian men, and this is because a relatively large proportion continued their studies beyond the age of 16. Nearly a quarter of Asian men continued their education into their twenties, compared with seven per cent of white men and two per cent of West Indian men. This extraordinarily broad distribution of leaving ages is largely due to the great mixture of backgrounds from which the Asian informants come. Those educated in Britain have on average a higher leaving age than those who grew up overseas, but even among these older immigrants there is a very wide variety of backgrounds, in terms of the relative wealth or poverty of their families, the urban or rural setting of their original towns or villages, their religion, and their previous experiences of the upheaval of migration. There is also within the Asian population a far greater difference between the educational background of men and women than within the rest of the population. Among Asian women, as among Asian men, there is a polarisation between a highly educated group and a group with little formal education, but in the case of women those with little

132

education are much more numerous than those with a great deal. Thirty-two per cent of Asian women left school before they were 12, or had no schooling, compared with about two per cent of West Indian and white women. The reasons for the wide range of educational experience of Asian women are the same as for the men, but the gap between women and men is the result of the position of women in the different social structures in India, Pakistan and Bangladesh, and, to a lesser extent, in Britain.

Qualifications

There are further differences between ethnic groups in terms of the qualifications they possess, and these are considered for three age groups in Tables 74, 75 and 76. There is such a strong relationship between age and qualifications that comparisons must be made within age groups. To make the comparisons we show only the informant's highest qualification, and rather than trying to equate academic and vocational qualifications we show a separate hierarchy for each; if, for example, an informant has an apprenticeship and GCE 'O' levels, neither of these very different qualifications is judged as higher than the other. The details of the classification are given in Appendix I.

In each age group the pattern of ethnic variation is different for men and women. In general, Asian men tend to be as well qualified academically as white men, but less qualified vocationally, while West Indian men tend to be less qualified than white men both in academic and vocational terms. Asian and West Indian women tend to have lower academic qualifications than white women, and Asian women to have lower vocational qualifications than white women; in the younger age groups, equal proportions of West Indian and white women have vocational qualifications. It should be noted that nearly half of the West Indian women with qualifications classed as 'professional or clerical' in fact have nursing qualifications.

Qualifications of informants aged 45 and over (Table 74). This age group contains 48 per cent of white adults, 35 per cent of West Indian adults and 26 per cent of Asian adults. Over two-thirds of all three ethnic groups have no academic or vocational qualifications in this age group, but this proportion is higher for blacks than for whites. Looking first at the qualifications of men, we see that the Asians are as well qualified academically as the whites, but fewer have manual job qualifications. West Indian men have fewer academic qualifications and fewer vocational qualifications than white men.

Although the percentages of West Indian men and Asian men with any vocational qualifications are the same, West Indians mostly hold manual job qualifications, while Asians mostly hold professional or clerical qualifications. Turning to the women, we see that the academic qualifications of whites, West Indians and Asians are similar, but this is not the case for vocational qualifications: 20 per cent of white women have some kind of vocational qualification, compared with 11 per cent of West Indian women and three per cent of Asian women.

Qualification of informants aged 25-44 (Table 75). This age group contains 34 per cent of white adults, 36 per cent of West Indian adults, and 54 per cent of Asian adults. White men are slightly better qualified than Asian men in academic terms and much better qualified in vocational terms, and they are in both ways better qualified than West Indian men. Thus the ethnic differences are the same as in the older age group, although a larger proportion of the younger men have qualifications. The proportion of West Indian women with academic qualifications is similar to that of white women, although they tend to be lower qualifications for West Indian women; the proportions with vocational qualifications are almost identical. Fewer Asian women have any academic qualifications, but the proportion with A-levels or a degree is almost level with white women (11 per cent, 14 per cent and 6 per cent of Asian, white and West Indian women respectively); as in the case of older women, the proportion with any vocational qualification is much lower than for whites and West Indians.

Qualifications of informants aged 16-24 (Table 76). This age group contains 18 per cent of white adults, 29 per cent of West Indian adults and 20 per cent of Asian adults. These younger informants are perhaps of greatest interest in these comparisons because a large percentage of them will have had some or all of their education in Britain and will have entered the job market without work experience overseas, and so their position is indicative of the direction of change. We shall see later that they have a different pattern of employment and unemployment from older people. Although many more young people have qualifications than older people, the pattern of ethnic differences has some elements in common with that observed in the previous tables. In vocational terms, Asian men are not as well qualified as white men, but West Indian men are much closer to white men in this respect than in the older age groups: 15 per cent

134

of West Indians have an apprenticeship or City and Guilds qualification, compared with 17 per cent of whites. In fact, there are signs that young Asian men are also closing the gap: the proportion of white men with manual job qualifications in the 16-24 age group is smaller than in the 25-44 age group, while for Asians it is larger in the younger group (seven per cent among 16-24 year-olds, and four per cent among 25-44 year olds). In the 16-24 age group a greater proportion of Asian and West Indian men than of white men have qualifications beyond CSE (Asians 47 per cent, West Indians 38 per cent, whites 33 per cent), but among the West Indians relatively few go beyond 'O' level.

The vocational qualifications of young women follow a similar pattern of ethnic differences as in the 25-44 year-old group: over 25 per cent of white and West Indian women have vocational qualifications compared to only eight per cent of Asian women. The proportions of young West Indian women and young white women with any academic qualifications are the same, but the level of the West Indians' qualifications tends to be lower (53 per cent of whites with 'O' levels and above, compared with 41 per cent of West Indians); fewer Asian women in this age group have academic qualifications, although almost as many have 'A' levels or above as white women. In fact, these figures hide a very big difference between Asian women in their teens and in their twenties: seventy per cent of Asian women aged 16-19 in our survey have academic qualifications, compared with only 42 per cent of those aged 20-24, and this difference comes mainly from the larger proportion with 'O' levels: this indicates that the trend is towards a reduction of the difference between young Asian women and other young women.

Among Asians, the level of academic and vocational qualifications is related very strongly to the informant's fluency in English, as we might expect. Table 77 shows the different distributions of qualifications for men with different levels of fluency. Nearly two-thirds of those who are fluent in English have some qualification, while none of those without any English has any qualification. The pattern for women is very similar.

Present full-time and part-time study
Because there is a higher proportion of young adults among the black population than among the white population, the percentage of adults still in full-time education is bound to be higher for the Asian and West Indian samples. However, comparison of the proportions still at school or college within the younger age groups

135

shows that black men and women are more likely to extend their education beyond the minimum school-leaving age than white men and women. This is particularly true of Asian men and women, and West Indian women; West Indian men, on the other hand, are very similar to white men in the proportions in each group at school or college (Table 78). Some of the differences in the 16-19 category could be due to a larger proportion of black people in the lower ages within that category, but this cannot go very far to explain them. One of the most interesting aspects of the greater likelihood of young blacks to be found in full-time education is that it is the case for Asian women almost as much as for Asian men, and this is in dramatic contrast to the finding that a large proportion of young Asian women have no academic or vocational qualifications; this is further evidence that there is a trend towards a larger proportion of Asian women becoming academically qualified.

We also asked informants whether they were studying part-time for any qualifications. It is notable that West Indian women are involved in part-time study to a greater extent than Asian and white women. In addition to those in full-time education, nine per cent of West Indian women are studying part-time, compared with two per cent of Asian women and white women. The spread of qualifications pursued by West Indian women is very broad: 18 per cent of them are studying for 'O' levels, 25 per cent for clerical or commercial qualifications, ten per cent for a degree, ten per cent for City and Guilds exams, and six per cent for nursing exams.

Table 65: Fluency in English

	All Asians	Men	Women
Informant speaks English....			
Fluently	41	48	32
Fairly Well	23	27	18
Slightly	21	17	27
Not at all	11	4	20
Not recorded	4	4	4
Base: Asian Adults			
(weighted)	6894	3870	3013
(unweighted)	3323	1836	1484

Table 66:   Per cent of Asian adults speaking English 'slightly' or 'not at all'

Bangladeshi women	76
Pakistani women	70
Bangladeshi men	50
Indian women	42
Pakistani men	27
African Asian women	23
Indian men	15
African Asian men	13
Sri Lankan women	(4)
Sri Lankan men	(-)
All men, 1974 survey	30
All men, 1982 survey (1974 survey areas)	23
All women, 1974 survey	59
All women, 1982 survey (1974 survey areas)	52
Age Group:	
16-24	19
25-34	26
35-44	36
45-54	42
55-64	53
65 and over	59
Concentration of Asian and West Indian Households in ED:	
Up to 4%	18
4%-12%	32
12%-30%	39
Over 30%	37

Table 67: Fluency in English by date of arrival in Britain

Per cent speaking English 'slightly' or 'not at all'

	Asian Men	Asian Women
Born in UK	-	(1)
Arrived in UK:		
before 1962	29	50
1962-1966	23	42
1967-1971	14	43
1972-1976	16	48
1977-1978	30	59
1979-1980	32	64
1981-1982	(34)	(75)

Table 68: Housing deprivation and unemployment rate by fluency in English

Percentages

	Per cent of households lacking exclusive use of bath, hot water, and inside WC	Male unemployment rate	Female unemployment rate
Informant speaks English...			
Fluently	4	16	15
Fairly well	8	20	25
Slightly or not at all	10	31	25

<u>Table 69:</u>   <u>Language problems and work</u>

	All Asian	Indian	Paki- stani	Bangla- deshi	African Asian
Had difficulty obtaining a job because of language (Base = all who have worked or tried to obtain job)	8	8	7	15	6
Had difficulty at work because of language (Base = all working or seeking work)	3	3	4	9	3

Table 70: Past attendance at English classes, and desire for opportunity to improve English

Column percentages

	All Asian	Men	Women	Indian	Paki-stani	Bangla-deshi	African Asian
Attended English Classes (not as part of school curriculum)	10	10	11	10	13	12	8
Would like more opportunity to improve English language skills	30	24	38	30	32	46	25
Base: Asian Adults (weighted) (unweighted)	6894 3323	3870 1836	3013 1484	2672 1241	1840 935	617 336	1634 743

Asian adults: attendance at English classes, and desire of opportunity to improve English, by age and English fluency

Row percentages

	Attended English Classes	Would like more opportunity to improve English
Aged under 25:		
Men	11	21
Women	10	32
Aged 25 and over:		
Men	10	25
Women	11	39
Speaks English:		
Fluently	7	14
Fairly Well	12	32
Slightly	16	55
Not at all	8	42

Table 72:   Attitudes towards mother-tongue

Column Percentages

	All Asian	Indian	Paki-stani	Bangla-deshi	African Asian
'It is a good thing to be able to speak the language of your family's area or origin'					
Agree strongly	46	42	49	43	59
Agree	49	51	47	51	47
Neither agree nor Disagree	2	4	1	1	1
Disagree	2	2	1	3	1
Disagree strongly	1	1	*	1	-
'Children should be taught the language of the family's area of origin'					
Agree strongly	55	48	62	51	60
Agree	39	43	34	39	37
Neither agree or Disagree	3	4	2	5	1
Disagree	2	3	1	4	1
Disagree strongly	1	1	-	1	1
Base: Asian Adults					
(weighted)	3471	1349	940	313	894
(unweighted)	1688	633	476	173	372

143

Table 73:   Age on completing full-time education

	Men			Women		
	White	West Indian	Asian	White	West Indian	Asian
Under 10	–	1	10	*	1	22
10-12	*	1	5	1	1	10
13-15	56	34	16	56	31	16
16	23	39	18	19	35	15
17-19	10	14	20	16	22	19
20 and over	7	2	23	5	3	12
Still in full-time education	3	6	6	2	7	5
DK/No Answer	*	3	2	*	2	2
Base: Adults						
(weighted)	2567	1630	3870	2802	1790	3013
(unweighted)	1001	781	1836	1262	876	1484

144

Table 74: Informants aged over 44: highest academic and vocational qualifications

Column percentages

| | Men | | | Women | | |
	White	West Indian	Asian	White	West Indian	Asian
Highest Academic Qualification:						
Degree or Higher Degree	2	-	3	2	1	1
GCE 'A' Level, HND/C, or above (no degree)	6	2	5	3	2	4
GCE 'O' Level, ONCD	8	3	11	6	4	8
CSE and other academic qualifications below 'O' level	-	3	4	*	4	1
No academic qual., but vocational or professional qual.	18	6	3	13	6	1
Highest Vocational Qualification:						
Professional or Clerical Qualification	9	2	6	17	8	3
Apprenticeship	17	6	2	2	1	-
City and Guilds	3	1	1	1	2	-
No vocational qual., but academic qual.	8	4	18	5	5	11
None of these quals.	64	87	74	75	84	86
Age of completing full-time education:						
under 13	1	4	31	1	7	54
17 and over	9	8	41	14	14	15
Base: All Adults						
(weighted)	1157	678	1212	1414	507	571
(unweighted)	487	335	529	624	252	237

Table 75:

Informants aged 25-44: highest academic and vocational qualifications

Column percentages

	Men			Women		
	White	West Indian	Asian	White	West Indian	Asian
Highest Academic Qualification:						
Degree or Higher Degree	10	3	6	4	1	4
GCE 'A' Level, HND/C, or above (no degree)	12	5	11	10	5	7
GCE 'O' Level, ONCD	18	13	15	21	18	12
CSE	4	8	7	5	12	6
No academic qual., but vocational or professional qual.	15	6	5	10	10	1
Highest Vocational Qualification:						
Professional or Clerical Qualification	18	4	9	26	28	6
Apprenticeship	20	11	2	2	*	-
City and Guilds	7	7	2	2	1	*
No vocational qual., but academic qual.	18	14	31	21	17	23
None of these quals.	38	64	56	50	54	71
Age on completing full-time education:						
Under 13	-	2	10	*	1	32
17 and over	29	22	50	27	29	36
Base: All Adults						
(weighted)	901	461	1933	886	755	1739
(unweighted)	379	251	1029	479	390	925

Table 76: Informants aged 16-24: highest academic and vocational qualifications

Column percentages

	Men			Women		
	White	West Indian	Asian	White	West Indian	Asian
Highest Academic Qualification:						
Degree or Higher Degree	4	*	5	1	-	1
GCE 'A' Level, HND/C, or above (no degree)	8	6	14	10	5	8
GCE 'O' Level, ONCD	21	32	28	42	36	28
CSE and other academic qualifications below 'O' level	34	24	18	22	36	14
No academic qual., but vocational or professional qual.	5	3	1	1	2	*
Highest Vocational Qualification:						
Professional or Clerical Qualification	5	3	3	19	22	7
Apprenticeship	9	7	4	2	-	1
City and Guilds	8	8	3	5	5	-
No vocational qual., but academic qual.	50	48	56	53	52	43
None of these quals.	27	35	35	22	21	50
Age on completing full-time education:						
Under 13	-	-	2	-	-	15
17 and over	29	41	58	47	51	50
Base: All Adults						
(weighted)	483	476	718	470	495	684
(unweighted)	123	185	272	146	219	311

147

Table 77: Asian Men: highest academic and vocational qualifications by fluency in English

Column percentages

		Informant speaks English:		
	Fluently	Fairly Well	Slightly	Not at All
Highest Academic Qualification:				
Degree or Higher Degree	10	1	–	–
GCE 'A' Level, HND/C, or above (no degree)	16	7	1	–
GCE 'O' Level, ONCD	22	13	8	–
CSE	11	8	2	–
Highest Vocational Qualification:				
Professional or Clerical Qualifications	14	1	*	–
Apprenticeship	4	1	1	–
City and Guilds	3	1	–	–
No qualifications	37	69	88	100
Base: Asian men				
(weighted)	1858	1055	646	159
(unweighted)	816	539	325	78

Table 78:   Present study by ethnic group

Column percentages

| | Men | | | Women | | |
	White	West Indian	Asian	White	West Indian	Asian
Full-Time Study:						
Aged 16-19	(25)	26	58	(24)	37	51
Aged 20-24	6	7	13	–	5	6
Aged 25-34	1	3	2	–	4	–
All ages	3	6	6	2	7	5
Part-Time Study for Examinations:						
All ages	6	6	4	2	9	2
Base: Adults						
(weighted)	2567	1630	3870	2802	1790	3013
(unweighted)	1001	781	1836	1262	876	1484

VII Employment

Economic activity

Comparisons of economic activity rates show up large differences between white people and black people, and between different groups of black people. Over 85 per cent of West Indian and Asian men are working or seeking work, compared to 80 per cent of white men (Table 79). The difference is due to the larger proportion of retired men among whites, although this is partially balanced by the group of men still in full-time education, which is larger among blacks than among whites. Although the rates of economic activity differ, the proportions of black and white men actually in work are fairly similar: 67 per cent of white men are in work, compared with 64 per cent of West Indians and 68 per cent of Asians. This is because of the wide differences in rates of unemployment, which are discussed in a later section.

While the overall economic activity rate of West Indian women is much higher than that of white women, this is partly the product of the different age distributions, (Tables 80 and 81). For those aged 16-19, the activity rate of West Indian women is lower than that of white women, and for the 20-24 age group it is only a little higher. For women aged 25 or over, the activity rate is much higher for West Indians than for whites. The pattern is different for Asian women. Overall, they are less likely to be found in the labour market than white women, but this comparison hides a big difference between Muslim women and other Asian women: only 18 per cent of Muslim women are working or unemployed, compared with 57 per cent of other Asian women. In most age groups, however, the activity rates of the non-Muslim Asian women are to varying degrees lower than those of white and West Indian women. The exception is in the 25-34 age group, in which 60 per cent of these Asian women are in the labour market, compared with 54 per cent of white women.

It should be noted that these are comparisons of the proportions of women unemployed or working, whether full-time or part-time. The ratio of full-time to part-time workers is very different for the three ethnic groups: 44 per cent of white women employees are part-time workers, compared with 29 per cent and 16 per cent for West Indian and Asian women respectively. This means that the difference between the positions of white and West Indian women in the labour market is even greater than that shown by the comparison of overall activity rates; it also means that non-Muslim Asian women are, in terms of full-time work, more active than white women.

Economic activity among Asian women is related very strongly to fluency in English. Fifty six per cent of those who speak English fluently are in the labour market, compared with 29 per cent of those who speak English only slightly, and eight per cent of those who speak no English (Table 82).

A small proportion of informants (up to two per cent) in each ethnic group report that they are participating in one of the schemes run by the Manpower Services Commission to provide training and work experience. At the time of the survey, the schemes in operation were the Training Opportunities Scheme (TOPS), the Youth Opportunities Programme (YOP) and the Community Enterprise Programme (CEP).

Unemployment
Unemployment rates
The present survey was carried out in the first half of 1982 at the end of a steep and sustained rise in the overall level of unemployment to about 3 million nationally, or 13 per cent of the working population, and overall unemployment has since remained at about the same very high level. In accordance with a general relationship established from previous research, the survey shows that the rate of unemployment among black people at this time of very high general unemployment is much higher than among white people: about twice as high among West Indians and about one-and-a-half times as high among Asians. The survey allows us to analyse the factors underlying this abnormally high level of unemployment in greater detail than has been possible before. First, it provides accurate data for men and women in particular minority groups. Secondly it provides a basis for controlled comparisons of unemployment rates between blacks and whites in the same age, sex and occupational groups. Thirdly, it allows us to address the question whether the high rate of unemployment among blacks is closely associated with the areas where they live and shared by that atypical part of the white population that lives in the same or similar areas.

Table 83 shows the registered unemployment rates among different ethnic groups. Among men in the PSI survey, the unemployment rates are 13 per cent for whites, 25 per cent for West Indians and 20 per cent for Asians. The overall Asian figure

151

hides important differences between the different Asian groups, however. The unemployment rate for Muslim men (a large proportion of whom are Pakistani or Bangladeshi) is 27 per cent, while for Hindu and Sikh men (most of whom are Indian or African Asian) the rate is half that, and is the same as for white men. For women there is also a large gap between the whites and blacks: Asian women have an unemployment rate twice as high as white women, and West Indian women have a rate one-and-a-half times that of white women. Although there are variations between the different Asian groups of a similar character to those among Asian men, none of them has a female unemployment rate lower than 18 per cent.

Despite the fact that unemployment rates within particular Asian ethnic groups are generally higher for women than for men, the overall rates for Asian men and women are both 20 per cent. This is because the rate is high among Pakistanis and Bangladeshis, who form a higher proportion of Asian men than of Asian women in the labour market. This tendency, among Asians, for women to be more vulnerable to unemployment than men, is not common to the other ethnic groups. Asian women work more commonly than white or West Indian women in jobs and industries that have suffered most in the recession: as we shall see later, they are often employed in manual jobs, in the private sector, in industrial manufacture and, in particular, in the textile and clothing industry, and this employment pattern has made Asian women particularly vulnerable to unemployment.

Within the population generally, different age groups suffer different rates of unemployment, with young people and older people having higher rates than people in the middle age ranges. In no age group, either for men or women, do the levels of Asian or West Indian unemployment fall below the white level, and the rates only come close for black and white men aged 25-34, and for West Indian and white women aged 35-44 (Table 84).

Table 85 shows regional unemployment rates, found within the survey; with one exception, the differences in rates of unemployment between whites, West Indians and Asians are not reduced when comparisons are made within regions. The exception is the Asian unemployment rate in the 'other regions', which is the same as the white rate. Only five per cent of the Asian population live in these areas - the North, East Anglia, Wales and the South West - but nearly all are concentrated in the South West, and in fact for this region on its own the Asian unemployment rate is higher than the white rate (17 per cent compared with 12 per cent). Overall, the regional distribution of black people tends to deflate their national unemployment rate rather than inflate it: if Asians and West Indians had the same regional distribution as whites then their unemployment rates would be even higher than they are already.

Given the very clustered residential patterns found among black people, it may be that within a region, or within a town, Asians and West Indians are to be found in areas of worst job shortage. To see to what extent this is the case, we have produced unemployment rates for the inner areas of the three main conurbations (London, Birmingham and Manchester), their outer areas and the rest of the country, and for areas with high and low concentrations of black households in the local population. The results are shown in Tables 86 and 87.

Over 40 per cent of West Indians and over 20 per cent of Asians live in the inner areas, compared with six per cent of whites. In these areas of generally high male unemployment the gap between black and white men is much reduced, although a distinct difference remains. Thirty per cent of black people live in the outer conurbation areas; here the general level of unemployment is much lower, and the rate is twice as high among black men as among white men. In the rest of the country the gap between the unemployment rates of black and white men is also wide. In the case of women the general unemployment rate varies in quite a different way between the three types of area, but the important point is that there is a large difference between the rates for black and white women within each group of areas. This analysis shows that the high rates of unemployment among black people are only partially associated with the residence of a relatively large proportion of black people in the inner-conurbation areas.

When the analysis is carried out at the micro level of the Census enumeration district (ED), a different pattern emerges. More than three-quarters of the black population live in EDs with a density of black households of more than four per cent, whereas only a tenth of the white population lives in these areas. In the case of men there is little difference between the unemployment rates for West Indians and whites, and the rate for Asians is the same as for whites. In the case of women, the gap remains but the sample size for white women here is rather small. In the areas of low black residential density there is still a strong contrast between the rates for white and black women, and for West Indian and white men, although the rate is the same for Asian and white men. However, a majority of black people live in the EDs of higher black residential density and the analysis does show that if these black people are compared with the small section of the white population who live close to them then the difference in the rate of male unemployment almost disappears.

Care is needed when interpreting these links between geography and unemployment, particulary at the ED level. The similarity between black and white unemployment rates in small areas is not necessarily the result of both groups suffering the effects of the same restricted local job markets. Enumeration

153

districts in residential areas are only a few hundred yards across - they each contain about 165 households - and it may be that the white people living in the EDs of relatively high black density are themselves economically disadvantaged: if this were the case it would be possible for such an ED to exist within an area with a relatively buoyant labour market. In other words, the parity of unemployment rates in these small areas could be due to blacks living among poor whites or it could be due to blacks and whites sharing a depressed local labour market. In fact, there is likely to be truth in both of these explanations, but it is difficult to disentangle their effects. It is certainly not the case that ethnic differences in unemployment rates can be explained away by ethnic differences of residential patterns, for many of the 'high unemployment EDs' are within travel-to-work distance of lower unemployment areas. The geographical distribution of black people is only one of a number of different factors that lead to their unemployment rates being higher than that of whites.

As we shall see later in this chapter, black workers have substantially lower job levels than white workers. Because workers with lower job levels are more vulnerable than others to unemployment, the gap between black and white unemployment rates is related to this occupational inequality. For men, the relationship between job level and unemployment is quite strong: among white men, for example, 52 per cent of the unemployed who had a job prior to registering were in semi-skilled or unskilled manual work, compared with only 14 per cent of those presently in work; the corresponding figures are 50 per cent and 33 per cent for West Indians, and 61 per cent and 33 per cent for Asians. Using information given by unemployed informants about their previous jobs, we can estimate what the white unemployment rate would be if white workers had the same job levels as black workers. The white unemployment rate for men would be about 17 per cent if job levels were generally the same as among Asians, and 19 per cent if job levels were generally the same as among West Indians(1). These hypothetical rates are not as high as the actual rates found among Asians and West Indians (20 per cent and 25 per cent respectively), but they are much higher than the actual rate among whites (13 per cent); this demonstrates that differences of job levels are partly responsible for the faster growth of unemployment among black men than among white men. The same is true for women, although in their case the relationship between unemployment and job level appears to be weaker and therefore explains less of the gap between black and white unemployment rates.

Over and above the effect of actual job levels, the industrial distribution of black workers has been only a limited factor in the disporportionate growth of their unemployment rate. Asians, however, have been badly affected by unemployment in the textile

154

and clothing industries, where a relatively large proportion have in the past found work: over a third of unemployed Asians' previous jobs were in these industries.

The rate of unemployment among Asians is strongly related to fluency in English. The rates for men and women who are fluent in English are 16 per cent and 15 per cent, but are 31 per cent and 25 per cent respectively among those who speak English slightly or not at all (Table 68 in the previous chapter).

Length of unemployment

The higher rates of unemployment among Asian and West Indian people are associated with longer durations of unemployment. From Table 88 it can be calculated that over half of the black unemployed men have been registered for over a year, compared with a third of white unemployed men. The proportion of black unemployed women who are long-term unemployed is over double that of white women.

Unregistered unemployment

Up to now we have only considered as unemployed the informants who have registered as unemployed with an employment office, job centre or careers office(2). However, there is a further proportion of the adult population who are seeking a job but for one reason or another are not registered. Table 89 shows the different proportions of people in this category. Contrary to frequent claims, unregistered unemployment is not more common among black people than among white people. Overall the figures for men are small in comparison with the registered unemployed figures; the simplest way to state them is to say that the proportions of white, West Indian and Asian men seeking work who are not registered are 16 per cent, three per cent and three per cent. Closer investigation reveals that almost all of the difference between white and black men in this respect is due to white full-time students who report that they are seeking work; these figures do not therefore indicate a higher level of the unregistered unemployment among white men. For women, these figures are much higher, at 31 per cent, 27 per cent and 22 per cent respectively. The unregistered unemployed group corresponds very closely in size with the unclassified ('other') group in the tables of economic activity, Tables 79 and 80, and further investigation confirms that they are largely the same group. As a proportion of all informants, rather than as a proportion of all seeking work, the unregistered unemployed are most common among West Indian women: four per cent of them are in this category, compared to two per cent of other women and men. We find that nearly half of these West Indian women are lone parents. A fifth give reasons for not signing on that are associated with children and looking after the house,

155

compared with a negligible proportion of unregistered white women.

For white, Asian and West Indian people aged under 25 the level of unregistered unemployment appears from the table to be higher than for older people, but after allowing for the number of people seeking work while finishing courses of full-time education, the unregistered unemployed are no more common as a proportion of the total seeking work in this age group than in other age groups.

Reasons for leaving last job

The formal terms of severance from previous employment are shown in Table 90 for all those seeking work. The reasons given by black and white men follow a common pattern; over 40 per cent were made redundant, and the next most common reasons were, jointly, 'leaving for own reason' and 'never had a job'. The proportion of Asians who were dismissed is half that for whites and West Indians, but the proportion of Asians who left of their own accord is correspondingly larger: it is likely that the latter group includes a number of men who had to vacate their jobs in order to make a visit to their country of origin, because extended leave was not available for this purpose. Two-thirds of Asian unemployed men who left jobs of their own accord have made visits to their country of origin in the past five years, compared with about half of Asian men in total. The patterns for women are very different: a large group of Asian and West Indian women have never had a job, but this is seldom the case for white unemployed women. White women are on average older than black women, and therefore fewer of them will be new to the labour market, but, even so, the scale of the difference suggests that black women in the labour market are frequently failing to obtain any work at all; the much higher level of long-term unemployment among blacks supports this theory.

In 1979 PSI carried out a survey of the registered unemployed from ethnic minority groups, and the informants were also asked about the formal terms on which they left their last job. The results obtained then were rather different to those obtained in 1982. The main change has been the growth in the proportion of redundancies among men of all ethnic origins; also, in the 1979 survey it was found that a substantially larger proportion of black men than white men had been dismissed from their previous job (and this was particularly the case for West Indian men), and this is not the case for the 1982 survey. For women, the number with redundancies has also risen - particularly for Asians: over 40 per cent of the unemployed who had a previous job were made redundant, while the corresponding figures for whites and West Indians are 26 per cent and 24 per cent.

156

Current occupations
Job levels
As well as differences in rates of unemployment, there are among those in work large differences between the jobs done by white people and people of Asian and West Indian origin. This can be seen immediately from a comparison of the socio-economic group (SEG) classification of the jobs of black and white employees (Tables 91 and 92): overall the job levels of whites are much higher than those of Asians and West Indians, but there is considerable variation between men and women, and between the different sections of the black population.

Looking first at men, we see that the proportion who are manual workers is larger for West Indians and Asians than for whites: 83 per cent of West Indian men and 73 per cent of Asian men, compared with 58 per cent of white men. Also, more of the blacks are doing unskilled and semi-skilled manual work than the whites, and this feature is more prominent within the Asian distribution. The proportion in the top SEG category in the table (employers, managers and professional workers) is 19 per cent for whites, 13 per cent for Asians and only five per cent for West Indians. The proportion of whites in 'other non-manual' jobs is double that for Asians and West Indians. There is variation between the different Asian groups: job levels are much higher for African Asians than for others, and in fact African Asians have a greater proportion in the top SEG category than whites; nearly 70 per cent of the Bangladeshi employees are semi-skilled or unskilled manual workers, compared with just over 40 per cent of Indian and Pakistani employees and 25 per cent of African Asian employees. Comparisons of the religious groups show that Hindus have overall much higher job levels than Muslims or Sikhs, and that among Sikhs there is a large proportion in skilled manual work.

It should be noted that although the Pakistani and Bangladeshi groups have, overall, the lowest job levels, their SEG profiles are quite distinct from each other. Pakistanis and Bangladeshis are often treated as a single ethnic group in survey analysis, and this practice hides different aspects of disadvantage which are observable for each group when they are separated. For example, the number of Pakistani men who are self-employed is much lower than for the Bangladeshis and other Asians but, as can be seen from this table, the proportion of semi-skilled and unskilled workers is very high among the Bangladeshis.

In the case of women, there is a very different overall pattern, with smaller proportions in professional and managerial jobs and in the skilled manual category; at the same time there is much less contrast between blacks and whites. There is a greater proportion of non-manual workers among whites, but the percentage of Asians in professional and managerial jobs is almost as high

157

as that of whites; the percentage of 'other non-manual' workers among West Indians is as high as among whites, with the Asian figure somewhat lower. And although the semi-skilled account for a larger section of the manual workforce among blacks than among whites, there is a higher percentage of unskilled workers among the whites; this is largely because of the higher proportion of white women in part-time employment.

We saw in the previous chapter that black people tend to have fewer formal qualifications than white people, and we might therefore expect this fact to explain their lower job levels. Table 93 shows that this is only true to a limited extent: analysis of job levels of people grouped according to educational qualifications changes the pattern but does not remove the Asians and West Indians from their position of overall disadvantage. Generally speaking, the disparity between black and white job levels is less among men and women with qualifications than among those without. In the group with qualifications of A-level standard or above, we see that white men have distinctly better jobs than Asians. Seven per cent of the Asians in this group have semi-skilled or unskilled manual jobs, compared with only two per cent of whites; 84 per cent of whites have non-manual jobs, while the figure for Asians is 75 per cent. It is not possible to make a reliable comparison of white and West Indian men in this category because the numbers for the latter are small, but the SEG distribution of the highly qualified West Indians in our sample is the same as that of the highly qualified whites. For those with O-levels there is a much larger gap between the black and white men. Among men without any qualifications at all (over a third of white men of working age, and over a half of black men) the proportions of whites who are non-manual workers is four times that of West Indians, and almost twice that of Asians.

Among women also we see that the disadvantage of Asians and West Indians is not removed by comparing informants in the same qualification groups, except in the case of West Indians with an academic qualification; in fact West Indian women with O-levels have a slightly higher overall job level than whites. This is a very interesting finding, but it should be remembered that the majority of black and white women with jobs have no academic qualifications, and it is in this group that the extent of racial inequality in terms of job level is greatest.

Among both men and women in the Asian sample there is a strong relationship between fluency in English and job level. As we have seen, English language ability is closely associated with educational attainment, so to some extent we are observing the same relationship with job level, but in fact job level is more closely linked with English fluency than with education level. Table 94 shows that 21 per cent of men fluent in English are in semi-skilled and unskilled manual jobs, compared with 70 per cent of men who speak English slightly or not at all; the corresponding figures for women are 24 per cent and 87 per cent.

To remove entirely the effect of poor English fluency on job levels we show in Table 93 the proportions of semi-skilled/unskilled workers and non-manual workers among Asian employees who are fluent in English. There is a closer resemblance between the Asian and white jobs in this comparison than in the overall comparison, but differences persist: Asian men with academic qualifications and Asian women without qualifications are found more frequently than their white counterparts in the lower manual jobs, and less frequently in non-manual jobs; and although the proportion of non-manual workers among Asian men without qualifications is a little higher than among white men without qualifications, there is a larger proportion with lower manual jobs among the Asians.

Supervisory responsibility

We have shown that job levels of Asian and West Indian workers are substantially lower than those of white workers, and it is therefore not surprising to find that white people more often have supervisory responsibilities than black people. But, as demonstrated by Table 95, even _within_ the SEG categories used for our analysis the black employees are less frequently than whites in supervisory posts. The largest difference exists for the 'skilled manual and foremen' group, in which 26 per cent of whites have people working under them, compared with only 17 per cent of Asians and West Indians. This suggests that the grouping of skilled workers with foremen into this single SEG category can be misleading, as the balance between the two is different for black and white workers; in fact further analysis shows that the balance between manual supervisors and skilled workers is about the same for West Indian men as for white men, but among Asian men there are proportionally fewer supervisors. Ten per cent of all white and West Indian male employees have jobs classed as supervisory manual, as opposed to four per cent of Asian male employees. Among women there are very few manual supervisors (one per cent) and this does not vary between whites, Asians and West Indians.

Less than one per cent of white employees have an immediate boss who is black, compared with five per cent of West Indians and 12 per cent of Asians; most of these Asians are supervised by other Asians, and most of these West Indians by other West Indians.

Industry sector and employer type

Tables 96 and 97 show the extent to which Asian and West Indian employees are found in different industries from white employees. Considering men first, we see that Asians, and particularly Pakistanis, are more often found in manufacturing industry than whites or West Indians, and that both Asians and West Indians are more often found in vehicle manufacturing than whites. Asians are also more commonly found in the textile, clothing and leather industries than whites or West Indians, and this is particularly the case for Pakistanis and Bangladeshis. Asians are less strongly represented in the construction industry than whites or West Indians. Although whites and West Indians have about the same proportion in the service industries, they are differently distributed within this sector: 24 per cent of West Indians work in transport or communications, compared with ten per cent of whites, while a greater proportion of whites than West Indians are in the 'other services' group, chiefly in financial services and in professional and scientific work. Within the service sector Indians are well represented in transport and communications, African Asians in the distributive trades, and Bangladeshis in the 'other services'. The proportion of men working in public administration is smaller among Asians and West Indians than among whites (three, two and seven per cent respectively).

The pattern is broadly similar for women. As in the case of men, West Indians and whites are divided between the manufacturing and service sector in a similar way, while Asians are more commonly found in the manufacturing sector than whites, especially in the textile and clothing industries. There is, however, a large variation in the proportions of the different groups within the 'professional and scientific' services, which accounts for 40 per cent of West Indian women, 25 per cent of white women, 19 per cent of Indian women and seven per cent of African Asian women: this reflects the relative size of the groups employed in the National Health Service.

To help further understand the different employment sectors occupied by the different ethnic groups we have classified employers according to a simple scheme which reflects whether a job is in the private or state sector, and which part of the state sector. The state sector is divided into three parts: the first covering local authorities (including education authorities) and health authorities, the second covering nationalised industries and state corporations and the third being the civil service. Table 97 shows that for men, the patterns are broadly similar, although there are more Asian men in the private sector than whites or West Indians, and the proportion of West Indians working for local authority bodies is larger than for Asians and whites. For women, the patterns for the three groups are very different: nearly half the West Indians work for local authority bodies, compared with 25 per cent of whites and 16 per cent of Asians, and this reflects again the large number of NHS employees among West Indian women. Seventy-five per cent of Asian women employees work in the private sector, compared to 64 per cent of white women and 43 per cent of West Indian women.

Job levels and industry sector in different areas of residence

Given the very different geographical distributions of black and white people in this country, it might be expected that residential location would help to explain the differences between the job levels of black and white workers and the industries in which they are found. In fact geographical distribution can only help explain differences of industrial sector, and then only to a limited extent; although there are some interesting geographical variations in job levels, they do not help to explain the overall differences between black and white workers.

Table 99 shows that within each region the differences in job levels between whites and blacks are largely preserved. In each area there is a smaller proportion of West Indian men than of white men in non-manual work, and a larger proportion in semi-skilled or unskilled manual work. The same is true for Asian women and Asian men, although in London the proportion of Asian men who are non-manual workers is almost the same as for whites (43 per cent compared with 46 per cent). The comparisons for West Indian women show a less consistent pattern: in the West Midlands and in the 'other regions' category the proportions of non-manual workers and lower manual workers are roughly the same as for whites, but in London the white women have substantially higher job levels than the West Indian women.

When the geographical focus is narrowed to the areas of different densities of black residence, most of the differences between blacks and white remain. In the EDs with relatively low densities of black residence, West Indian men and women have lower job levels than whites, but among Asian men and women the proportions in the non-manual and lower manual categories are rather similar to those among whites. In the EDs of relatively high density, where we find over three-quarters of the black population, but only a tenth of the white population, the job levels of blacks are lower than in the low-density areas, particularly among Asians. There are not enough white employees in our sample for us to say with confidence what their job levels are in these areas, but there is no evidence in the table to suggest that job levels in these areas are as low for whites as they are for blacks.

Table 100 shows a regional breakdown of the proportions of employees in selected industrial sectors. Comparisons in this table are confined to features that we identified earlier as ethnically characteristic: for example, we compare the proportions of white and Asian employees in the textile and clothing industry in different regions, to see whether it is the regional distribution of Asians that produces the relatively large proportion of these workers among Asians nationally. For each of the industrial categories in the analysis, the characteristic ethnic differences persist in nearly all of the regional comparisons, and we can

161

therefore conclude that the differences of industrial distribution are not merely a product of the different regional distribution. However, the table shows that in some respects the regional distributions do reinforce these ethnic differences: for example, the concentration of Asian workers in the East Midlands and in Yorkshire, where the textile and clothing industries are well represented, tends to add to the tendency for Asians to be found in these industries. The same is true for Asians and West Indians in the West Midlands (vehicle manufacture), and for West Indians in London (transport and communications). On the other hand, regional differences tend to dilute the contrast between blacks and whites in terms of job levels: in other words, if black people were distributed between regions in the same proportions as white people, then the difference in job levels between blacks and whites would be even greater than it actually is.

Job levels in different industry sectors
So far we have seen, in separate analyses, that the jobs of black and white employees differ both in terms of their SEG levels and in terms of the industrial sector in which they are found. However, the gap between the job levels of blacks and whites is not the same for each industrial sector; in other words, there is a further order of differences between the employment patterns of blacks and whites which is only revealed when we make a combined analysis of job level and industry sector. If we do this by comparing job-level distributions within different industry sectors, we see that the representation of black workers in non-manual jobs is very uneven. In some industries - notably in transport and communications and in the 'professional and scientific' sector - black employees have job levels that are much closer to those of whites than is the case generally, while in other industries - notably manufacturing industry - the gap between whites and blacks is much larger.

Table 101 shows the SEG distributions of men employed in the engineering industries, in other manufacturing industries, in transport and communications and in the rest of the service sector. In this table we also show separately the proportions in skilled manual and supervisory manual jobs. In the manufacturing industries the proportions of non-manual workers among West Indian and Asian men are much smaller than those among whites, and the proportions of black workers having lower manual jobs are much larger; West Indian men in these industries have the same proportion of skilled manual jobs as whites, but the proportion among Asians is smaller; the proportions of blacks with manual supervisory jobs is smaller than for whites, with the exception of West Indian men in manufacturing outside the engineering industries, among whom the proportion is almost the same as among whites.

162

In the transport and communications sector, the job levels of black and white men are much closer together. Although the proportion of lower manual jobs is a little larger among blacks than among whites, the size of the non-manual group among West Indians is relatively close to that among whites (11 per cent compared with 16 per cent) and among Asians it is larger (19 per cent); and an important feature of the West Indians' jobs in this sector is that the proportion of manual supervisors is a little higher than it is among whites. In the rest of the service sector, there is a close correspondence between the job levels of Asians and the job levels of whites (although again the lower non-manual jobs are more common among Asians) but West Indians have lower overall job levels: the whites and West Indians have the same proportions of lower non-manual, manual supervisory and skilled manual jobs, but the whites have a larger proportion of higher non-manual jobs and a smaller proportion of semi-skilled and unskilled manual jobs.

Table 102 shows the same comparison for women employed in manufacturing in the 'professional and scientific' sector, and in the rest of the service sector. In manufacturing the gap between whites and blacks is very large: the proportions in lower non-manual jobs are 38 per cent for whites, 66 per cent for West Indians and 82 per cent for Asians. In this sector only seven per cent of Asian women and 19 per cent of West Indian women have non-manual jobs, compared with 40 per cent of white women. The professional and scientific sector is quite different. Here the job levels of white and West Indian women are almost identical, with nearly 70 per cent in non-manual work; among the Asians over 80 per cent are in non-manual work. In the rest of the service sector the job levels of Asian women are, overall, rather higher than those of white women, but West Indian women have lower job levels than white women; the differences between white and Asian women in this sector are a product of the larger proportion of Asian women working in the distributive trades (90 per cent of women in the distributive trades have non-manual jobs, and, within the 'other services' category in the table, 55 per cent of Asian women, compared with 39 per cent of white women, have jobs in this area).

Table 103 compares the proportions of non-manual workers among blacks and whites in the private sector and the public sectors. Broadly speaking the findings show that blacks are on a more equal footing with whites within the public sector than within the private sector. Figures are given separately for local authorities (including health authorities), nationalised industries and for private firms. The numbers of black employees in the civil service in our survey are small, and this sector is therefore not shown in the table. The difference between the local authority sector and the private sector is considerable, particularly in the case of women: broadly speaking, the difference is like that found between

163

the manufacturing sector and the parts of the service sector in which black workers have higher job levels, although this is not the case for West Indian men. In the private sector there are much larger proportions of non-manual workers among white employees than among Asian and West Indian employees, and there are correspondingly smaller proportions of lower manual workers among whites. In the local authority sector, job levels are much closer together: among West Indian women and Asian men the figures come close to those of whites, and among Asian women the figures are better than among whites. For West Indian men in this sector, however, job levels are considerably lower than those of white men. In the nationalised industries and state corporations (for which we only give figures for men, because of the small numbers of women in our survey working for these employers) the pattern is different for Asians and West Indians: the proportion of non-manual workers among the Asians is as large as it is among whites, but there are proportionally more lower manual workers among the Asians; West Indians have generally lower job levels.

It is interesting to note that for Asian and West Indian men job levels are similar in private firms and in the nationalised industries, but for whites the proportion of non-manual workers is twice as high in private firms as in publicly-owned firms.

Our findings show that the British labour market has absorbed blacks in a very uneven way. For the most part, black workers have been taken into manual jobs, and unskilled manual jobs in particular. Only in specific areas of the service sector have blacks obtained non-manual jobs in the same proportions as whites. For West Indians, these are the employers that recruited blacks during the earlier periods of immigration, that is to say the health service and the transport services. It should be noted that even in these sectors the similarity between the SEG patterns of whites and West Indians may be partly an artifact of the way different jobs are classified: for example, the 'other non-manual' group among women in the 'professional and scientific' services (which covers the NHS) is made up of a combination of categories covering supervisory and junior administrative staff and nursing staff, and therefore hides any differences between the proportions in nursing jobs and in junior and middle-range administrative jobs (in our survey over 25 per cent of the 'other non-manual' group among white women were administrative workers, compared with only five per cent among West Indian women). For Asians also the health service and transport services are areas in which their employment patterns resemble those of whites more closely than elsewhere; additionally, the relatively small proportion of Asian employees in the other parts of the service sector have overall SEG distributions similar to whites. Outside the service sector, the jobs of both West Indians and Asians are heavily concentrated in manual work, and the same is true for West Indian men in service industries other than transport and communication, and for West Indian women in service industries other than the 'professional and scientific services'.

One of the interesting features of Table 101 and 102 is the relatively large proportion of Asians in the professional/employer /manager group in the service sector. Among Asian women the large proportion in this category (12 per cent) in the professional and scientific services are likely to be senior medical staff; although it is not shown in the table, the figure for Asian men in this part of the service sector is also high (22 per cent). Further analysis of the job characteristics of the Asian workers in this SEG category shows that the remainder are more concentrated in the distributive services and miscellaneous services than whites in the same category, and that a larger than average proportion have Asians as their immediate supervisors. This suggests that in many cases they are employed in retail and other businesses that are run by Asians. It is therefore unlikely that the size of the professional /employer/manager group among Asians is generally an accurate gauge of movement into higher jobs with white employers; this is further evidenced by the fact that half of the Asian men in this group within the manufacturing sector are in the food and drink industry, where Asian businesses are relatively well represented, compared with less than one in ten among white men.

Self-employment
Self-employed workers account for 18 per cent of Asian men in employment; the corresponding figures for West Indian men and white men are seven per cent and 14 per cent respectively. A similar pattern is observable for women: the percentages are respectively fourteen, one, and seven (Table 104). Thus the self-employed form a larger proportion of Asians than whites, and are very much less commonly found among West Indians. Within the Asian group the Pakistani men are least likely to be self-employed (10 per cent), and the Bangladeshis most likely (26 per cent); this again demonstrates the importance of considering these two groups separately, rather than as a single ethnic group, in this kind of survey.

The types of business run by self-employed people vary a great deal between Asians, West Indians and whites (Table 104). We have to treat the percentages for the West Indian group with some caution, for there are only 38 self-employed people in the West Indian sample, but nearly half of them work in the construction industry; 28 per cent of the white self-employed, and only two per cent of the Asian self-employed, are in this industry sector. Two-thirds of Asian self-employed workers are in the sector covering 'distribution, catering, hotels and repairs'. Although this

165

figure is much higher than those for white or West Indian self-employed workers (26 and 21 per cent respectively), and must therefore be taken seriously into account when discussing Asian employment patterns, the size of the self-employed catering and retail sector among Asians is still small in relation to the rest of the Asian workforce. Eleven per cent of all Asian workers are self-employed with a business in this sector (the figure is the same for men and women) compared with three per cent of white workers and one per cent of West Indian workers; thus it is correct to say that Asians are more strongly represented among the self-employed in the retail and catering trades than whites or West Indians, but it is wrong to suggest that this type of employment is typical for Asians: the majority of Asian workers are employees and work outside of this sector.

More Asian self-employed workers have employees than whites or West Indians (Table 105). Over sixty per cent of the Asian self-employed have employees, compared with under 40 per cent of whites and West Indians. A relatively large proportion of Asian self-employed workers have between one and four employees, while the proportions of the Asian and white self-employed with five or more employees are about the same.

Working hours and shifts
Table 106 shows the pattern of hours and shiftwork among employees of different ethnic origins. Average numbers of hours worked per week are very similar for white, Asian and West Indian full-time workers. There is a greater variation in the hours of part-time women workers, among whom the average is 18.4 hours for whites, compared with 22.3 hours for Asians and 24.1 hours for West Indians. The Asian and West Indian employees work shifts more commonly than white employees: just under a third of all black men work shifts on a regular basis, compared with a fifth of white men; the figures for women are 18 per cent for West Indians, 14 per cent for Asians and 11 per cent for whites. The differences are even greater when night shifts are considered: one per cent of white male employees work only night shifts, compared with four per cent of West Indians and seven per cent of Asians. For women workers the night-shift figures are also one per cent for whites and four per cent for West Indians, but among Asian women only one per cent work nights. The greater likelihood of working shifts among black employees is related in part to their lower job levels, but Table 107 shows that in each job level category the proportion of black employees on shiftwork is greater than that of white employees. The differences also persist if different industrial sectors are compared. For example, 27 per cent of white male employees in vehicle construction and shipbuilding work shifts, compared to 35 per cent of black male employees; in textiles the

figures are respectively 21 and 51 per cent, and in transport and communication, 33 and 58 per cent.

Within the Asian group, the incidence of shiftwork is strongly related to English language ability. Table 107 shows that although the pattern is not regular, the informants who speak English fluently are less likely to work shifts, and less likely to work only nights, than those who speak English only slightly or not at all.

Earnings
On average white men earn substantially more than black men, whereas there is little difference in the case of women (Table 109). The median figure for white men is about £20 higher than for West Indian men and about £18 higher than for Asian men. The median for white women is £4 higher than for Asians, but is actually £3 lower than for West Indians. This pattern is associated with the pattern of job levels. There is a much larger difference between white and black men than between white and black women in terms of job levels and in terms of earnings.

Table 110 shows that an earnings differential for men is maintained if the samples are broken down by region. The differential is larger in areas outside London and the South East.

The difference between the overall earnings levels of black and white men is partly the result of their different job levels. However, if we compare the median earnings of blacks and whites in the different SEG groups, we see that there is a pattern of inequality even within these categories (Table 111). The median for white men is higher in each category than the median for black men, although they are closer together than for the overall comparison. They are closest in the 'other non-manual' and the 'unskilled manual' groups; because of the small sample size of the latter group in the white survey and the small size of the differential (£2.10 per week), it is best to regard the unskilled manual earnings of blacks and whites as the same. However, as the table also shows, the different age distributions of black and white workers have an effect on wage differentials. If we confine the analysis to men aged 25-54, thus removing the age groups where earnings are relatively low for manual workers, we see that the differential in the unskilled group rises. We also see that in the top group, 'professional workers, employers and managers', the gap between blacks and whites closes, from £35.90 to £15.80 per week: this is because men aged over 54 are more common among whites than blacks, and are within this job category the highest earners, so the removal of these older workers lowers the white median relative to the black median.

We noted above that the proportion of Asian and West Indian employees working shifts is much larger than among whites. Table 112 shows that among manual workers the wages of those who work

167

shifts are higher than those who do not; this is true for both white and black workers, although it is interesting to see that shifts attract a different premium when whites and blacks are compared. White manual workers on alternating shifts receive a median £139.20 per week, and those on nights receive £137.40, these being respectively £27.00 and £25.20 more than the median wages of those not working shifts; Asian and West Indian manual workers on alternating shifts receive £119.70, and those on nights receive £104.50, these being respectively £20.50 and £5.30 more than the median wages of those not working shifts. Thus, overall, shiftwork premiums are smaller in absolute terms for black workers than for white workers, and black night-shift workers are particularly badly paid. This does not necessarily imply that shiftwork premiums vary between black and white workers in the same jobs in the same workplace: it is more likely that this difference results from the different job levels and industries in which black and white workers are found.

The fact that shiftworkers are on the whole paid considerably more than other manual workers, coupled with the fact that shiftwork is more common among black workers than white workers, would lead us to expect the wages of manual workers to be higher for blacks than whites, other things being equal. Since we find the reverse is true (for men), it follows that the difference in basic wages between black and white workers is greater than the difference in total wages, even at similar SEG levels.

As we saw earlier, the median earnings of white women are greater than those of Asian women, but less than those of West Indian women, although all three are within a range of about £7, and are much lower than the earnings of men. Table 113 shows that if we compare the earnings of black and white women within job level categories, the earnings of black women are higher in each category. As in the case of men, the different age structure of the two groups rather confuses matters, and a comparison confined to the 25-54 year-old group shows earnings levels that are much closer in all but the top SEG group, and shows an overall earnings differential in favour of white women for all jobs taken together. This reversal of the overall differential, from £1.50 in favour of black women to £10.40 in favour of white women occurs when under-25s and over 54s are excluded because of a real difference in the nature of the female workforce among the ethnic minorities: 47 per cent of white women workers are in these two age groups, compared with only 28 per cent of black women workers, and as it is the women from these age groups that are the lowest paid in each job level, they have a large effect of the relative earnings of black and white women. However, the most important finding in terms of earnings is that within job-level categories black women are not paid less than white women, as was the case for men. In the report of the 1974 PEP survey David Smith suggested that part of the explanation for the similarity in the overall levels of wages among white and black women was that the enormous disparity between men and women in this respect left little scope for racial disadvantage to have a further, additive effect. Other explanatory factors may be that black women are more commonly than white women found in large workplaces (over half of white women work in establishments with fewer than 50 employees, compared with only a third of Asian and West Indian women) and West Indian women are very much more likely to be with public sector employers. In large firms and in the public sector, wages tend to be higher than in small firms in the private sector. West Indian women tend also to be found more often in unionised workplaces than white women, and this would also tend to result in their wages being higher.

Within the black sample, we have seen that West Indian and Asian men have very similar overall median earnings while Asian women earn less that West Indian women, there being about £6.80 difference between their median earnings. Within the Asian group, however, we can see further differences. Table 114 shows that among men and women the Pakistanis and Bangladeshis earn less than others; the position of the Bangladeshis is particularly bad, their median earnings for men being about £25 lower than for Indians and African Asians, and even £17 lower than for Pakistanis.

These ethnic differences are related to the association between fluency in English and earnings: male manual workers who speak English fluently have a median of £110.80, compared with £94.20 for those who speak English only slightly or not at all, and the differences are even greater for non-manual occupations.

Trade union membership and activity
Overall, 56 per cent of Asian and West Indian employees are union members, compared with 47 per cent of white employees. This overall comparison hides considerable differences between men and women, and between Asians and West Indians. Table 115 shows that among male employees, 57 per cent of whites are union members, compared with 64 per cent of West Indians and 59 per cent of Asians; among female employees, 34 per cent of whites are union members, compared with 57 per cent of West Indians and 38 per cent of Asians. Thus, although both West Indians and Asians are found to be members more often than whites, the difference is mainly between West Indians and whites. Attendance at union meetings over the previous six months is about equal for white and Asian men: just over 40 per cent of members have attended a meeting (it should be noted that these are any union meetings, whether held at the workplace or outside). For West Indian men, this figure is a little lower, at 36 per cent. Among women, the

169

level of attendance of West Indians is greater (33 per cent) than among Asians or whites (26 per cent). Despite the fact that black people are generally more likely to join unions than white people, and attend meetings with about the same frequency, black members are much less likely than white members to hold an elected post. Eleven per cent of white male union members say they hold some kind of post, compared with four per cent both of Asians and of West Indians. The proportions of women with elected posts is generally lower, but again, the proportion for whites (six per cent) is higher than for Asians or West Indians (three per cent).

The greater propensity of black workers to join unions is largely a feature of the types of job they do: when comparisons are made within job level categories, the overall difference between white, Asian and West Indian men is very much reduced; for women the pattern remains when comparisons are made within job levels, but the incidence of part-time working among black women is less than among white women, and, as part-time workers are much less likely to join unions, this has the effect of raising the level of membership among black women generally. A comparison of the membership levels among workers in jobs for which unions are recognised by the employer shows no differences between white, West Indian and Asian men, but again shows higher levels of membership among black women than among white women.

Racial discrimination by employers: reported experience and beliefs

Asian and West Indian informants were asked whether they had ever been refused a job, or a promotion, for reasons that were to do with race or colour. Table 116 shows that of those currently in the job market, or who have worked in the last 10 years, about a quarter of West Indian men and a tenth of Asian men report that they had been refused a job on grounds they suspect were racial; among women the proportions are similar. Far fewer report having been refused promotion on racial grounds: 11 per cent of West Indian men and eight per cent of Asian men, and even smaller proportions of women. In about 60 per cent of these cases the last reported incident of discrimination was within the past eight years. In nine per cent of these incidents the employer actually mentioned the ethnic origin of the informant when refusing the application, or the informant overheard a conversation about his or her ethnic origin. In 19 per cent of the cases the informant was told the job had gone but later discovered it was still available.

The interviewers asked both white and black informants whether they thought there were employers who would refuse a job to a person on racial grounds. The results are shown in Table 117, and several important points emerge. First, there is a considerable difference between the responses of the Asians and the West

Indians: 77 per cent of West Indian men and women say that there are employers who discriminate, compared with 48 per cent of Asian men and only 29 per cent of Asian women. The proportions of white men and women giving this response are, at 73 and 69 per cent respectively, similar to those of the West Indians. Secondly, the way the remaining responses are distributed varies between the different groups. The proportion saying employers do not discriminate is much larger among whites than among West Indians and among Asian women; Asian men are an exception among black informants, for the proportion saying employers do not discriminate is the same as among whites. The proportions giving 'don't know' responses is much larger among black people than white people; it is particularly large among Asians - 28 per cent of Asian men and 56 per cent of Asian women say they do not know whether employers discriminate. The third point to note is that although the white informants are almost as likely to acknowledge the problem as West Indian informants, they think it is far less widespread; comparison of the overall proportions saying half or more employers discriminate shows that white people's views are closer to those of Asians than those of West Indians in this respect: over 35 per cent of West Indians give this response, compared with under 20 per cent of whites and Asians.

Informants were also asked whether there were firms or organisations where promotion was less likely for black people with the same qualifications as white people. The pattern of responses among black people is much the same as in the case of the recruitment question. White people, however, are markedly less likely to agree that discrimination takes place in promotion than in recruitment: most of the difference between their responses to these two questions is located in the larger number of 'don't knows' in the answers to the promotion question. One might expect to find differences between the responses of younger and older people within the black sample, but this is true only to a limited extent. If we split the Asians and West Indians into groups aged up to and over 24, the proportions who say there are employers who discriminate in recruitment are very similar, except among West Indian men. Among Asians, the figure for the younger group is five percentage points larger than for the older group, and among West Indian women it is eight points larger. Among West Indian men, however, the proportion of the younger group who say employers discriminate in recruitment is 90 per cent, compared with 72 per cent of the older group. The views of the two age groups are uniformly close together when it comes to the question on promotion discrimination (the proportions saying there is discrimination come within seven per cent of each other in each ethnic group) and except among Asian women it is the older group that is slightly more likely to say discrimination exists. The differences

171

between the views of younger and older black people are discussed further in Chapters IX and X.

Table 118 shows the responses to the same questions from Asian and West Indian informants who are in the labour market. The pattern is much the same as among all adults, except that Asian women in the labour market are more likely to give a definite response, and therefore a larger proportion say that employers discriminate. It should be remembered that only about 40 per cent of Asian women are in the labour market, compared with over 70 per cent of West Indian women and about 90 per cent of Asian and West Indian men. This largely accounts for the high percentage of 'don't know' responses among Asian women generally.

Research carried out by making test applications for advertised jobs has shown that large numbers of employers are more likely to reject black applicants than white applicants even when they have equivalent qualifications and experience(3). In 1973 and 1974, when PEP carried out such a study in six different towns, it was found that the black applicants were discriminated against in 30 per cent of cases involving non-manual jobs, 20 per cent of cases involving skilled manual jobs and 37 per cent of cases involving unskilled and semi-skilled jobs. A study carried out by Nottingham Community Relations Council between 1974 and 1979 in that city showed that discrimination occurred in 46 per cent of tests on advertised non-manual vacancies. Given the levels of discrimination that have been shown to exist by this and other research, it is extraordinary that, of Asian respondents in the labour market, under half report a belief that employers discriminate in recruitment and only just over half report a belief that employers discriminate in promotion; it is all the more noteworthy that white people are more likely than Asians to acknowledge the existence of discrimination by employers.

A question was also asked about the way employers treat black people in general: avoiding any specific reference to recruitment or promotion, informants were asked whether employers treated Asian and West Indian people the same, better or worse than white people. For white informants, the wording of the question was 'people of Asian and West Indian origin', while for the Asian and West Indian informants it referred to people of their own ethnic origin. This question produced a different pattern of response: both Asians and West Indians are more likely than white people to give the view that blacks are treated worse than whites (Table 119). Nearly half of West Indians, and over a third of Asians, say this, compared with about a quarter of whites. Over half of white informants say black and white people are treated the same by employers compared with about 35 per cent of West Indians and 40 per cent of Asians. Very few informants in any ethnic group say black people are treated better than whites. The

172

explanation for the different pattern of responses to this question when compared with the specific questions on discrimination and recruitment is not clear. It may lie in the emphasis within the specific questions on discrimination by 'any employers', rather than by employers in general: this emphasis on 'any employers' would tend to produce higher proportions acknowledging discrimination because in order to give an affirmative reply an informant would theoretically only need to be aware of a single employer where this occurred. However, the proportion acknowledging discrimination is higher for the specific questions only for whites and West Indians. Among Asian men the proportions are roughly the same for the general and specific cases, and among women the proportion is larger in the case of the general question.

The pattern of change

No mention has been made so far in this chapter of the changes in the patterns of employment of Asian and West Indian people. Because the two questionnaires have much in common, the 1974 PEP survey and the 1982 PSI survey provide a good basis for comparison in order to assess the changes that have occurred over the intervening eight years. In some respects there have been sizeable and important changes, while in others the situation has remained remarkably stable: for example, the proportions out of work have grown to make a high level of unemployment a major feature of the economic position of blacks, while the sectors of industry in which black workers are found are very similar to those in 1974.

It is vital to remember that we are not comparing the same group of Asian and West Indian people at two different points in time. The adult population with family origins in the Caribbean, India, Pakistan and Bangladesh grew by over a third between 1974 and 1982, by natural increase and by immigration, so we are now dealing with a black labour force that is composed of a large proportion of the workforce in 1974, a group of young adults who have recently come into the labour market, a group of immigrants who have recently come into the labour market, and, finally, a group of people who were adults and living in Britain in 1974, but who were not then working or seeking work and have subsequently entered the labour market. Some people, although they will have been few, will have retired or moved away from Britain since 1974. We must therefore be very careful in our analysis of change: contrasts between the 'snapshots' of black employment taken in 1974 and 1982 will not necessarily be made up of changes in the lives of individual people - they are just as likely to arise from the presence of groups that were not in the British labour market in 1974.

173

Unemployment

Undoubtedly the most important change has been the rise of unemployment rates among Asian and West Indian men and women to very high levels. The faster growth of unemployment among blacks than among whites has opened up an area of massive racial disadvantage that was absent in 1974. At the time of the PEP survey the unemployment rate for both white and black people was around four per cent, although there was evidence that young West Indian men and all black women suffered a higher rate. In the 1982 survey we find that the white unemployment rate has risen to 13 per cent for men and 10 per cent for women, while over the same period the rates have risen for West Indians to 25 per cent and 16 per cent respectively, and for Asians to 20 per cent for both men and women. Although unemployment is particularly bad among young people, the survey shows that this source of racial disadvantage has also affected older people and it is therefore correct to identify unemployment as a major new factor of racial inequality for both young and old. Analysis of Department of Employment figures over a period shows that ethnic minorities are particularly disadvantaged in this respect because their position in the labour market is very sensitive to overall changes in job supply. When unemployment rises nationally, it rises much faster for black people, and the gap between whites and blacks widens. This is illustrated in Figure 1 which shows the trends between 1963 and 1981.

The overall proportions of adults in the labour market, either working or unemployed, follow a pattern which is very similar to that found in 1974: activity rates for Asian men and West Indian men and women are higher than corresponding rates for whites, and the same is true for Asian women who are not Muslims. Black people are more often economically active than whites because there are still relatively few who are old enough to retire. Muslim women are an exception, probably because of cultural factors and, possibly, also because of factors associated with English language fluency.

Self-employment

Among those who are working, there has been a substantial growth in the proportion of Asians who are self-employed. Overall, 18 per cent of Asian men, and 14 per cent of Asian women are now self-employed. To make a comparison with the 1974 survey we have to exclude the geographical areas that were omitted from the sample in 1974, because self-employment is rather more common in those areas. On this basis we see that among Asians the proportions who are self-employed have risen from eight per cent to 14 per cent for men, and from seven per cent to 12 per cent for women. This is an important change, because it means that self-employment is now

174

more common among Asians than among whites; the reverse was true in 1974. Self-employment is still much less common among West Indians than among whites. There has been a substantial degree of individual movement from employed to self-employed occupations among Asian men and women between 1974 and 1982: 11 per cent of those who were employees in 1974 have since then become self-employed, and the corresponding figure for Asian women is seven per cent.

Job levels
The differences between the job levels of white and black workers make up an important indicator of racial disadvantage: earnings, job security and health are all related to job level, and we have seen that Asian and West Indian people have distinctly worse jobs than white people. It is of great interest, therefore, to know whether there has been any narrowing of this gap between white people and people of Asian and West Indian origin in the period between the two surveys. An overall comparison of the figures from the two studies is shown in Table 120, which excludes from the 1982 sample all black people living outside the types of geographical area included in the 1974 sample. As explained earlier in the report, a comparison of this kind, which takes account of the different geographical bases of the two surveys, is preferable to a straightforward comparison of the overall figures. The 1974 study did not give job level figures for the employed and self-employed separately; the 1982 figures in this table are therefore also based on these groups added together.

The table shows that the socio-economic group distributions of West Indians and Asians are different to those found in the 1974 survey. Overall there appears to have been a shift towards non-manual work: eight per cent of black men, and ten per cent of black women, have 'moved' from manual to non-manual jobs, and this aspect of the change is the same for Asians and West Indians. But there are other differences between the 1974 and 1982 distributions, and these are not the same for Asians and West Indians, nor for men and women. For West Indian men, all of the manual to non-manual shift has appears to have occurred at the expense of the skilled manual group, which accounts for 48 per cent in the 1982 survey as opposed to 59 per cent in 1974; the unskilled manual group is even a little larger now than in 1974. The non-manual growth has, for Asian men, been accompanied by a decline of both the skilled and unskilled groups. For both Asian and West Indian men the non-manual growth has been mainly in the top SEG grouping, the 'professional, employer, manager' category; for Asian women the growth has been in both non-manual categories, and for West Indian women it has been only in the lower non-manual category. The categories that have become smaller for

175

West Indian women are the skilled and semi-skilled manual workers, while for Asian women they are the semi-skilled and unskilled workers. The table also shows that the job levels of white people have changed over this period, but to a much smaller extent. There has been a shift from manual to non-manual work, but the scale of this change has been, in the case of women, only half that found among blacks and, in the case of men, less than half. The upwards shift of the white SEG distribution comes mainly from a reduction in the proportions in the lowest categories, and is therefore more aligned with the changes among Asians than among West Indians.

Using this very broad comparison we can therefore say that the working populations of Asian and West Indian men and women now have higher overall job levels than in 1974, and, although there is still a large gap between their job levels and those of white people, this gap has closed slightly. There are several possible components of this change. The first is individual job mobility: people in the labour market in 1974 and 1982 may have changed their jobs for the better. The second is the contribution of young adults to the overall pattern: these and other people new to the labour market may have a different SEG distribution from other workers. The third is the contribution of recent arrivals to this country, for they too may have an SEG pattern that is distinctive. The fourth is the effect that unemployment will have had on the distribution of jobs among those still at work: we know that the people who have lost their jobs in the period between the two surveys have come disproportionately from the lower SEG categories, so the net effect will have to be move the overall distribution of job levels upwards. We can see just how important each of these factors is by further analysis of the 1982 survey data.

We shall consider the four possible explanations in reverse order, starting with the effect of unemployment. The simplest way to test the theory that it is the loss of low SEG workers through unemployment that has changed the overall SEG distribution is to re-include the unemployed in the analysis, classifying them by the SEG of their last job. Table 121 shows the resulting distributions, alongside the 1974 figures. The patterns for the two surveys are, as expected, closer together, but the changes noted earlier are still apparent. There is a shift from manual to non-manual work which is not explained by the loss of jobs through unemployment.

Table 122 shows the job levels of the people who are new to the job market since 1974. They are shown as two groups for the Asians: those aged over 25 who came to Britain after 1974, and all others new to the job market. There are very few West Indians in the 'recent immigrant' category (about one per cent of all workers) and, as their job levels could not therefore noticeably affect the overall pattern, they are not shown separately on the table. It can be seen that the Asian recent immigrants have jobs which are distributed in a very similar way to those of other Asians; they make up about ten per cent of Asian workers, and clearly their job levels do not affect the overall pattern. The other people who are new to the labour market, however, do have a pattern of employment which is different to other workers, and this is true for both Asians and West Indians. This group is composed mainly of young adults - about 60 per cent are aged under 25 - but also includes others who for any other reason were not in the labour market in 1974. The non-manual group is larger among Asians and West Indians who are new to the labour market than among those who were working in 1974. For West Indian men and women, and for Asian women, it is the lower non-manual group that is larger among new workers than among those who have been working longer. But for Asian men, it is the top SEG category which is larger in the new group. Nineteen per cent of Asian men who have started work since 1974 are in the 'professional, employer, manager' group, compared with 13 per cent of other Asian men. The new workers are no more likely to be self-employed than those who have been in work longer, so this trend is not associated with the general trend towards self-employment among Asians.

Thus much of the upward movement in the job levels of Asian and West Indian workers is the result of different distributions of jobs among younger workers. This leads us to consider the question of whether young black workers have similar jobs to young white workers. In fact the job levels of black and white workers aged under 25 are closer together than for other age groups, but even among young workers there remains a definite gap (Table 123). Overall, there are more black men in this age group with low job levels than among whites, but the proportions of non-manual workers are similar, and among Asians more of these non-manual workers have senior positions. The job levels of young white and West Indian women are very close together; Asian women, however, are twice as likely to have semi-skilled manual jobs as whites and West Indians, and the total proportion in white-collar jobs is substantially smaller.

These findings are evidence of a convergence of employment patterns among young black and white people, but this convergence must be seen in a context of diverging rates of unemployment and economic activity. Far fewer young Asians and West Indians than young whites actually have jobs, because more of them have stayed on in full-time education or are unemployed. The proportions of white, West Indian and Asian men working, within the 16-24 age group, are 61 per cent, 42 per cent and 48 per cent, and the corresponding figures for women are 56 per cent, 38 per cent and 25 per cent. The coming together of the job-level distributions of young black and white workers may therefore be largely the result of the erosion of opportunities for young black people to obtain the manual jobs in which older black people are disproportionately employed; as a proportion of all those economically active, non-manual workers are in fact no more common among blacks aged under 25 than in the black population generally.

Returning to the analysis of the whole samples, we have seen part of the explanation for the SEG distribution change in the generally higher job levels of entrants to the labour market, and part of the explanation in the effects of unemployment. It is also important to know whether any of the change is due to actual job mobility among the people who were in the labour market both in 1974 and 1982. Comparison of the 1982 job levels of those who were working in 1974 (Table 122) with job levels found in the 1974 survey (Table 120) suggests that there may have been some movement of this kind. All of the comparisons show a degree of movement into the non-manual occupations, but this is not large, and further analysis shows that it is reduced if the effect of unemployment is taken into account by including in the 1982 figures the most recent job levels of people now unemployed but who were working in 1974. Making the comparison on this basis, we estimate that the non-manual sector now takes in three per cent more of the Asian men and women and West Indian men who were working in 1974, and five per cent more of the West Indian women who were working in 1974.

Comparisons of this type may be vulnerable to differences in the coding practices between different surveys. Even though the 1982 fieldwork for the black and the white surveys was carried out by two organisations, we had both the black and the white informant's jobs coded by the same organisation, in order to ensure that different practices did not create artificial differences between the job levels of the different ethnic groups. Comparisons over time, between surveys carried out by different organisations, have no guarantee against such problems. As a guard against the possibility of distortion from this source, we asked informants about the job they had back in 1974, so that we could compare these with their present jobs. The findings of this comparison are given in Table 124, where we can see support for the suggestion that there has been a small movement from manual to non-manual work among Asians and West Indians, at an individual level, over the period between 1974 and 1982. There have been movements in both directions, but a net three per cent of men and women have moved into non-manual jobs in this period in the areas covered by the 1974 survey.

It should be noted that further analysis of the 1974 jobs reported in this retrospective way suggests that the present sample of Asian and West Indian men had fewer skilled manual workers among them in 1974 than would be expected from the 1974 PEP survey figures (40 per cent, rather than 48 per cent). In the light of this, it is important to treat with caution the earlier finding that the growth of the non-manual sector among West Indian men has been entirely at the expense of the skilled manual group: the shrinkage of this group observed in Tables 120 and 121 may well be a feature of the technical differences between the 1974 and 1982 surveys. The other changes discussed in this section are not likely to have been caused in this way, for we have been able to corroborate the changes observed between the two surveys with data from within the 1982 survey.

In discussing the occupational mobility of black people we have so far restricted the analysis to the geographical areas covered by the 1974 survey, and have therefore omitted changes that may have taken place in the areas of less dense Asian and West Indian residence. Working from data within the 1982 survey we find that the pattern is the same, but is perhaps stronger: the main element of the move from manual to non-manual jobs is found in the occupational distribution of people who are new to the labour market, rather than the individual job mobility of other workers.

It is worth summarising at this point the conclusions of the analysis of the changes in job levels: (i) Among Asians and West Indians the rise in the proportion of those in the labour market who are now jobless has been much larger than among whites; (ii) Asian and West Indian workers still find themselves in jobs that are generally of a lower level than the jobs of white people, and the difference cannot be explained away by differences in geographical distribution or qualifications; (iii) overall, the gap between white and black workers has closed a little over the period 1974-1982; (iv) much of this change is caused by the fact that many black people in the poorest jobs have become unemployed and those in the better jobs have therefore become a larger proportion of all blacks in employment; (v) there has been a very small amount of individual mobility from manual jobs to non-manual jobs over this period; (vi) most of the improvement in the job levels comes from the entry of new workers to the job market, for these new workers have a very different distribution of jobs from that of the people who have been working since 1974; (vii) even the rise in the job levels of black workers new to the labour market may be due in large part to the collapse of job opportunities in the lower-SEG categories, as it has been accompanied by a reduction in the proportion who actually have jobs.

Industry
The types of industry in which black people are found are broadly similar to those in 1974, although there have been changes which are part of the movements discussed so far in this section. The

179

proportions of both black and white workers found in the services sector have grown, but they have grown faster among black people. In this respect Asian and West Indian patterns appear to be converging towards those of white people, but this is an illusion, for within the service sector the types of job done by black people are very different from those done be whites, as shown earlier in this chapter. Among men, this growth of the service sector has been accompanied by a decline, of a smaller scale, in manufacturing industry, and some smaller declines within some other sectors, but no particular difference between these changes for black and white men emerges. Among women, the decline of manufacturing matches the growth of the service sector among blacks and whites.

Earnings

Turning now to changes in the earnings of the different ethnic groups, we see that the 1982 survey findings are still very much in line with those of the 1974 survey. Overall, West Indian and Asian men earn less than white men, and in percentage terms the gap between them appears not to have closed: in 1974 the median earnings figure for Asian and West Indian men was 10 per cent lower than the white figure, and the comparison in 1982 puts the Asian and West Indian men 15 per cent lower than white men. As explained in the appendix, some of the difference shown in the 1982 survey may be the result of different non-response rates, and for this reason it would be unwise to conclude that the change from 10 to 15 per cent represented a real widening of the gap. It is clear, however, that there has been no overall improvement in the situation. As explained earlier, much of the earnings differential between black and white men is caused by differences between their job levels, but comparison of men in the 25-54 age group in the different job level categories shows that some of the gap persists within these categories. The findings of this comparison are slightly different to those of the 1974 survey. The earnings differential appears to have diminished in the non-manual occupations, remained static in the the skilled manual occupations, and grown in the semi-skilled and unskilled occupations. In all, the earnings differentials within these three job levels are now very similar to each other: in 1974 the non-manual differential was much larger than that for skilled manual workers, and there was no differential between white and black semi-skilled and unskilled workers.

Within the Asian and West Indian sample there are, as in 1974, differences between the various ethnic groups in this respect. Indians and African Asians earn more than West Indians, and Pakistanis and Bangladeshis less. The position of the African Asians has changed: in 1974 they had the lowest earnings median, but they are now one of the highest-earning black groups. In 1974 the Bangladeshi group was too small for separate analysis, and they were included with the Pakistanis. In the present survey we are able to look at their position separately, and we find that their median earnings figure is over £22 lower than that of other black men. The median earnings figure for Bangladeshis is only 69 per cent of the white figure; there is a gap of £40 between them.

It is hard to compare the earnings position of black women in 1982 with that in 1974 because the white comparison survey in 1974 was of men only, and as a consequence there was very little analysis of female earnings. The findings suggested that white and ethnic minority women earned similar wages, both overall in the manual and non-manual groups. In the 1982 survey the earnings are quite close overall, with white women earning £4 more than Asian women, and about £4 less than West Indian women. Within the different job level categories, however, black women's median earnings are consistently higher than white women's, although this pattern is weakened considerably if the comparison is limited to women in the age range 25-54. It is not possible to say whether this is a real change over time or a feature of the different sources of information on the white women's earnings used in the two studies. The 1974 study used figures from the New Earnings Survey (NES) for white women.

Hours and shiftwork
The ethnic variations in the patterns of hours and shifts worked in 1974 and 1982 are very similar. Total hours worked by white and black employees are very similar, although not identical, as in 1974. The averages have fallen from 47.5 hours for all men in 1974 to 43.9, 42.5 and 43.5 hours for white, West Indian and Asian men respectively. The questionnaire items concerning shiftwork were not identical in 1974 and 1982 (the present survey distinguishes between occasional and regular shiftwork, and has a different classification of shift types) so we have to be cautious in our inferences of trends over time. The incidence of shiftwork appears to have increased among black and white people since 1974, but there is still a large difference between them: in 1974, 15 per cent of white men worked shifts compared with 31 per cent of Asian and West Indian men, while in 1982 we find these figures have risen to 23 per cent and 35 per cent respectively(4). Night shifts and alternating shifts are, among those regularly working shifts, more commonly worked by Asian and West Indian men than white men. As found in 1974, among black workers the incidence of shiftwork, and night work in particular, is greatest for the Pakistanis. Broadly, then, we see that the ethnic variations in working hours and shiftwork have changed little since 1974.

181

Union membership

The level of trade union membership among Asian and West Indian workers is higher than among white workers, for both men and women. We find that this is primarily due to differences in the type of work and the industrial sectors in which black workers are found. Whilst the overall finding of higher membership levels among blacks is in line with the 1974 survey results, it was the case in 1974 that the higher membership level could not be explained by occupational differences: there was then an apparently greater propensity to join unions among Asian and West Indian workers than among black workers. As this no longer seems to be the case, we must infer a closing of the gap between the levels of membership of white and black workers in equivalent employment situations. It certainly appears that the overall proportion of working white men in membership has risen, from 47 per cent in the 1974 survey to 57 per cent in 1982, while the level for Asian and West Indian men has remained level at 61 per cent in the areas common to both surveys. Trends to the contrary may be apparent for women, however, for we see that the membership level has risen from 36 per cent to 48 per cent among Asian and West Indian women, while it has remained level, at about 35 per cent, for white women. The factors giving rise to these changes may be very complex, as trade union membership levels are associated with the workplace situation of employees and with the strength of individual and collective commitment to union organisation. We have seen that there are many people in the 1982 survey who are new to the labour force since 1974, and that they often have different types of job from those they are joining: their circumstances at work or attitudes to trade unions may be different from those of longer established workers.

English fluency and local density of black residents

One of the most important persisting relationships is that between employment and fluency in English among Asians. Asian men and women who speak English poorly occupy a very disadvantaged position in the labour market. They have higher rates of unemployment, lower job levels, lower wages and more often work shifts. Compared to other Asians, their employers are more commonly private firms, and their employment is far more concentrated in manufacturing. Among Asian men, the likelihood of being self-employed is related strongly to English fluency: in a period when a greater proportion of Asians than of any other group have moved to self-employment, perhaps as a response to difficulties of maintaining employment in the face of racial discrimination and economic recession, those least able to make this move have been those who are also the most disadvantaged at work.

182

Coupled with this relationship between disadvantage in employment and English language fluency is the general relationship between disadvantage and local concentration of Asian and West Indian households. In the 1974 survey it was shown that, for most indicators of racial disadvantage, the situation worsened as higher levels of concentration were analysed; this association was shown to be very much stronger for Asians than for West Indians. In the 1982 survey we find the same feature within the Asian sample: unemployment, job levels, industrial sector and earnings are all related to local concentration in such a way as to make the individuals and households living in the denser areas worse off than others. Among West Indians this tendency is much weaker, except in the case of unemployment, which is very much worse in the areas of high concentration.

Experience of and beliefs about discrimination
The results of the questions on experience of and belief in racial discrimination are not substantially different to those of the 1974 survey. However, among West Indian men and women, and among Asian women, the proportions reporting personal experience of racial discrimination when applying for a job are between five and ten percentage points higher than they were in 1974, but, curiously, the proportion of Asian men reporting experience of discrimination is now smaller (10 per cent, compared with 14 per cent). The proportions reporting experience of discrimination in promotion have not risen: the pattern is very similar to that found in 1974, and in fact overall the figures are now about two per cent lower. The proportions who believe in the existence of discrimination in recruitment and discrimination in promotion have risen among black women by about ten percentage points, but among Asian men the figures have only risen a little (from 47 to 49 per cent for recruitment, and from 55 to 59 per cent for promotion) and among West Indian men the figure has risen more for promotion (from 67 to 78 per cent) than for recruitment (from 74 to 78 per cent). Among white men the proportions who say there is discrimination in recruitment and in promotion are the same as in 1974.

183

Notes

(1)   This is done by first calculating the white unemployment rate for each job-level category, based on all those presently working at that level plus all registered unemployed whose last job was at that level, then combining these into an overall unemployment rate using the job-level distribution of the black sample.

(2)   Note that since the survey was carried out the official basis for unemployment statistics has changed. Official unemployment figures are now based on persons who register to claim benefit, not on persons who register as seeking a job.

(3)   W.W. Daniel, Racial Discrimination in England, Penguin, 1968; M. Firth, 'Racial Discrimination in the British Labour Market', Industrial and Labour Relations Review, Vol. 34, No. 2, January, 1981, pp. 265-72; J. Hubbuck and S. Carter, Half a Chance?, Commission for Racial Equality, 1980; R. Jowell and P. Prescott-Clarke, 'Racial Discrimination and White-Collar Workers in Britain', Race, Vol. XI, No. 4, April 1970, pp. 397-417; N. McIntosh and D.J. Smith, The Extent of Racial Discrimination, PEP Report 547, 1974.

(4)   This comparison is based on the Asian and West Indians living in the areas as defined for the 1974 survey, and uses for the 1982 figure the total of those working shifts 'regularly' and 'sometimes'.

Table 79: Economic activity by ethnic origin: men

Column percentages

	White		West Indian		Asian	
Employee (full-time)	54		57		54	
(part-time)	5	67	3	64	2	68
Self-Employed	9		5		12	
Registered Unemployed	10		21		17	
Government Scheme	1		2		1	
Seeking work, not registered	2		1		1	
Total in labour market	80		88		87	
Keeping House	*		–		*	
Full-time Education	3		6		6	
Retired	15		4		4	
Unable to Work	3		2		1	
Other	2		3		3	
Base: Adults						
(weighted)	2567		1630		3870	
(unweighted)	1001		781		1836	

<u>Table 80:</u>　　　<u>Economic activity by ethnic origin: women</u>

Column percentages

	White	West Indian	Asian	Muslim	Hindu	Sikh
Employee (full-time)	21	41	21	6	32	32
(part-time)	17	17	4	1	7	5
Self-Employed	3	1	4	3	8	4
Registered Unemployed	4	11	8	5	10	12
Government Scheme	*	1	*	*	*	-
Seeking work, not registered	2	4	2	3	1	2
Total in labour market	46	74	39	18	59	54
Keeping House	33	11	53	78	32	38
Full-time Education	2	7	5	4	6	5
Retired	17	4	2	1	4	2
Unable to Work	2	1	*	*	-	1
Other	2	7	2	3	2	2
Base: Adults						
(weighted)	2802	1790	3013	1328	830	618
(unweighted)	1262	876	1484	704	387	290

Table 81:   Economic activity by age and ethnic group

Per cent of age group in labour market

	Whites	West Indians	Asians	
Men aged..:				
16-19	(84)	73	42	
20-24	94	92	85	
25-34	99	96	97	
35-44	99	99	95	
45-54	96	94	95	
55-64	78	90	79	
			Muslims	Other Asians
Women aged..:				
16-19	(71)	59	(42)	(36)
20-24	74	78	20	65
25-34	54	75	17	60
35-44	70	88	14	64
45-54	65	83	(11)	58
55-64	34	40	(1)	(21)

Table 82:   Asian women: Those in the labour market and in full-time education, by fluency in English

	Informant Speaks English –			
	Fluently	Fairly Well	Slightly	Not at All
In Labour Market	56	55	29	8
In Full-Time Education	11	3	1	-
Base				
(weighted)	966	542	807	594
(unweighted)	449	280	397	307

188

Table 83:   Unemployment rate by sex and ethnic group

Per cent

	Men	Women
White	13	10
West Indian	25	16
Asian	20	20
Indian	14	18
Pakistani	29	(28)
Bangladeshi	29	(52)
African Asian	17	21
Muslim	27	31
Hindu	14	18
Sikh	14	22

Note: Unemployment rate is calculated as the registered
        unemployed as a percentage of all those in the labour
            market (omitting those on government schemes and
        unregistered unemployed):

$$\frac{\text{registered unemployed}}{\text{employed \& self-employed \& registered unemployed}} \times 100\%$$

Table 84:   Unemployment rates by sex, age and ethnic group

Per cent

	White	West Indian	Asian
Men aged..			
16-19	(30)	46	(35)
20-24	22	42	26
25-34	15	17	17
35-44	5	15	17
45-54	7	16	22
55-64	13	26	26
Women aged..			
16-19	(23)	50	(47)
20-24	17	26	30
25-34	10	18	15
35-44	5	6	17
45-54	1	9	18
55-64	8	(15)	(11)

Table 85:   Male unemployment rates in different regions

Per cent

	North West	Yorkshire and Humber- side	West Mid- lands	East Mid- lands	South East (excl.) London	London	Other Regions
PSI survey							
White	17	21	19	-	8	11	14
West Indian	40	(15)	34	(29)	(19)	19	30
Asian	32	25	32	20	12	16	14
Department of Employment figure, March 1982, All men, including school leavers	18	16	18	13	12	11	16

191

Table 86:   Unemployment in inner cities by ethnic group

Per cent

	Inner London, Inner Birmingham Inner Manchester	Rest of London, West Midlands Metropolitan County and Greater Manchester	Rest of Country
Unemployment Rate			
Men:			
White	23	8	12
West Indian	29	18	26
Asian	26	18	19
Women:			
White	(4)	8	10
West Indian	18	14	18
Asian	24	17	21
Per cent of ethnic group that lives in these areas:			
White	6	13	81
West Indian	41	30	28
Asian	23	30	47

Table 87: Unemployment in areas of different levels of black residence

Per cent

	Concentration of Asian and West Indian Households in Enumeration District	
	Up to 4 per cent	Over 4 per cent
Unemployment Rate		
Men:		
White	12	22
West Indian	26	25
Asian	12	22
Women:		
White	9	(11)
West Indian	15	17
Asian	18	21
Per cent of ethnic group that lives in these areas:		
White	90	10
West Indian	23	77
Asian	21	79

Table 88:   Registered unemployed: how long ago informant registered, by ethnic group and sex

Column percentages

	Men			Women		
	White	West Indian	Asian	White	West Indian	Asian
Up to 6 weeks	*	3	1	1	3	1
7-13 weeks	1	2	1	2	2	3
4-6 months	3	3	2	2	1	3
7-12 months	4	4	3	3	3	5
Over a year	5	13	13	2	9	9
Base: All working or unemployed (weighted)	1999	1417	3336	1246	1255	1120

194

Table 89:   Registered and unregistered unemployment, by ethnic group

	Men			Women		
	White	West Indian	Asian	White	West Indian	Asian
Per cent of whole adult population who are ...						
Registered Unemployed	10	21	17	4	11	8
Seeking work but not registered	2	1	1	2	4	2
Per cent of population aged under 25 who are...						
Registered Unemployed	20	33	19	13	21	29
Seeking work but not registered	5	5	3	3	9	5

Table 90: All those seeking work: formal terms of leaving last job in 1982 and 1979

Column percentages

	Men			Women		
	White	West Indian	Asian	White	West Indian	Asian
Made redundant	42	46	46	25	16	24
Dismissed	12	13	6	2	9	7
Retired	3	-	-	1	1	-
Left, for own reason	17	16	23	54	37	26
End of temporary job	8	2	2	13	2	-
Other reason	3	3	5	1	2	1
Never had a job	16	21	18	4	32	43
Base: All seeking work who gave formal terms of learning last job (weighted)	305	356	692	168	292	279

Comparison with 1979, excluding from base those who have never had a job:

	Men						Women					
	White		West Indian		Asian		White		West Indian		Asian	
	79	82	79	82	79	82	79	82	79	82	79	82
Made redundant	25	49	24	58	27	56	18	26	22	24	22	42
Dismissed	19	14	31	16	26	7	17	2	20	13	12	12
Retired	4	4	-	-	1	-	3	1	3	1	1	-
Left, own reason	45	20	40	20	43	28	61	56	53	54	65	46
Other	5	13	5	6	2	9	1	15	2	6	3	2

196

Table 91: Job levels of men: all employees by ethnic group

Column percentages

Job Level	White	West Indian	Asian	Indian	Paki-stani	Bangla-deshi	African Asian	Muslim	Hindu	Sikh
Professional, Employer, Management	19	5	13	11	10	10	22	11	20	4
Other non-manual	23	10	13	13	8	7	21	8	26	8
Skilled Manual and Foreman	42	48	33	34	39	13	31	33	20	48
Semi-skilled Manual	13	26	34	36	35	57	22	39	28	33
Unskilled Manual	3	9	6	5	8	12	3	8	3	6
Base: Male employees										
(weighted)	1490	972	2167	847	611	177	495	998	571	452
(unweighted)	591	467	1041	401	298	96	227	507	258	213

197

Table 92: Job levels of women: all employees by ethnic group

Column percentages

Job Level	White	West Indian	Asian	Indian	African Asian	Muslim	Hindu	Sikh
Professional, Employer, Manager	7	1	6	5	7	(7)	8	3
Other non-manual	55	52	42	35	52	(36)	49	19
Skilled manual and foreman	5	4	6	8	3	(1)	4	10
Semi-skilled Manual	21	36	44	50	36	(52)	37	66
Unskilled Manual	11	7	2	1	3	(5)	2	2
Base: Female employees								
(weighted)	1050	1020	760	431	237	102	322	229
(unweighted)	495	502	340	195	102	45	146	105

198

	Men				Women			
	White	West Indian	Asian		White	West Indian	Asian	
			All Asians	Asians Fluent in English			All Asians	Asians Fluent in English
Per cent in non-manual jobs:								
All employees	41	16	27	40	62	53	48	60
A-level and above/ Professional qual.	84	(85)	75	76	90	87	(78)	(79)
O-level	61	42	29	34	80	90	78	80
No qualifications	22	5	13	24	42	29	22	34
Per cent in semi-skilled and unskilled manual jobs:								
All employees	16	36	39	27	32	43	46	35
A-level and above/ Professional qual.	2	(2)	7	4	8	10	(21)	(19)
O-level	5	17	34	28	14	10	15	13
No qualifications	28	43	50	38	51	66	70	60

Note: The figure in each cell of the table is the number of non-manual workers as a percentage of all informants in a given ethnic group with given qualifications. For example, 84 per cent of white male employees with qualifications of A-level or above are non-manual workers.

Table 94:   Asians: job level by fluency in English

Column percentages

	Men			Women		
	Fluent-ly	Fair-ly Well	Slight-ly/Not at all	Fluent-ly	Fair-ly Well	Slight-ly/Not at all
Professional, Employer, Manager	25	5	1	10	3	1
Other Non-Manual	18	13	2	61	32	4
Skilled Manual and Foreman	34	34	25	4	6	7
Semi-skilled Manual	19	41	56	24	53	82
Unskilled Manual	2	5	14	-	4	5
Base: All employees						
(weighted)	996	657	430	387	172	167
(unweighted)	447	340	210	169	85	72

Table 95: Employees: Supervision of other workers

percentages

Per cent who supervise others	White	West Indian	Asian
Men	35	18	17
Women	20	17	8
Professionals, Employers, Managers	76	62	
Other Non-Manual	27	22	
Skilled Manual and Foremen	26	17	
Semi-skilled Manual	5	3	
Unskilled Manual	3	–	

Table 96:   Industry sector by ethnic group: men

	White	West Indian	Asian	Indian	Pakistani	Bangla-deshi	African Asian
Mining, Chemicals and Metal Manufacture	9	4	7	7	8	2	6
Engineering and Metals	15	9	13	14	13	8	14
Vehicles and Shipbuilding	5	12	11	13	10	9	7
Textiles, Clothing and Leather	2	3	13	8	20	32	7
All other Manufacturing	10	14	14	13	19	7	10
All Manufacturing and mining industries	41	41	57	55	70	59	45
Construction	8	7	3	3	2	-	4
Transport and communication	10	24	12	16	9	4	12
Distributive Trades	8	6	6	4	3	2	13
All other service industries	23	14	17	16	13	31	18
All service industries	41	45	35	36	25	37	43
Public Administration and Defence	7	3	2	2	-	2	3
Base: All employees (weighted)	1490	972	2167	847	611	177	495
(unweighted)	591	467	1041	401	298	96	227

202

Table 97: Industry sector by ethnic group: women

Column percentages

	White	West Indian	Asian	Indian	African Asian
Textiles, Clothing and Leather	4	4	21	24	14
All Manufacturing and Mining Industries	21	20	44	52	35
Transport and Communication	4	6	2	2	2
Distributive Trades	17	8	14	9	23
Professional and Scientific	25	41	16	19	7
All Service Industries	70	72	41	36	43
Public Administration and Defence	6	6	8	7	12
Base: All Employees (weighted)	1050	1020	760	431	237
(unweighted)	495	502	340	195	102

Table 98:   Employer type: all employees

	Men			Women		
	White	West Indian	Asian	White	West Indian	Asian
Local Authority, Health Authority	12	17	11	25	48	16
Nationalised Industry or State Corporation	14	14	9	3	3	1
Civil Service	3	1	2	4	2	5
Private Firm	68	66	77	64	43	75
Police, Prison Service or Armed Forces	2	1	*	1	*	*
Other	1	*	1	3	2	*
Base: All Employees						
(weighted)	1490	972	2167	1050	1020	760
(unweighted)	591	467	1041	495	502	340

Percentages

| | Region | | | | | | Concentration of Asian and West Indian households in Enumeration districts | |
	Yorkshire and Humberside	West Midlands	East Midlands	South East (excl. London)	London	Other Regions	Up to 4 per cent	Over 4 per cent
Per cent in non-manual jobs								
Men								
White	34	37	33	43	46	45	42	(31)
West Indian	(7)	4	(-)	(19)	20	14	21	14
Asian	7	10	23	26	43	32	50	21
Women								
White	63	53	(61)	66	86	55	61	(75)
West Indian	(60)	52	(27)	(58)	53	57	56	52
Asian	(28)	(44)	20	44	66	(44)	62	43
Per cent in semi-skilled and unskilled manual jobs								
Men								
White	18	17	23	17	11	13	15	(21)
West Indian	(39)	31	(53)	(27)	34	41	33	37
Asian	54	38	38	36	33	50	23	43
Women								
White	33	43	(21)	28	12	40	33	(22)
West Indian	(40)	44	(73)	(35)	44	36	39	44
Asian	(68)	(48)	70	43	31	(53)	30	51

Table 100:   Industry sector in different regions

Percentages

	Yorkshire and Humber-side	West Midlands	East Midlands	South East (excl. London)	London	Other Regions
Men						
Per cent in manufacturing and mining						
White	53	55	46	38	23	40
Asian	79	68	59	63	38	57
Per cent in textiles, cloting and leather						
White	10	-	6	1	-	2
Asian	40	1	19	2	10	19
Per cent in vehicles and ship-building						
White	3	11	1	4	5	5
West Indian	(-)	19	(31)	(21)	8	11
Asian	5	27	8	13	7	3
Per cent in transport and communications						
White	5	3	9	12	21	9
West Indian	(-)	25	(14)	(16)	32	12
Women						
Per cent in manufacturing and mining						
White	20	22	(39)	10	20	25
Asian	(67)	(44)	72	50	27	(45)
per cent in textiles, clothing and leather						
White	6	4	(21)	-	-	6
Asian	(62)	(26)	38	14	5	(21)
Per cent in professional and scientific services						
White	21	30	(29)	29	27	21
West Indian	(53)	44	(42)	(47)	34	55

Column percentages

	Engineering, Vehicles Shipbuilding	Other Manufacturing and Mining	Transport and Communications	Other Services
White men				
Professional/Employer/Manager	13	13	3	33
Other Non-Manual	16	14	12	33
Manual Supervisors	12	14	11	5
Skilled Manual	41	39	50	19
Semi-skilled/Unskilled Manual	16	18	24	9
Base: (weighted)	285	327	151	461
West Indian Men				
Professional/Employer/Manager	5	1	4	9
Other Non-Manual	3	1	7	30
Manual Supervisors	7	11	16	7
Skilled Manual	45	41	43	22
Semi-skilled/Unskilled Manual	43	44	30	33
Base: (weighted)	200	198	234	199
Asian Men				
Professional/Employer/Manager	4	6	7	32
Other Non-Manual	5	3	12	34
Manual Supervisors	6	4	3	3
Skilled Manual	36	30	45	12
Semi-skilled/Unskilled Manual	49	56	33	16
Base: (weighted)	502	725	262	505

Table 102:   Female employees: job levels by industry by ethnic
group

Column percentages

	All manufacturing and Mining	Professional and Scientific Services	Other Services
White Women			
Professional/Employer/Manager	6	1	10
Other Non-Manual	35	68	57
Manual Supervisors	2	-	1
Skilled Manual	17	1	*
Semi-skilled/Unskilled Manual	38	28	31
Base: (weighted)	217	263	474
West Indian Women			
Professional/Employer/Manager	-	1	1
Other Non-Manual	19	67	48
Manual Supervisors	4	-	-
Skilled Manual	14	2	1
Semi-skilled/Unskilled Manual	66	31	49
Base: (weighted)	200	417	316
Asian Women			
Professional/Employer/Manager	1	12	7
Other Non-Manual	6	71	69
Manual Supervisors	2	-	-
Skilled Manual	9	-	2
Semi-skilled/Unskilled Manual	82	15	23
Base: (weighted)	341	122	186

208

Table 103:   Employees: job levels in the public and private
             sectors

Percentages

	Local Authority Health Authority	Nationalised Industry, State Corporation	Private Firm
Per cent in non-manual jobs			
Men			
White	62	20	40
West Indian	22	9	14
Asian	54	19	22
Women			
White	67		61
West Indian	62		44
Asian	84		33
Per cent in semi-skilled and unskilled manual jobs			
Men			
White	17	21	15
West Indian	28	42	38
Asian	15	37	45
Women			
White	30		31
West Indian	37		47
Asian	16		58

Notes: (1) The table shows the number of non-manual workers
           as a percentage of all employees in a given sector in
           a given ethnic group. For example, 62 per cent of
           white men employed by local authority bodies are
           non-manual workers.
      (2) The nationalised industry/state corporation sector is
           not shown for women because the base for each
           ethnic group is less than 50.

Table 104:   Self-employment by ethnic group

	White	West Indian	Asian	Indian	Paki-stani	Bangla-deshi	African Asian
Men	14	7	18	18	10	26	23
Women	7	1	14	12	(25)	-	18

Table 105:   Self-employment: type of Business, and number of employees

Column percentages

	White	West Indian	Asian
Industry Group:			
Agriculture	4	-	-
Manufacturing	14	(18)	10
Construction	28	(47)	2
Distribution, Catering	26	(21)	67
Hotels, Repairs			
other services	26	(14)	21
Number of Employees			
(excluding self):			
None	55	(59)	27
Under 5	20	(26)	43
5 or more	16	(12)	20
Don't know	10	(2)	11
Base: All Self-employed			
(weighted)	302	83	600
(unweighted)	120	38	265

Table 106:   Employees' hours of work and shiftwork

	Men			Women		
	White	West Indian	Asian	White	West Indian	Asian
Mean Hours per Week:						
Full-time workers	43.9	42.5	43.5	38.5	38.8	39.6
Part-time workers	20.1	21.9	22.4	18.4	24.1	22.3
Per cent regularly working shifts	20	29	33	11	18	14
Per cent working alternating shifts	12	19	16	6	9	4
Per cent working nights only	1	4	7	1	4	1
Base: Employees						
(weighted)	1490	972	2167	1050	1020	760
(unweighted)	591	467	1041	495	502	340

Table 107:   Shiftwork by job level

Percentage of SEG category
regularly working shifts

	Profess- ional, Employer, Manager	Other Non- Manual	Skilled Manual and Foreman	Semi- Skilled Manual	Un- skilled Manual
All white Employees	5	15	25	17	10
All Asian and West Indian employees	12	18	35	29	32

Table 108:   Asian Employees: shiftwork by fluency in English

Column percentages

	Fluently	Fairly Well	Slightly/ Not at all
Men:			
Regularly Works Shifts	26	43	38
Works Nights Only	5	6	10
Women:			
Regularly Works Shifts	13	11	22
Works Nights Only	1	-	2

Table 109:   Gross earnings of full-time employees

		Median Weekly Earnings	Unweighted Base
Men:	White	£ 129.00	526
	West Indian	£ 109.20	383
	Asian	£ 110.70	862
Women:	White	£ 77.50	247
	West Indian	£ 81.20	319
	Asian	£ 73.00	237

Table 110:   Gross earnings of full-time employees by region

£ median weekly earnings

	England and Wales	North West	Yorks/ Humberside	West Midlands	East Midlands	South West	South East (excl. London)	London
White men	128.90	141.50	116.20	130.20	135.40	129.20	126.90	129.90
Asian and West Indian men	110.20	98.60	103.70	105.90	96.00	107.50	115.20	118.70

Note: Because of small base sizes, the North, East Anglia and Wales regions have been omitted from this table. In each of these regions, the Asian and West Indian earnings were lower than those of the whites.

213

Table 111:   Gross earnings of male full-time employees by job
level

£ median weekly earnings

	All		Aged 25-54	
	White	Asian and West Indian	White	Asian and West Indian
All	129.00	110.20	136.50	114.50
Professional, Employer Manager	184.70	151.80	187.10	171.30
Other Non-Manual	135.80	130.40	143.90	137.90
Skilled Manual and Foreman	121.70	112.20	126.70	114.80
Semi-skilled Manual	111.20	101.00	(115.30)	104.00
Unskilled Manual	(99.90)	97.80	(117.10)	110.80

Table 112:   Gross earnings of full-time male manual workers, by
shiftwork

£ Median weekly pay

	White	Asian and West Indian
All	118.90	105.9
Never work shifts	112.20	99.20
Regularly work shifts	132.00	113.80
Alternating shifts	139.20	119.70
Nights only	137.40	104.50

214

Table 113:   Gross earnings of female full-time employees by job level

| | All | | Aged 25-54 | |
	White	Asian and West Indian	White	Asian and West Indian
All	77.50	78.50	91.50	81.90
Professional, Employer, Manager	(106.80)	(122.10)	104.70	(129.50)
Other non-manual	81.70	86.00	98.60	97.30
Skilled Manual	(66.90)	(74.40)	(70.60)	(74.20)
Semi-skilled and Unskilled Manual	(66.50)	72.40	(72.00)	75.60

Table 114: Asians: full-time employees' gross earnings

£ Median weekly pay

	Men	Women
All Asians	110.70	73.00
Indian	115.40	72.80
Pakistani	106.20	(64.30)
Bangladeshi	88.50	(43.80)
African Asian	114.20	76.80
Muslim	103.30	(67.10)
Hindu	117.20	79.60
Sikh	116.10	68.90

Speaks English:

	Men	
	Manual	Non-Manual
Fluently	110.80	147.90
Fairly well	108.80	120.50
Slightly/Not at all	94.20	(109.30)

Table 115:   Trade union membership and activity

Column percentages

	Men			Women		
	White	West Indian	Asian	White	West Indian	Asian
Trade Union Member	57	64	59	34	57	38
Attended Union Meeting in last 6 months	25	23	25	9	19	10
Hold Elected Post	6	2	3	2	2	2
Base: All employees (weighted)	1490	972	2167	1050	1020	760
(unweighted)	591	467	1041	495	502	340

Table 116:   Experience of racial discrimination in employment

Column percentages

	Men		Women	
	West Indian	Asian	West Indian	Asian
Have you yourself ever been refused a job for reasons which you think were to do with race or colour?				
Yes	26	10	23	8
No	45	32	49	33
Other/DK	29	57	28	59
Have you ever been treated unfairly at work with regard to promotion or a move to a better position, for reasons which you think were to do with race of colour?				
Yes	11	8	5	3
No	84	76	91	79
Other/DK	5	16	5	19
Base: Adults in labour market, or have worked in last 10 years				
(weighted)	1544	3563	1621	1462
(unweighted)	745	1709	804	679

218

Table 117:   Belief in racial discrimination in employment

Column percentages

	Men			Women		
	White	West Indian	Asian	White	West Indian	Asian
Do you think there are employers in Britain who would refuse a job to a person because of their race or colour						
Yes	73	77	48	69	77	29
No	23	7	25	28	5	15
Other/DK	4	16	28	4	18	56
If yes, how many?						
Most	5	14	8	3	15	5
About half	14	22	14	14	26	10
Fewer than half	32	31	19	29	28	10
Hardly any	18	4	2	16	2	2
Other/DK	5	6	3	7	6	3
Do you believe there are firms or organisations in Britain where promotion is less likely for Asian or West Indian people than for white people, even though their experience and qualifications are the same?						
Yes	55	78	57	49	73	34
No	28	8	17	30	8	12
Other/DK	17	15	26	21	19	60
Base: Adults						
(weighted)	2567	1630	3870	2802	1790	3013
(unweighted)	1001	781	1836	1262	876	1484

219

Table 118:   Belief in racial discrimination in employment: Asians and West Indians in the labour market

	Men		Women	
	West Indian	Asian	West Indian	Asian
Do you think there are employers in Britain who would refuse a job to a person because of their race or colour				
Yes	78	49	80	42
No	7	26	4	18
Other/DK	15	26	16	40
Do you believe there are firms or organisations in Britain where promotion is less likely for Asian or West Indian people than for white people, even though their experience and qualifications are the same?				
Yes	78	59	76	50
No	8	17	7	14
Other/DK	14	25	17	36
Base: All working or unemployed (weighted)	1417	3336	1255	1120

Beliefs about treatment of ethnic minorities by employers

Column percentages

	Men			Women		
	White	West Indian	Asian	White	West Indian	Asian
Are people of Asian/ West Indian origin treated the same, better or worse than white people by employers?						
Same	59	38	44	57	33	38
Better	4	1	2	3	*	*
Worse	28	49	42	25	48	34
DK	9	10	11	15	17	27
Base: Adults						
(weighted)	2567	864	1970	2802	951	1493
(unweighted)	1001	415	926	1262	467	760

Note: This question was on the interview schedule administered to a sample of <u>half</u> of the ethnic minority informants.

Figure 1. Registered unemployment rate among general population and ethnic minorites. Moving average, males and females, 1963-1981

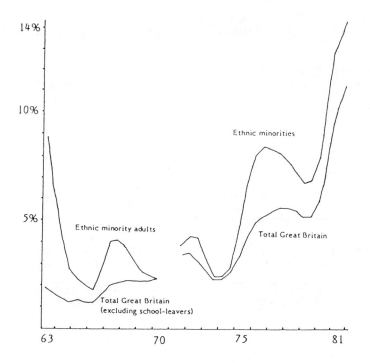

This figure is based on Figure 9 in Ethnic Minorities in Britain: a study of trends in their position since 1961 by S. Field et al., Home Office Research Study No.68, 1981, HMSO, with additional information for 1981 supplied by the Home Office.

Table 120: Job levels of whites, Asians and West Indians in 1974 and 1982

NB: Geographical areas as for 1974 survey only.

Column percentages

| | Men | | | | | | Women | | | | | |
| | White | | West Indian | | Asian | | White | | West Indian | | Asian | |
	1974	1982	1974	1982	1974	1982	1975/6	1982	1974	1982	1974	1982
Professional, Employer, Manager	23	22	2	7	7	14	5	9	1	1	2	7
Other non-manual	17	20	6	9	11	12	51	52	42	53	30	35
Skilled Manual and Foreman	42	44	59	48	40	36	7	9	8	3	13	14
Semi-skilled Manual	12	11	23	23	30	31	36	19	41	36	47	42
Unskilled Manual	6	3	9	11	11	5		11	6	6	8	3
Base: (weighted)	1594	1664	2896	748	4308	1931	9822	1079	2345	720	1207	566
(unweighted)	996	647	634	391	1229	985		508	429	380	237	286

Notes: (1) Figures for white women in 1975/6 derived from General Household Survey (Table 5.9, Social Trends No. 8, 1975)
(2) Bases for the 1974 survey include all people in the job market who have worked, whether employed or self-employed.
(3) Bases for the 1982 survey include only those in work, whether employed or self-employed.
(4) White figures are for all areas (nationally representative).

223

Table 121:   Job levels in 1974 and 1982, including the unemployed

N.B. Geographical areas as for 1974 survey only.

Column percentages

	Men				Women			
	West Indian		Asian		West Indian		Asian	
	1974	1982	1974	1982	1974	1982	1974	1982
Professional, Employer, Manager	2	7	7	12	1	1	2	6
Other Non-Manual	6	9	11	11	42	52	30	33
Skilled Manual and Foreman	59	47	40	34	8	4	13	12
Semi-skilled Manual	23	25	30	35	41	37	47	44
Unskilled Manual	9	11	11	7	6	5	8	3
Weighted Base:	2896	974	4308	2281	2345	866	1207	677

Table 122: 1982 job levels of Asians and West Indians by whether working in 1974

N.B. Geographical areas as for 1974 survey only.

Column percentages

| | Asian Immigrants | | All others new to labour market since 1974 | | | | All those in the labour market in 1974 | | | |
| | | | West Indian | | Asian | | West Indian | | Asian | |
	Men	Women	Men	Women	Men	Women	Men	Women	Men	Women
Professional, Employer, Manager	13	(9)	7	3	19	6	8	1	13	7
Other Non-Manual	14	(31)	24	59	11	41	5	51	12	29
Skilled Manual and Foreman	31	(11)	41	5	43	9	50	3	34	20
Semi-skilled Manual	35	(46)	19	31	23	41	25	39	34	42
Unskilled Manual	4	(4)	8	4	3	2	12	7	6	3
Base: (weighted)	208	87	177	236	460	244	569	483	1264	236
(unweighted)	118	45	80	118	204	111	310	261	663	130

Table 123:   Job levels of those aged under 25

	Men			Women		
	White	West Indian	Asian	White	West Indian	Asian
(a) Employees and self-Employed						
Professional, Employer, Manager	7	5	18	6	2	5
Other Non-Manual	25	27	10	69	72	57
Skilled Manual and Foreman	51	38	42	6	9	7
Semi-skilled Manual	10	22	26	14	15	32
Unskilled Manual	4	7	3	3	3	-
Base: All Working, Aged 16-25						
(weighted)	296	198	344	264	188	167
(unweighted)	76	76	130	79	85	66
(b) Employees only						
Professional, Employer, Manager	7	4	17	4	2	3
Other Non-Manual	30	27	11	73	72	61
Skilled Manual and Foreman	48	38	38	5	9	3
Semi-skilled Manual	11	23	30	15	15	35
Unskilled Manual	3	7	3	3	3	-
Base: Employees, Aged 16-25						
(weighted)	235	191	300	251	188	155
(unweighted)	65	72	116	75	85	59

Asians and West Indians: reported job mobility over period 1974-1982

Column percentages

| | Men | | Women | |
	All Areas	1974 Survey areas	All Areas	1974 Survey areas
Manual to non-manual	5.1	4.3	4.0	4.3
Non-manual to manual	2.1	1.7	3.0	1.3
Net manual to non-manual	3.0	2.6	1.0	3.0
Manual throughout	72.3	78.0	49.6	52.3
Non-manual throughout	20.4	16.1	43.3	42.0
Base: All Working in 1974 and 1982				
(weighted)	2331	1728	960	686
(unweighted)	1135	918	475	374

VIII Support and Care

Financial support

<u>Earned income</u>
In the previous chapter we made a comparison of the wage levels of black and white employees. Although this basic comparison is important, it should be placed in the context of a broader analysis of the extent to which different households receive financial support from earned income and from other sources. As a first step in this analysis we show in Table 125 the proportions of households lacking a person in paid employment and the average numbers of persons in paid employment per household. Here we see that among Asian and West Indian households these overall indicators of levels of support from earned income are rather better than among white households: there are fewer black households without an earner, and a larger average number of earners per household among blacks. These simple facts hide a much more complicated pattern, however. First, the much older average age of the white adult population means that there are many more households made up only of pensioners than among black people: 29 per cent of white households are pensioners only, compared with two per cent of Asian and West Indian households. Secondly, there are on average more people in black households than in white households; black households therefore require more earners to maintain the same level of earned income per person as white households. Thirdly, there are considerable differences between the different groups in the black population: in particular, the Muslims have on average fewer earners per household than other Asians, and over twice as many households without any earners.

To allow for the different household sizes we have calculated the average number of dependants supported by each earner within each ethnic group as a whole (the 'dependency ratio'). It can be seen that despite their higher average numbers of earners and lower proportions of households without an earner, the black groups have more dependants per earner than the whites. This is partly a result of ethnic differences in household structure and partly a reflection of the higher unemployment rates among blacks; an idea of the impact of unemployment on black families can be obtained by a comparison of the dependency ratios found in the 1974 PEP survey and this survey. Confining the comparison to the limited geographical boundaries of the 1974 survey, we see that the overall dependency ratio has risen from 1.57 to 2.23. Over the same period, the dependency ratio for whites has risen from 1.17 to 1.36; the rise for blacks has therefore been, in the areas of the 1974 survey, over three times the size of the rise experienced by white people. The changes in household size experienced by Asians and West Indians over this period would lead us to expect dependency ratios to have fallen but for the rise in unemployment. Within the black sample the West Indian households have 'lost' so many children that their dependency ratio has remained static, so all of the growth is located within the Asian part of the sample; if however, we take account of the fall in the average number of children by looking at the adult dependency ratio - the number of adult dependants divided by the number of earners - we find that the West Indian ratio has grown more than either the white or Asian ratio, in line with the different growth of unemployment.

The dependency ratio tends also to vary within each ethnic group according to differences in household structure, so it is important to consider different types of household separately if we are interested in how their financial needs are met. Table 126 shows for each household type the proportion of households without an earner and the ratio of dependants to earners. As we noted above, the large proportion of pensioner-only households in the white sample results in a larger proportion of white households than black households lacking an earner. When we look at other types of household the picture is very different. The proportion of West Indian households lacking an earner is very similar to that of whites (for lone parents, 'others with children' and single adults it is a little higher, and for extended households and 'other households' a little lower) while the relative position of Asians varies between household types. The proportion of Asian extended households that have no earner is lower than for whites and West Indians, the proportion of single adults who have no job is about the same as for West indians and a little larger than for whites, and the proportions of lone parent households and 'others with children' with no earner are distinctly larger than for whites or West Indians. This last group of households - the nuclear families - accounts for over half of the Asian households in the survey, and the proportion lacking an earner (19 per cent) is over twice as large as that for whites (eight per cent).

229

We show the ratio of dependants to earners in different types of household in two ways: first, we show the overall dependency ratio for all the households irrespective of whether they contain anyone in paid employment, in other words the total number of dependants in the sample divided by the total number of earners; secondly, we show the dependency ratio just for households that have at least one person in employment. Although the first of these measures gives a good summary of the support from earnings for the sample as a whole, it takes no account of the different position of households with and without any earned income, by allowing earners in multiple-earner households to compensate for their absence in other households. The second measure gives a more accurate picture of the position of households that are supported by earned income, but it must be seen in conjunction with the percentage of households lacking an earner.

Not only do a greater proportion of Asian households than white households (other than pensioner-only households) lack earned income, but in those households where someone is working, each earner has more people to support. It can be seen that for all types of household the Asians have more dependants per earner, and this is true for both versions of the measure. The dependency ratios for West Indians are, for households with one or more earner, similar to those for whites, with the exception of lone parent households, where each West Indian earner supports on average 2.1 dependants compared with 1.7 for each white earner, and 'other households' where the averages are 0.8 and 0.6 respectively. Thus we see that although for some types of household a slightly higher proportion of West Indians lack an earner than whites, those with any earners have a similar average ratio of dependants to earners.

These patterns fit well with our knowledge of the employment status of men and women in the three ethnic groups, and the numbers of adults and children in their households. Excluding pensioners from the analysis, we know that among Asian and West Indian men there are fewer employed and self-employed than among white men because of their higher rate of unemployment, but among West Indian women the total in the labour market is sufficiently large, relative to that for white women, to offset the effect of unemployment on the total percentage working. Asian women are less likely to be found in the labour market and are also affected by higher unemployment, so far fewer are working than among white or West Indian women. The total impact of this pattern is to make the average number of people in paid employment in West Indian households rather similar to that in white households, but much lower in Asian households. The household sizes of West Indians are for the different household types somewhere between those of whites and Asians. Therefore we should expect to find a general pattern of support from earned income that is similar for whites and West Indians (although for some types of households, West Indians should be worse off) but inferior for Asians, and this is the case.

The lower earnings levels of blacks generally compound the effects of these differences in dependency ratios. This can be demonstrated if we make a calculation of the likely order of earnings per person in the household, using the figures from the survey. If for each earner in the household we allow the median earnings for their ethnic group, and divide this total among all the members of the household, we obtain figures for weekly earned income for each household member as follows:

	Extended Households	Lone Parents	Others with Children	Adults without Children
White	£46	£20	£37	£59
West Indian	£37	£24	£32	£51
Asian	£27	£21	£27	£50

In each case the median is based on all employees in the ethnic group living in the given type of household, irrespective of sex, and includes part-time workers; in this way we automatically take into account the differing mix of male and female workers and of full-time and part-time workers in the different categories. The comparison is necessarily confined to households that contain at least one earner. We see that in extended households and in nuclear families the earned income per person is lower among West Indians than among whites, but is particularly low among Asians: the Asian figure is only 59 per cent of the white figure in the case of extended households, and 73 per cent of the white figure in the case of nuclear families. For both Asians and West Indians the figure for adults without children is also lower than for whites, by over ten per cent. The earned income per person for the lone parent households is, for all three groups, lower than for other types of household, partly because of the large proportion of women and part-time employees among them, but the white figure is level with the Asian figure and lower than the West Indian figure, and this is a reflection of the fact that two-thirds of employed lone parents in the white sample are part-time workers, compared with a third in the black sample.

These figures assume that all workers - including the self-employed - are earning the median wages for their ethnic and household-type group as a whole, and are meant as a demonstration of how lower wage levels combine with varying dependency ratios to produce a pattern of ethnic disadvantage that is far greater than can be seen from the individual earnings medians alone. They are not intended to be used as statistically reliable estimates of average income per head. It should also be remembered that these comparisons omit reference to the households lacking any earners, in respect of which we have seen further ethnic differences.

Support between households

Some households receive regular or occasional financial support from other households, and this is strongly related to household type (Table 127). Among whites it is lone parents who most commonly receive this source of income, but a much smaller proportion of Asian and West Indian than of white lone parents have financial support from another household. This reflects a difference in the circumstances of the lone parents in the three groups. The support for white lone parents is mainly support from estranged husbands; about 70 per cent of white lone parents are divorced or separated, and only six per cent of them are single. Over half of West Indian lone parents are single, and less than 40 per cent are divorced or separated. This helps explain the difference in the proportions supported by people outside the households: more of the white lone parents receive legally agreed maintenance for the children. The Asian lone parents are more often widows or widowers (30 per cent) or are married but living alone, while less than a third are divorced or separated. It is something of a puzzle why over half of the Asian single parents are married but living alone; because divorce and separation are less accepted within their group they may be reluctant to give their marital status as 'separated', if that is their position, but another explanation may be that for some reason their partner is currently living abroad.

The proportion of vertically or horizontally extended households receiving any financial support from outside is not very large among whites or West Indians (ten and eight per cent respectively) but is even lower among Asians (three per cent). Among the pensioner-only households, a greater proportion of the Asian and West Indians than of the whites receive support from other people. For other types of household the proportions receiving support from another household are small and are comparable for the three ethnic groups.

There is a very large difference between black and white households in the practice of sending financial support to other households. Forty per cent of West Indian households and 30 per cent of Asian households send money to dependants living elsewhere, compared with five per cent of white households. Among households sending money to support dependants the average amounts sent per month are £44.50 for white households, £17.10 for West Indian households and £26.20 for Asian households.

Over four-fifths of the sums sent by Asians and West Indians goes to help relatives in their family's country of origin, over half going to parents. Nearly half of the money sent by white households goes towards the support of their children, and this ties in with the finding that most of this type of support reported as coming into white households is maintenance for children. Among West Indian households, far fewer report that they are sending money to support children (10 per cent of those sending money) and the proportion among Asians is negligible.

Support from state benefit schemes

We asked all heads of households what state benefits were received by members of the household. As can be seen from Table 128, the proportions claiming the various benefits vary considerably with the type of household, so the value of comparing the overall proportions in receipt of benefit between white, West Indian and Asian households is limited: this comparison mainly reflects the differences between the populations in terms of age, childbearing and unemployment. Twice as many Asian and West Indian households receive child benefit as white houeholds, and over six times as many white households receive a pension as Asian and West Indian households. Twice as many black households as white households receive unemployment benefit. Family income supplement and supplementary benefit are received more often by West Indian households than white or Asian households.

When comparisons are made within particular types of household we still find that a larger proportion of Asians and West Indians than of whites are receiving unemployment benefit. Nearly all lone parents and 'others with children' are receiving child benefit. Although the take-up of child benefit among these households should in theory be 100 per cent, claimants are sometimes without benefit because of temporary administrative complications, and we must also allow for a small degree of non-response to the question, so the shortfalls in the survey figures are unlikely to represent any real, permanent level of underclaiming of child benefit. Among extended households, the different proportions in receipt of child benefit are exactly in line with the relative numbers that have children in the household.

The proportions of households receiving supplementary benefit (supplementary allowance or supplementary pension) and family income supplement vary between the ethnic groups in a more complex way. Supplementary allowance is paid to people who have no full-time job and whose incomes are too low to meet basic domestic costs. About half of all lone parents receive supplementary allowance, irrespective of ethnic group. For white and West Indian extended families the proportions claiming supplementary allowance are the same as those claiming

233

unemployment benefit, but among Asians the proportion of supplementary allowance claimants is lower than the proportion of unemployment benefit claimants (14 per cent of households compared with 21 per cent of households). This may be associated with the fact that only nine per cent of Asian extended households lack an earner, compared with 16 per cent of West Indian extended households and 18 per cent of white extended households. Among nuclear families we also find that the proportion of Asian households receiving supplementary allowance is much lower than the proportion receiving unemployment benefit (8 per cent compared with 18 per cent) but in this case the proportion of wageless Asian households is 19 per cent: the low proportion of supplementary allowance claimants is therefore puzzling. There is no way we can assess whether this is the result of families falling outside entitlement for various reasons (for example, because of their level of savings) or the result of their failing to receive benefits to which they are entitled. Nevertheless the fact is that the proportion of wageless families who receive supplementary benefit is smaller among Asians than it is among whites or West Indians.

Family income supplement is paid to families with children where the male parent (or lone parent of either sex) is in full-time employment but their income is low. In total, very few of the households in the survey are in receipt of FIS, but the proportion among West Indian households is higher than among white households, for each household type. This might be expected, because West Indians at work earn, on average, less than whites and therefore there is a higher percentage of low-income families among the West Indians. But it is surprising that a smaller proportion of Asian than West Indian households are in receipt of FIS, since their level of support from earnings is lower than for West Indians. In fact, the proportion of Asian households claiming FIS is, for each household type, about the same as for white households, and this does not reflect the large gap between them in terms of earnings and household size. It is not possible to calculate with any accuracy the proportions of households that, according to the qualifying rules, should be in receipt of FIS, and we cannot therefore assess the extent of under-claiming among the different ethnic groups. However, levels of earnings and household sizes among Asians would lead one to expect the proportion claiming FIS to be larger than we find in the survey.

Comparisons of the benefits paid to households that contain only people of pensionable age have to be made with some caution because of the small sample sizes among Asians and West Indians. However, we find differences between the ethnic groups with are understandable in terms of the qualifying rules for the benefits: fewer Asians and West Indians than whites are claiming retirement pension, and this is because qualification is by past national insurance contributions, which a proportion of elderly Asians and West Indians have not paid because they are relatively recent immigrants. Supplementary pension (the pensioners' equivalent to supplementary allowance) is not subject to qualification by previous contributions, and this is claimed by about a quarter of pensioner households in each ethnic group.

Views on treatment by DHSS offices

As part of the series of questions on the treatment of black and white people by different organisations, we asked whether people of Asian and West Indian origin were treated the same, better or worse than white people by DHSS offices. The responses of the white informants differ from those of the Asian and West Indian informants in a similar way to that found in the corresponding question on council housing departments, as discussed earlier. We see first of all that of Asians and West Indians only two-thirds are prepared to give a view, compared with nearly 90 per cent of whites (Table 129). A majority of those in each ethnic group who give a view say that DHSS offices treat white and black people the same. Of the remaining informants - about 25 per cent of all men and 20 per cent of women - most of the white people say they think Asian and West Indian people are treated better, and most black people say they think white people are treated better. It is interesting to note that there is no association between the answers given to this question and the informant's status as a claimant or non-claimant of benefits, except for a weak tendency for those not in receipt of any benefits to give a 'don't know' response; this is the case for whites and blacks alike. We have no objective evidence within the survey results to assess the actual treatment of different informants by DHSS offices; there is certainly no evidence to suggest that Asian or West Indian households are receiving benefits beyond their entitlement, and we have already noted that the proportions of Asian households receiving supplementary benefit and family income supplement are lower than we might have expected them to be.

Health care

A limited number of questions dealing with contact with the health service were included in the interview. These were to assess the levels of registration with a GP, the use of hospital facilities in preference to a GP for everyday medical care, and the take-up of ante-natal care services. We also sought informants' views on whether white and black people received different treatment from hospitals.

Table 130 shows that nearly all white, West Indian and Asian adults are registered with a doctor; the proportion saying they were not registered, or did not know whether they were registered, was only one per cent of whites and two per cent of Asians and West Indians, and there were no differences between the different Asian groups. The proportion of informants who say they use their local hospital rather than their GP for everyday medical care is negligible.

In households where there were children, mothers were asked whether they had attended an ante-natal clinic or had any other ante-natal care before the birth of their last child in Britain. Table 131 shows that at least 95 per cent of white, West Indian and Asian women had ante-natal care at a clinic or elsewhere (usually their doctor). Among white women, the pattern of care was different for older women (who were more likely to have had their last child some time ago), in that older women were slightly more likely to say they had no ante-natal care, and were more likely to have been seen by their doctor (rather than a clinic) than younger women. The proportion of Asian women saying they had no ante-natal care is slightly larger than for West Indian women and young white women (five per cent as opposed to two per cent). It is interesting to look closer at the group who said they had no ante-natal care, to see if there are any relationships with other variables. There is no clear relationship with fluency in English (those who speak English 'not at all' are as likely as those who speak English fluently to have had ante-natal care), nor is there any clear relationship with local concentration of black households, and the relationship with age is contrary to that which might be expected - the older women are less likely to say they had no ante-natal care. Among the different Asian groups the Pakistanis give this response most commonly (seven per cent) and the Bangladeshis least commonly (two per cent). There is therefore no evidence to suggest that failure to use ante-natal care facilities fits in with the general pattern of ethnic disadvantages. When those who had no ante-natal care were asked why, two thirds said they had no particular reason or did not know about the available services, and a quarter said they were 'too busy'.

The views of white, Asian and West Indian informants on the relative quality of service given by hospitals to white and black people are shown in Table 132. A majority of all three groups say that equal treatment is given, although, as for other questions in this format in the survey, the Asian and West Indian informants give a 'don't know' response more often than white informants. A small minority of white informants feel that hospitals treat black people better (under four per cent), and this is matched by a similar proportion within the Asian sample giving the same response. About five per cent of West Indians and ten per cent of Asians feel that white people are treated better by hospitals. The views of black and white informants on equality of treatment by various institutions and organisations are discussed further in Chapter X.

Table 125:   Household support from earned income

	White	West Indian	Asian	Indian	Paki-stani	Bangla-deshi	African Asian	Muslim	Hindu	Sikh
Per cent of households without an earner	37	22	19	14	28	27	13	25	10	12
Average number of earners	1.1	1.4	1.3	1.4	1.0	1.0	1.5	1.1	1.6	1.5
Average number of dependants	1.5	2.1	3.3	2.9	4.2	4.0	2.6	3.9	2.4	3.2
Overall dependency ratio	1.4	1.5	2.5	2.1	3.2	2.9	1.8	3.6	1.5	2.1
Base: Households (weighted) (unweighted)	2694 2305	1834 1189	2851 1893	1150 726	751 518	277 197	604 411	1339 937	748 481	520 349

Note: The dependency ratio is defined as the total number of persons (of all ages) not in paid employment in all the households in the sample divided by the total number in paid employment in all the households in the sample.   It is equivalent to the average number of dependants divided by the average number of earners.   'In paid employment' includes the self-employed.

238

Table 126: Support from earned income by household type

	All Households			Pensioners			Extended Households			Lone Parents		
	White	West Indian	Asian	White	West Indian	Asian	White	West Indian	Asian	White	West Indian	Asian
Per cent of households without an earner	37	22	19	93	(85)	(100)	18	16	9	47	51	61
Overall dependency ratio	1.4	1.5	2.5	13.0	(5.0)		1.2	1.4	2.2	3.7	4.6	7.6
Dependency ratio for households with one or more earners	1.1	1.3	2.3	0.5	(0.2)		1.3	1.4	2.5	1.7	2.1	2.5
Base: Households (weighted)	2694	1834	2851	778	39	42	114	154	518	85	324	101
(unweighted)	2305	1189	1983	389	27	28	114	97	360	85	203	71

.../Contd.

239

126 contd/...

	Others with Children			Single Adults			Adults without children		
	White	West Indian	Asian	White	West Indian	Asian	White	West Indian	Asian
Per cent of households without an earner	8	10	19	27	33	32	13	9	10
Overall dependency ratio	1.7	1.7	3.3	0.4	0.5	0.5	0.6	0.7	1.0
Dependency ratio for households with one or more earners	1.9	1.8	2.8	0.0	0.0	0.0	0.6	0.8	1.1
Base (weighted)	699	656	1582	154	201	115	864	460	496
(unweighted)	699	415	1041	154	133	77	864	314	318

Notes: (1) Overall dependency ratio: see definition for previous table.
(2) Dependency ratio for households with one or more earners is calculated in the same way, but excluding the no-earner households altogether.
(3) As there are no earners among the Asian pensioner-only households, a dependancy ratio cannot be calculated; similarly, the dependancy ratio is always zero for single-person households where the person is employed, because there are no dependants.

Table 127:   Support provided from, and for persons outside the household

Percentages

	White	West Indian	Asian
Percent of Households that Receive Support from Someone Outside Household:			
Pensioners Only	4	(8)	(17)
Extended Household	10	8	3
Lone Parent	33	13	9
Others with Children	3	1	2
Single Adult (not pensioner)	3	5	5
Others	2	1	2
Percent of Households Sending Money to Someone Outside Household (column percent):			
Sometimes	1	25	21
Regularly	4	15	9

<u>Table 128:</u>   <u>Support from state benefits by household type</u>

	White	West Indian	Asian
All Households:			
Per cent in receipt of...			
Child Benefit	34	60	75
Unemployment Benefit	7	17	16
Family Income Supplement	1	5	2
Supplementary Benefit/			
Pension	14	20	11
Retirement/Widow's Pension	35	6	6
Extended Households:			
Per cent in receipt of...			
Child Benefit	45	47	78
Unemployment Benefit	15	18	21
Family Income Supplement	3	3	2
Supplementary Benefit	15	19	14
Lone Parents:			
Per cent in receipt of...			
Child Benefit	98	95	97
Unemployment Benefit	7	11	10
Family Income Supplement	6	15	7
Supplementary Benefit	45	50	45
Others with Children:			
Per cent in receipt of...			
Child Benefit	99	97	98
Unemployment Benefit	9	15	18
Family Income Supplement	1	4	2
Supplementary Benefit	7	10	8
'Pensioner Only' Households:			
Per cent in receipt of...			
Retirement Pension	95	(80)	(74)
Supplementary Pension	25	(31)	(26)

Table 129:   Beliefs about treatment of ethnic minorities by DHSS offices

Column percentages

	Men			Women		
	White	West Indian	Asian	White	West Indian	Asian
Are people of Asian/ West Indian origin treated the same, better or worse than white people by Social Security Offices (DHSS)?						
Same	65	46	51	65	46	46
Better	20	2	2	18	1	1
Worse	5	24	21	4	21	14
DK	10	27	27	13	33	37
Base: Adults						
(weighted)	2567	864	1970	2802	951	1493
(unweighted)	1001	415	926	1262	467	760

243

Table 130: Registration with a GP, and normal first source of medical care

Column percentages

	White	West Indian	Asian	Indian	Paki-stani	Bangla-deshi	African Asian
"Are you yourself registered with a doctor?"							
Yes	99	98	98	99	98	98	98
No/Don't know	1	2	2	1	2	2	2
"When you want a medical check-up or medical treatment because you are unwell or have hurt yourself, where do you normally go first? Do you go to..."							
Your local hospital	*	1	*	*	*	-	*
Your local doctor, that is you G.P.	96	94	97	96	97	97	96
Don't know/No answer	3	5	3	3	2	3	4
Base: Adults							
(weighted)	5369	3465	6894	2672	1840	617	1634
(unweighted)	2263	1678	3323	1241	935	336	743

244

Table 131:   Women with children who have given birth in Britain: ante-natal care

	White		West Indian	Asian
	Aged 16-24	Aged 25+		
Before you last child was born, did you attend an ante-natal clinic or have any ante-natal care?				
Yes, clinic/hospital	94	87	94	92
Yes, other	4	8	4	2
No	2	4	2	5
Base: Mothers who have given birth in Britain				
(weighted)	112	866	1184	1875
(unweighted)	43	447	590	1013

Table 132: Belief about treatment of ethnic minorities by hospitals

Column percentages

	Men			Women		
	White	West Indian	Asian	White	West Indian	Asian
Are people of Asian/West Indian origin treated the same, better or worse than white people by hospitals?						
Same	90	77	74	90	81	72
Better	4	3	6	3	2	6
Worse	1	5	9	2	6	11
DK	5	14	10	5	9	9
Base: Adults						
(weighted)	2567	864	1970	2802	951	1493
(unweighted)	1001	415	926	1262	467	760

IX Racial Attacks

No assessment of the impact of racialism on the lives of British blacks can be made without taking into account their experience and fears of racially-motivated harassment and physical attacks. These most brutal manifestations of racial hatred were the subject of a Home Office report published just before the PSI survey was carried out, and it reached the following conclusion:

> Our study clearly indicates that the incidence of racial attacks presents a significant problem. The frequency of such attacks, often of a particularly insidious nature, and the depth of feeling and concern which they generate in the ethnic minority communities, are a matter of fact and not of opinion(1).

One of the main features of the Home Office study was a survey of inter-racial incidents reported by police officers in thirteen police areas, including London, Greater Manchester and the West Midlands, during two months early in the summer of 1981. This provided the first available estimates of the incidence of racially motivated offences, and they indicated that the rate of racial victimisation was much higher for black people than white people: the rate for Asians was 50 times the rate for white people, and the rate for West Indian and African people was over 36 times that for white people. The main limitation of the survey was that it could only cover incidents that came to the attention of the police, and there are many incidents of personal assault and other victimisation that are not reported to them. Further, such incidents were only reported to the research team when a special form was filled in by a police officer: it was not practicable for every incident, whether inter-racial or not, to be covered by the survey, and so the researchers had to rely on the initial assessment, and effort, on the part of officers. There may therefore have been a number of incidents that were not included in the Home Office Survey. For these reasons it was felt by researchers at PSI and at the Home Office that it would be useful to obtain some measure of the extent of racial harrassment from the PSI survey which can provide information from all potential victims, and not just those who contacted the police. Therefore we asked informants about any incidents of assault, deliberate property damage and burglary of which they had been the victims in the period between 1 January 1981 and their interview. The interviewing took place in the spring and summer of 1982, and for the majority of informants the period in question was between 16 and 18 months long. In the survey of Asian and West Indian people, the questions were located on the 'alternate schedule' which was used for half of all individual interviews. The numbers asked about victimisation were therefore 2265 white informants, 882 West Indian informants and 1688 Asian informants.

The most useful information from these questions concerns the incidence of physical assault, and most of this chapter will therefore deal with this. The figures for property damage and burglary are interesting but very often lack any information about the person or persons alleged to have committed the offence, while in most of the cases of physical assault a description has been given. Descriptions of assailants are of course necessary if any attempt is to be made to evaluate the racial connotations of the incident. The proportions of white, Asian and West Indian households that had a burglary or attempted burglary over the specified period were four, eight and seven per cent respectively. The proportions of informants who had property deliberately damaged were closer together, at ten per cent of whites and eight per cent of West Indians and Asians.

The first question asked about physical attacks was:

The next few questions are about things that may have happened to you since 1 January 1981 - that is since the beginning of last year. (Questions about burglary and damage of property were asked here). Since 1 January 1981, that is since the beginning of last year, has anyone physically attacked or assaulted you or molested you in any way?

If the informant said yes, the interviewer went on to find out how many times he or she had been assaulted in this period and to obtain details of the most serious incident. It can be seen that the question aimed to include all incidents, even those that were not particularly serious. The resulting descriptions therefore range from incidents involving little violence through to very serious attacks with weapons. The incidence of any kind of assault as picked up by this question is shown in Table 133. Altogether, three per cent of white and Asian informants, and five per cent of West

248

Indian informants had been assaulted during the specified period. For whites and West Indians, the figure is a little higher among men than among women. The incidence of assault is higher in the major conurbations than elsewhere, and higher still in the inner parts of the conurbations. This relationship is stronger for white people than for Asians and West Indians. Overall, the proportions of black and white informants assaulted in the 16-18 month period before their interview are very similar; but the proportion assaulted is higher among whites than among blacks in the inner-city areas and, if anything, higher among blacks than among whites outside these areas. Among both whites and blacks younger people are more likely to have been attacked than older people, although again this association seems to be stronger within the white sample.

To assess which of the assaults reported in the survey were racially motivated the author inspected the description of each incident in detail. The quality of the description varied a great deal, from lengthy accounts of the entire incident and its background through to a few cases where no details were given at all. This unevenness in the data, coupled with the fact that we only had the victim's view of the incident to work with, meant that any classification of incidents into those that did and did not have a racial motivation would have to be cautious. As the Home Office report points out, the only reliable source of information on racial motivation would be from the offender, and this is generally not available; evidence from the police and from any witnesses would have been helpful to us, but it was not feasible within our survey to attempt to obtain this. The Home Office study collected the assessments of the police officer concerned and of the victim as to whether the incident was racially motivated (the views of the victims were, however, recorded by the police officers).

We first identified all attacks on Asian and West Indian people where the assailant was white, and all those on white people where the assailant was Asian or West Indian; we shall refer to these as inter-racial incidents. These were then classified into three categories as follows:

(a) Descriptions of inter-racial incidents where the victim specifically mentions a racial motive, a racialist organisation or an obvious background of racial hostility.
(b) Descriptions of inter-racial incidents where the attack was apparently unprovoked and where no motive is stated or apparent from the description.
(c) Other inter-racial incidents. This covers all attacks where motives other than racial hatred are stated or are otherwise clear from the description. It includes attacks that involve theft or attempted theft, and incidents where there was a prior dispute.

249

The actual numbers of informants reporting each type of incident are given in Table 133. Given the difficulties of classification involved, the seriousness of the subject and the small numbers of incidents, we felt that merely to group the incidents in this way would not present the findings in the most useful way, and we therefore give below the verbatim description of each of the incidents in categories (a) and (b), and some examples from (c).

Type (a). Descriptions of inter-racial incidents where the victim specifically mentions a racial motive, a racialist organisation or an obvious background of racial hostility

Case 1. West Indian informant
'We were just coming back from roller skating and they had this space invader place and they wanted for all the blacks to come out and leave the whites, so I started arguing and the next thing I know I was hit in the face with a bottle.'

Case 2. West Indian informant
'I was walking down the road in .... with two of my friends and a white man started shouting abuse at us. He called us racialist names. We had a scuffle. He didn't actually hit me but he hit my two friends and they hit him back.'

Case 3. Asian informant
'In my last school English lads had gangs to beat up Pakistanis. Once they attacked me when I was coming home.'

Case 4. Asian informant
'I was going to the bank, there were four lads, they started shouting 'Paki'. I told them don't be silly, then they hit me. They jumped on me, four of them, then we had a punch-up.'

Case 5. Asian informant
'I was talking to an Asian friend when a person came from behind me and slashed my face with a knife. I hit him with my hand in self defence. I was told by assailant 'this is how the National Front is going to get shot of all coons from England.'

Case 6. Asian informant
'Being attacked by gangs of white youths after saying prayers at the Mosque.'

250

Case 7. Asian informant
'I was going in the street; a few white people started shouting Paki, and abuse etc., and later on there was a punch-up and the Police were called and a man was removed from the street.'

Case 8. Asian informant
'Incident took place in bus station. Several skinheads who claimed to be N.F. members ran after me and my young brother. We ran away.'

Case 9. Asian informant
'Neighbour called at front door and banged the door on my head. The same neighbour called me racialist names and slapped me.'

Case 10. White informant
'Youth club outing to .... ice rink. Seven girls attacked me on the rink, followed me to the cloakroom and beat me up. I was very bruised. Had been agro there but I wasn't involved. I think it started with something between black boys and some boys in our group and then these black girls started on me.'

Type (b). Descriptions of inter-racial incidents where the attack was apparently unprovoked and where no motive is stated or apparent from the description

Case 11. West Indian informant
'Getting jumped on by a couple of skinheads. They started to fight so I retaliated.'

Case 12. West Indian informant
'Was walking down a road four white unknown men in a car started calling me names. One got out and started fighting. They drove off when they saw other blacks coming down the road.'

Case 13. West Indian informant
'Walking home, five youths attacked me.'

Case 14. West Indian informant
'I was walking home from work and some white people attacked me. The people were between 18 and 20.

251

Case 15. West Indian informant
'A white man spat on me and started to beat me and said he was going to kill me.'

Case 16. West Indian informant
'It happened at my place of work but it was dealt with by the police. Three white youths tried to pull me off the stool that I was sitting on.'

Case 17. West Indian informant
'I was stabbed.'

Case 18. West Indian informant
'I was hit at the supermarket by a white girl. When I confronted her she just walked away. I was ill for a week.'

Case 19. West Indian informant
'You're walking along the left-hand side of pavement - you see someone approaching in middle - you move off or away and they still come towards you - nine times out of ten they give you a 'haunch'-shoulder you into the road.'

Case 20. West Indian informant
'I was sitting in a car and one youth come up and kicked me and his friend came and pulled him away.'

Case 21. Asian informant
'A white person came up to me and punched me in the face. I fell down and broke my watch.'

Case 22. Asian informant
'They threw eggs and flour, stones at me'.

Case 23. Asian informant
'I was just going in the building, block of flats, when somebody threw a bottle, luckily nothing happened and I escaped.'

Case 24. Asian informant
'Skinheads threw stones at me. They called me names and swore.'

Case 25. Asian informant
'Skinheads beat me up. About six of them. Moved into the flat and did not like us.'

Case 26. Asian informant
'Assaulted with a big stick on the head, in two places, and there was a lot of bleeding. They wanted to kill me, and a few stiches were made. They were skinheads.'

Case 27. Asian informant
'I was standing in the garden and my next door neighbour threw a stone at me - it hit me in my back. I turned round and she was just standing there with her hands on her hips calling me names.'

Case 28. Asian informant
'I was beaten up in the street.'

Case 29. Asian informant
'I was in a phone booth and someone gave a knock on the window, I opened the door, this girl said 'Excuse me', kicked me in the leg and ran off. It was late at night.

Case 30. Asian informant
'Two boys, about 18 years, white, hit me and punched and kicked another boy, same age.'

Case 31. Asian informant
'Me and my two other friends went to meet another friend. When we were coming back from his house we were attacked by about 20 or 30 white hooligans and beaten up. No weapons were used but they used their fists and kicked everything, for no reaon at all.'

Case 32. Asian informant
'Many youths come and disturb and shout at us. One of many cases. They kick the back-yard doors and I ran after them and they surrounded me. They had knives in their hands and insulted me but I managed to get away from them.'

Case 33. Asian informant
'The skinheads tried to open the door and grab me out.'

Case 34. Asian informant
'Coming home from work. White youths started swearing and then threw stones. I showed them a milk bottle and they scattered.'

253

Case 35. Asian informants
'Gang of skinheads just attacked without any cause.'

Case 36. Asian informant
'Skinheads kicked me on the back and bottom when I was coming home.'

Case 37. White informant
'I was beaten up and got bruises and cuts on my head and lips.'

Case 38. White informant
'There were six West Indians and they took up the whole width of the pavement so that as I tried to walk by, continue my line, I was given a shoulder charge - walked into me - pushed me.'

Type (c). Other inter-racial incidents (examples)

West Indian informant
'Someone came from behind and hit me in the back. They grabbed my bag and my glasses were broken.'

West Indian informant
'Standing outside my gate. Before I had advised a coloured girl, his girlfriend, to try and find a single man - he is married. He blamed me for trying to muck up his life. I was punched several times in the face.'

Asian informant
'Had a knife, pointed it at my stomach. Asked for all money, in pocket and cash till. 'Don't shout'. Threatened my life.'

Asian informant
'A white man asked me to lift some stuff at work. I did not so he hit me in the chest.'

White informant
'Walking along when three black boys pushed me on the ground because I wouldn't give them my bag. It was dark at the time.'

254

  'Club brawl on three occasions.'

Several points emerge from a close look at these descriptions. The first is that a number of the attacks on black people without any stated motive are almost certainly racial attacks. The number of motiveless attacks on white people (by blacks or whites) is not large (about one fifth of assaults) and these are often incidents where there is just an insufficient description to be able to set the assault in any context (for example: 'Got beaten up by three lads in a pub'; 'Black eye, received in fight'). Many of the attacks on Asians and West Indians are attacks in the street where there is clearly no background of a prior argument or misunderstanding. In other words, we can tell from the white survey that not many assaults are of the kind where unknown people just approach others in the street and hit them, kick them or throw stones at them, but a large proportion of attacks by white people on Asians and West Indians are of this type. Secondly, a large proportion of these attacks are by gangs of youths, often identified as 'skinheads'. Eight of the black victims specifically mentioned skinheads, and a further eight mentioned gangs of young white people who attacked them in the street. Thirdly, we should note that these assaults are often of a serious nature: a third of those attacks by whites on Asians and West Indians listed above involve the use of weapons, including knives and bottles, or missiles such as stones and bottles. None of the assaults by black people on white informants involved weapons or missiles.

Thus, we find nine cases of attacks by white people on black informants where a racialist motive or background of racial conflict was given in the description of the incident, while many of the 26 'motiveless' and unprovoked attacks are likely to be racial attacks, and a large proportion are assaults with intent to do serious physical harm to the victim. By contrast we find one case of attack by black people on a white informant where there is a background of racial conflict and a further two 'motiveless' assaults. We cannot give estimates for the overall levels of racial attacks on black and white people from our survey because of the large area of doubt around the majority of assaults that might be suspected to be racially motivated. In particular, we feel that it would be difficult to assess from our evidence whether Asians are more likely than West Indians to suffer these attacks, as found by the Home Office Study. We can, however, make a comparison with the number of racial attacks we might have predicted in our samples using the Home Office report's figures. Such a comparison seems at first rather crude; the geographical areas covered by the two surveys are different, and the definitions of racial attacks are different. In fact the careful choice of areas included in the Home Office study meant that they gave 'an adequately representative national picture' of England and Wales, and should therefore be sufficiently well matched with the PSI national sample for England and Wales, and a close look at the definition used by the Home Office shows that it embraces more types of incident than our 'racial motive or context stated by informant' category, and this is therefore a good basis for comparison, the PSI figure being the more cautious of the two. The PSI figures need a further adjustment for this comparison because all of the Home Office cases came to the attention of the police and this does not apply to the cases in the PSI survey. Only four of the nine black victims (three Asians and one West Indian) reported their attacks to the police; the white victim did not report her attack.

The Home Office report shows rates of racial victimisation per hundred thousand of the population of 1.4 for whites, 51.2 for West Indians and Africans, and 69.7 for Asians, all over a three-month period. These refer to all incidents, not just those involving violence against the person, and include incidents that do not amount to criminal offences; all of them are defined as incidents where there is strong evidence, or some indications, of a racial motive. If adjustments are made for the longer time period covered by the PSI survey (about 18 months) and the proportion of incidents involving violence against the person, as shown in the Home Office report, one would expect to find in the PSI survey fewer than two black people, and less than one white person (0.06) who have been victims of racial attacks and reported them to the police. In fact we find four black people and no white people. This suggests that the Home Office report did not overestimate the frequency of racial attacks on black people. But the four cases that we are citing as equivalent to those picked up by the Home Office study represent only a small fraction of the cases of attacks that are likely to have been racially motivated. If only half of the 'motiveless' unprovoked attacks (cases 11 to 38) were racial attacks - and if anything this is an underestimate - then the actual frequency of racial attacks is over ten times the figure calculated using the Home Office figures. This is partly because only 40 per cent of the incidents mentioned in the survey (types (a) and (b)) were reported to the police, but presumably also because of the different way the information was collected and classified in the two studies.

Further analysis of the inter-racial incidents in category (c), those where another motive or prior dispute is involved, shows that three of the four white informants were victims of bag snatches, and one was involved in several brawls in a club. Of the 14 black informants in this category, six were victims of robbery in the street or in their shop, two were attacked after discovering persons attempting to break into their homes, two were involved in arguments at their workplace, one was involved in a domestic dispute, one was assaulted by a police officer, one was in a fight at a party and one was sexually assaulted.

The Home Office report concluded that racial attacks were growing in frequency. We have no way of testing this within our survey, or by comparison with the Home Office study, which covered a period of time within that covered by our own. We do have data, however, on the views of black informants on the trend in the frequency of racial attacks and racialist insults. This is not presented here as an indicator of the actual growth of these incidents, but rather as evidence of the widespread concern clearly felt among Asian and West Indian people. Table 135 shows the proportions who feel these problems have got better, worse or stayed the same over the past five years. About a fifth give no opinion on the subject, but nearly half of all informants say they feel the problem of racial attacks has worsened. Only about one in seven West Indians and one in twenty Asians say they feel the problem has eased. A fifth of all informants say the situation has not changed. Their views of the problem of racialist insults are similar, although a small proportion of the West Indian sample can be seen to hold a different view of the two problems: they give a more optimistic view regarding insults than regarding attacks. The greater concern about the increase in the frequency of attacks and insults among the Asian informants is understandable in the light of the evidence from the Home Office study that Asians are subject to more attacks than West Indians.

The Home Office report stated that, for a number of reasons, black people had a lack of confidence in the capacity of the police to respond to offences of a racial character. It further commented that such a lack of faith in the protection of the police from these attacks is likely to lead to pressure for the formation of self-defence or vigilante groups. In the PSI survey we asked black informants two questions about their attitudes towards this issue. The first was whether they thought people from their own ethnic group could rely on the police to protect them from racialist violence, and the second whether people from their own group should organise self-defence groups to protect themselves. The responses are shown in Table 136, and they show that despite the greater concern among Asians about racial attacks, it is the West Indians who have less confidence in the protection of the police; Asians, however, are more likely than West Indians to agree with the idea of self-defence groups. About half of West Indian men and women think it is 'definitely not true' that they can rely on the protection of the police, compared with about a fifth of Asians. About half of the Asians say it is 'definitely true' or 'probably true', compared with about a quarter of the West Indians. Although these

257

responses could be interpreted as assessments of the ability, rather than of the willingness, of the police to react to racial attacks, it must be of concern that a majority of West Indians and a large minority of Asians say 'definitely' or 'probably' that they cannot rely on the police for protection against racial violence. Just over half of Asian informants, and just under half of West Indian informants agree with the statement that self-defence groups should be set up if necessary to protect members of their ethnic group against racial attacks. Just under 30 per cent of Asians, and just over 40 per cent of West Indians, disagree.

As one might expect, there is a tendency for younger informants to give responses that are more critical of the police and more favourable towards self-defence groups, but this is not a strong relationship (Table 137). The biggest difference is between younger and older West Indian men, but it should be noted that the proportion of young West Indian men agreeing with the statement about self-defence groups (63 per cent) is not much larger than that of Asian young men and women (57 per cent and 60 per cent). The proportion of young West Indian men who say they can rely on police protection against racialist violence is very small (17 per cent) when compared with older West Indian men (32 per cent) and with Asian men and women of both age groups (43-52 per cent), but is not much smaller than among West Indian women of both age groups. We can therefore say that there is a particular lack of confidence in the police among young West Indian men and among West Indian women generally, but this is not reflected by a particularly high level of militancy among them with regard to their views on self-defence groups. Altogether, however, these results show that there is among black people an alarmingly low level of confidence in the support from the police against racial attacks, and that this is particularly the case among West Indians.

Notes
(1)   Racial Attacks.   Report of a Home Office Study, Home Office, 1981.

Table 133:   Victims of assault over past 16-18 months

Percentages

	White	West Indian	Asian
Per cent of informants that have been 'physically attacked, assaulted or molested in any way':			
All	3	5	3
Men	4	6	3
Women	2	3	3
Inner London, Inner Birmingham, Inner Manchester	10	5	
Rest of London, W. Midlands M.C and Greater Manchester M.C	3	4	
Elsewhere	2	3	
Age group:			
16-24	10	7	
25-34	3	4	
35-64	1	2	
65+	1	2	

Numbers of cases

	Ethnic Origin of Informants		
	West Indian	Asian	White
Inter-racial assaults reported by informants:			
(a) Racial motive or racial background specifically mentioned	2	7	1
(b) Unprovoked attack, no stated motive	10	16	2
(c) Other incidents	8	6	4
Unweighted Base	882	1686	2265

Note: No attacks involving groups of assailants that included both whites and blacks are in this table. All of these are of type (c), and they would add 1, 3 and 2 cases to the West Indian, Asian and white columns respectively.

Racial attacks and racialist insults - beliefs about trends

Column Percentages

	Men		Women	
	West Indian	Asian	West Indian	Asian
Would you say the following problems have got better than they were five years ago, about the same, or would you say the situation has got worse?				
Physical attacks for racial reasons on people of Asian/West Indian origin:				
Better	15	6	13	4
Same	24	22	20	17
Worse	43	52	46	50
DK	18	20	20	29
Racialist insults directed at people of Asian/West Indian origin:				
Better	18	5	17	3
Same	35	24	27	19
Worse	32	54	40	50
DK	15	17	16	28
Base: Adults				
(weighted)	864	1970	951	1493
(unweighted)	415	926	467	760

Table 136:   Racial attacks: attitudes towards protection by police and self-defence groups

	Men		Women	
	West Indian	Asian	West Indian	Asian
'People of Asian/West Indian origin can rely on the police to protect them from racialist violence'				
Definitely true	11	13	5	11
Probably true	17	36	17	40
Probably not true	18	19	15	16
Definitely not true	46	23	50	17
DK	7	9	12	15
'People of Asian/West Indian origin should if necessary organise self-defence groups to protect themselves from racialist violence'				
Agree strongly	17	16	18	14
Agree	27	36	28	44
Neither agree of disagree	10	15	12	15
Disagree	21	23	26	18
Disagree strongly	22	9	16	8
DK	3	1	1	2
Base: Adults				
(weighted)	864	1970	951	1493
(unweighted)	415	926	467	760

Table 137: Racial attacks: attitudes by age group

	Men		Women	
	West Indian	Asian	West Indian	Asian
Per cent who say it is definitely or probably true that Asian/West Indian people can rely on police to protect them from racialist vilence				
Aged 16-24	17	43	23	50
Aged over 24	32	50	21	52
Per cent who agree or strongly agree that people of Asian/West Indian origin should if necessary organise self-defence groups to protect themselves from racialist violence				
Aged 16-24	63	57	47	60
Aged over 24	38	51	45	57

X Views on Race Relations

The main task of this study is to provide a factual base for the discussion and understanding of racial discrimination and racial disadvantage, and most of the report has therefore been devoted to establishing, from the survey data, the objective circumstances of black people in relation to those of white people. But it is also useful to have some indications of the beliefs and attitudes of black and white people in this subject area. The interview schedule contained a number of items designed to tap informants' beliefs and attitudes, and the responses to some of these have been discussed where they were of direct relevance to the substance of the earlier chapters. Here we shall consider in a more general way the views expressed about racialism, racial discrimination and disadvantage, and race relations; we shall also look at informants' views on the race relations laws and their knowledge of the organisations set up to counter racial discrimination and promote good community relations.

Two points should be made clear. First, we are not attempting here to chart in detail the psychology of white racialism or of the response of black people to it. The simplicity of the questions asked, and of the methods we have employed to analyse the responses, prevent us from attempting anything so grand; rather, the aim is to draw out some of the more obvious patterns of reported opinions in order to help set a context for the discussion of the survey findings as a whole in the next chapter. Secondly, it is important to remember that most of the attitude and belief questions demand by their very structure that the informant evaluate an idea or a supposed fact in a passive way: the uniformly worded questions do not allow the informant to freely articulate their own views on the subject. We should therefore always be cautious when interpreting the attitudes of informants as seen through these devices, for they are unavoidably focused for the convenience of the researchers' own vision, however hard he or she may try to design the questions to reflect the concerns of those being interviewed. A good deal of effort went into the piloting of the attitude and belief questions in the PSI survey, and much of this involved open-ended, unstructured enquiries about which issues matter to Asian and West Indian people, but it is nevertheless the case that the views presented in this chapter are, for the most part, limited in scope and sensitivity by our own interpretation of those issues.

The general response of blacks to the questions on racial bias

One of the most important features of the response to the attitudes and beliefs questions among the majority of Asians and West Indians is the lack of any blanket condemnation of white people and institutions as racially biased.   This reluctance to express a general view complaining about the treatment of black people is visible in several respects. In the answers to the question about differential treatment of blacks and whites by a list of thirteen institutions, the proportion who say that blacks are treated worse exceeds a half only once among West Indians, and never among Asians. Secondly, the actual proportions vary a great deal between the evaluations of the different institutions in this question, so the informants are clearly prepared to evaluate the conduct of different bodies separately, rather than repeat the same answer for each. The proportion of West Indians saying that six or more of these institutions treat blacks worse than whites is less than a tenth; very few black informants (less than two per cent) say that ten or more institutions out of the thirteen treat blacks worse than whites.   Thirdly, we see a reluctance to make any judgement at all in some cases: for many of the items in this question the 'don't know' category is larger for the Asian and West Indian samples than for the whites.   In the answers to other questions about discrimination and acceptance by white people the proportion of Asians or West Indians who respond with an answer critical of the conduct of white individuals or institutions is rarely a majority.   There are two conclusions we must draw from this finding which are important for our interpretation of the substantive responses to the attitude questions: one is that the majority of Asian and West Indian people do not use these questions to express a generalised complaint about their position and treatment relative to white people; the other follows from this, and it is that the questions eliciting a critical response from Asians or West Indians are reflecting a real concern about a specific issue.

Issues of importance to black informants

There is clear concern among Asians and West Indians about racial discrimination in employment.   About three-quarters of West Indian men and women, and about half of Asian men say there are employers who would refuse jobs to people on the grounds of colour or race, and although the figure is much lower for Asian women, this is largely due to the reluctance of those not in the labour market to give any assessment, and in fact over 40 per cent of Asian women in the labour market say there are employers who discriminate in this way (Tables 117 and 118). The proportions who say there are employers who discriminate in promotion are equally high. Although proportions who say that in general employers treat black people worse than white people are lower, they are relatively high when compared with those given for other bodies in the same question: about half of West Indian men and women, 42 per cent of Asian men and 34 per cent of Asian women say their ethnic group receives worse treatment than whites. Although, as we suggested in Chapter VII, these results show a very cautious response in the light of the established facts of discrimination in recruitment, they show, in the context of an even greater reluctance to claim there is discrimination in other fields, a definite feeling of injustice within a large section of the Asian and West Indian population over the issue of employment.

We saw in Chapter V that over two-thirds of West Indian informants say they think that there are white landlords who discriminate on racial grounds, and a third say that council housing departments treat West Indian people worse than white people (Tables 52 and 53). Among Asians only a third say they think there are white landlords who discriminate, and 22 per cent feel that council housing departments treat them worse than white people. Thus West Indian informants are more likely to express concern about discrimination over rented housing than Asians, although the proportion of Asians saying that they are treated worse by council housing departments is large in comparison to the average Asian response to the 'better-worse' question. A fifth of West Indian informants are critical of their treatment by estate agents and banks, compared with under ten per cent of Asians.

Treatment by the police is criticised as being discriminatory by two-thirds of West Indian informants and a third of Asian informants: these are the proportions saying their group is treated worse than white people (Table 138). Among West Indians, this criticism extends to the courts, but not among Asians; the proportions saying they are treated worse than white people by the courts are 38 per cent and nine per cent respectively. Although these views are particularly widely held among the West Indian informants, the belief that the police give discriminatory treatment is among Asians more widespread than the belief in discriminatory treatment by any other body or institution except by employers. These results have to be seen in conjunction with the responses of Asians and West Indians as to whether they could rely on the police for protection from racial attacks: nearly half of the West Indian informants, and a fifth of the Asian informants, said that this was 'definitely not true' (Table 136), and about half of the Asian and West Indian sample together said they agreed that self-defence groups should be set up if necessary to protect their communities.

A third of West Indian informants said they thought that schools treated them worse than white people, and this reflects a clear dissatisfaction, among a large minority of West Indians, with their own or their children's education. The proportion giving this response among Asians is much smaller (12 per cent). When, in another question, we asked parents with school-age children whether they were happy with their children's education to date, 25 per cent of West Indians said they were 'fairly unhappy' or 'very unhappy', compared with 10 per cent of Asians. When West Indian parents were asked what they were unhappy about, the most common responses were that the children were not being encouraged enough, not 'being pushed', that the teachers were not concerned to help them, and that there was not enough concentration on learning basic skills (the 'three R's'). They were usually comments of a general nature and seldom specifically mention any racial bias: in all there was very little spontaneous complaint about racially biased teaching. Six per cent of West Indian households with school age children said their children had some form of supplementary schooling (other than religious education classes) compared with one per cent of Asian households, and this must also be a reflection of the concern felt by West Indian parents over their children's education.

Black informants' views on trends in race relations
We asked whether life in Britain for people of Asian and West Indian origin has improved over the last five years. Fifteen per cent of Asians and twenty per cent of West Indians say they think it has, and a similar proportion say they think there has been no change, but half of all Asian and West Indian informants say they think life has become worse for their ethnic group (Table 139). The same question was asked in the 1974 PEP survey, and the results then were totally different. Over half of the West Indians, and over a third of the Asians, said things had got better, and fewer than 20 per cent of informants said things were worse. However, this question is phrased without any reference to racial discrimination or disadvantage, and it might be argued that the general economic decline of the last few years may alone have produced this very grim change of view among black people. We probed this by asking all those who said life was worse to explain why. The responses are shown in Table 140, and it can be seen that 67 per cent mention the recession as a general reason, while racial discrimination and disadvantage is mentioned by 41 per cent of West Indians and 49 per cent of Asians (note that these responses are not exclusive - more than one answer could be given). It is

therefore true to say that a large part of the turn-about from the relatively optimistic answers of the 1974 survey is due to feelings of general economic decline, but it is also true that a substantial proportion of informants volunteered an explanation in terms of a worsening of their position relative to white people, under the heading of differential unemployment, racial discrimination, racialism and racialist organisations, or racial attacks.

Among the informants who said life had become better over the past five years, a variety of reasons were cited. Forty-four per cent of West Indians who gave this response said that it was because black people were now more accepted by white people, although only 14 per cent of the Asians gave this answer. Forty-seven per cent of Asians said that increased living standards were the reason, but only 20 per cent of the West Indians said this (Table 141).

Returning to the extent to which informants feel that discrimination and other manifestations of racialism have changed over the last five years, we see in Table 142 that when asked directly about the trend in discrimination, over 40 per cent of Asians and West Indians say that this is now worse. A quarter of Asians and West Indians say that the level of discrimination has remained the same, but 21 per cent of West Indians say there is less discrimination compared with seven per cent of Asians. It should be noted that a relatively large proportion of Asians declined to give a view as to the change in the extent of racial discrimination. We saw in the previous chapter that half of Asian informants thought the problems of racial attacks and racialist insults were getting worse, and that only about five per cent felt there was any improvement (Table 135); among West Indian informants the picture given was not quite as bad, but those saying the problems were worse (over 40 per cent for attacks, and over 30 per cent for insults) far outweighed those saying they were better (between 13 and 18 per cent).

We asked whether informants agreed with the ideas of enforcing the present laws against discrimination more effectively and bringing in new laws that were more strict. In the light of the views expressed on the trends in discrimination, attacks and insults, it is not surprising that a majority of blacks agreed with both propositions (Table 143). Among both Asians and West Indians there was slightly less agreement with the suggestion for new laws than with the suggestion for more effective enforcement.

Black informants' views on living in multi-racial Britain
Table 144 shows that at least 80 per cent of Asians and West Indians express agreement with three statements to the effect that blacks should have white friends and colleagues in trade unions and political organisations, and over 80 per cent express disagreement

with two statements to the effect that blacks should avoid living in white areas and keep apart from white people generally. The contrast between the strength of this view among West Indians with regard to white friends and white trade union colleagues on one hand, and white colleagues in political organisations on the other, is rather interesting: there is a small but distinct group who are less enthusiastic about participation in political organisations. It should also be noted that eight per cent of West Indian informants, and seven per cent of Asian respondents, agree with the statement about avoiding living in mainly white areas. This is likely to be the effect of fears of racial harassment: during the pilot interviews, at the design stage of the survey, some informants answered this question by pointing out that they would be happy to live in a mainly white area if they could be sure they were safe from attacks from organised racialists.

In all, we can conclude from these responses that if 'integration' means having white friends and colleagues, and living among white people, the overwhelming majority of Asian and West Indian people favour it.

Black informants' views on the preservation of their culture

While a majority of Asians and West Indians are in favour of white and black people living together in Britain, they also agree that their own culture and way of life should be defended. Eighty per cent of West Indians and 88 per cent of Asians say they agree with this proposition in its most general form, as shown in Table 145. When this is put specifically in terms of preservation of their mother tongue, the proportion of Asians who say it is a 'good thing' to be able to speak it is very large, at 95 per cent (93 per cent agree that it 'should be taught to children'). It is perhaps equally noteworthy that nearly two-thirds of West Indian informants express their agreement with the statement that it is a 'good thing' to be able to 'speak the patois or dialect of your family's country of origin', and that when this is hardened to the proposition that the dialect or patois should be taught to children, half the informants agree. There is a group of West Indians who disagree with these statements: a fifth disagree that it is a 'good thing', and this rises to a third when it comes to the suggestion of teaching children. However, given that traditionally a very negative attitude has been expressed by white people and by educational and administrative bodies, both in Britain and in the West Indies, towards anything at variance with standard English, these results show considerable support for the preservation of this linguistic heritage.

It is important to note that although most Asians and West Indians agree they should preserve their own way of life and culture, over a third also agree that they should adopt the way of life and culture of white people (Table 145). About 30 per cent of

269

all black informants agree with both statements. However, a larger proportion in total (over 40 per cent) say they disagree with the statement about adoption of white culture, and a substantial proportion record a neutral position. Perhaps the best way to sum these results up is to say that a majority of black people are committed to the cultural survival of their ethnic group, but they are divided in their opinions on whether the adoption of white culture represents a threat to the survival of their own.

Table 146 shows the extent to which Asians and West Indians believe that white people have accepted them as part of British society and understand their way of life. The figures are similar for the two groups, showing that about half say it is true that white people have accepted them (although most of these say 'probably true', not 'definitely true'), but, by contrast, over two-thirds say that it is true that white people do not understand their way of life or culture (and a larger proportion of these say 'definitely' true). We shall see later that these rather different views of the extent of acceptance and understanding are repeated among the white respondents.

The views of white informants on the existence of racial discrimination

As we saw earlier in the report, 73 per cent of white men and 69 per cent of white women say that at least some employers discriminate racially when recruiting, and this means that almost as many white people as West Indian people acknowledge that this kind of discrimination exists (Table 117). The proportion of whites who say that employers discriminate in this way is much larger than among Asians. Almost all of the remainder of the white sample, however, say that there are no employers who discriminate, and few give a 'don't know' response. In general, more of the white informants tend to give a firm answer to the attitude and belief questions than the Asian and West Indian informants, so the proportion in the 'don't know' category is usually smallest among whites. Four-fifths of white informants say that there are landlords who discriminate on racial grounds, and this proportion is larger than among Asians and West Indians. Over 60 per cent of white informants acknowledge that discrimination occurs both in employment recruitment and in private lettings.

The responses to other questions about racial bias were different. Only half of the white informants say they think there are firms where promotion is less likely for black people than white people with equivalent qualifications. For all of the items in the question on whether blacks are treated the same as whites by different organisations, over 50 per cent say blacks and whites are treated equally (Table 147). A substantial minority say that blacks are treated worse by employers (26 per cent), estate agents (20 per cent), the police (21 per cent) and pubs (26 per cent), but for most of the other bodies and institutions mentioned, under ten per cent feel blacks received worse treatment. Very few white informants say that Asians and West Indians receive better treatment than whites: this group is no larger than two per cent for building societies, banks, estate agents, insurance companies, trade unions and pubs, and is between three and six per cent for employers, hospitals, the police, the courts and schools. But there is a larger group of whites who say they think black people receive better treatment from council housing departments (15 per cent) and DHSS offices (19 per cent); there is a group of a similar size who think blacks receive worse treatment from housing departments (13 per cent) but the group saying that blacks are treated worse than whites by DHSS offices is much smaller (4 per cent).

White informants' views on trends in race relations and on race relations laws
Table 148 shows that a third of white informants say there is now less discrimination than there was five years ago, but over a third say there is more discrimination. Half agree with the statement that the laws against discrimination should be enforced more effectively, but a third disagree. There is less agreement with the statement that there should be new laws that are more strict than the present ones; 43 per cent of white informants are still in agreement with this idea, although they are balanced by 41 per cent who disagree.

The concept of racial discrimination has some ambiguity when used in general context such as a question about its increase or decrease: it could be interpreted as discrimination against whites as well as against blacks. A query therefore arises over the interpretation of the results of Table 148: might a large proportion of those who say they agree with a tougher legal response to discrimination be those who feel that some organisations give better treatment to blacks than to whites? In fact, this is not the case. Table 149 shows that there is almost no relationship between the views of white people on the treatment of different ethnic groups by different organisations and their views on the trend over time in racial discrimination: of those who think there is more discrimination now, only 17 per cent also say that council housing departments treat black people better than whites, and this is roughly the same as for the sample as a whole. Close scrutiny of the table shows that white informants who say blacks receive worse treatment and those who say blacks receive better treatment are both slightly better represented in the group claiming there is more discrimination; nevertheless, this relationship is weak, and the important conclusion is that the view reported by whites of the trend in discrimination is not dependent

271

on their responses to the question about differential treatment by different organisations. Table 150 shows the same analysis for the groups agreeing and disagreeing with more effective law enforcement and this confirms that the support for legal action against discrimination is not the result of anxiety about 'reverse discrimination' in favour of blacks: for example, only 11 per cent of those in favour of more effective legal action also feel that housing departments treat blacks better than whites, compared with 21 per cent of those against more effective legal action.

White informants' views on living in multi-racial Britain

The number of the attitude questions from the Asian and West Indian interview schedule that were repeated in the white interview was limited, but the results show an interesting contrast. We see from a comparison of Tables 151 and 144 that a similar, small minority of whites and blacks (under ten per cent) agree with the statement that black people should keep apart from white people. However, a larger proportion of whites than of blacks agree that Asian and West Indian people should avoid living in mainly white areas: 18 per cent, as opposed to eight per cent of West Indians and seven per cent of Asians. No question was asked to follow this up, so we have no indication as to why these informants give this response; they could be giving a blatantly racialist view that white areas should be kept white, or they could be motivated by a general concern about difficulties of race relations, or even by a concern for the safety of black families in the face of racial attacks. None of these explanations should be rejected out of hand, even the last: it should be remembered that 19 per cent of white informants say it is not true that Asian people can rely on the police to protect them, and this figure is as high as 25 per cent when referring to West Indian people; and 16 per cent of whites say they agree that Asians and West Indians should set up self-defence groups to protect themselves against racialist violence. When we asked whether it was true that white and black people could live in the same area without any problems of race relations, 39 per cent of whites said they thought it was not, compared with 20 per cent of Asians and West Indians; this probably reflects the same concern shown by the fact that 18 per cent of whites agree with the 'avoid white areas' statement, but does not help us to see the motivation behind it. We should remember that the survey was carried out in the first half of 1982, not long after the Scarman report and the Home Office report on racial attacks were published (and, in fact, not a year had passed since the disturbances in the inner areas of Britain's towns and cities in the summer of 1981): these may well have had an impact on the views of a number of the white informants.

Over half of white informants say it is true that white people have accepted Asian and West Indian people as part of British society, but three quarters say it is true that white people do not understand Asians' and West Indians' ways of life (Table 152). The answers to these questions match rather closely with those given by the Asian and West Indian informants, although the proportion of whites who say that black people have been accepted is larger.

White people are clearly divided over the statement about Asians and West Indians preserving their own culture and way of life: 50 per cent agree and 40 per cent disagree (Table 152). This contrasts with the wholehearted agreement of black people, and, if we take these responses at face value, they show that although nearly all black people and half the white population accept the view that black citizens should be accepted as part of a multi-cultural society where ethnic identities are not lost, there is a large minority of white opinion that resists this idea.

The views of young people

Surprisingly, we do not find that there are large differences between the views of informants aged 16-24 and those aged 25 and over, in any of the ethnic groups. This is despite the fact that 87 per cent of West Indian informants and 82 per cent of Asian informants say they think it is true that in their community 'there are large differences of views between young people and older people'. The similarity of the responses of younger and older informants is particularly marked among Asians. However, there are some differences, and not all of them are in the direction that might be expected. As we saw in the previous chapter, young West Indian men are more critical of the ability of the police to defend blacks from racial attacks than older West Indian men, and are more in agreement with self-defence groups; this same criticism of the police is seen in the answers to the question on differential treatment, when 73 per cent of young West Indians say the police treat them worse that whites, compared with 60 per cent of older West Indians (the corresponding percentages for the courts are 47 and 35). Young West Indians are also more critical of their treatment by pubs: 24 per cent of them say pubs treat them worse than whites, compared with 17 per cent of older West Indians.

Perhaps the most significant differences between young and old Asians and West Indians are seen in the answers to the questions on whether, and how, life has changed for their ethnic group over the last five years. Fewer young people say that life has deteriorated, and more say it has improved, although the latter difference is much stronger among Asians than among West Indians (Table 153). There is a further difference among those who say life has become worse: young people are less likely to give as a reason the general changes in the economy and job supply than are the

273

older people, and young West Indians are more likely to mention an aspect of racialism or racial disadvantage.

The general similarity of the views of old and young is repeated in the white sample, but young people are often more likely to say that organisations treat black people worse than whites. This is true for employers (36 and 24 per cent respectively), schools (14 and 7 per cent), pubs (34 and 24 per cent), DHSS offices (8 and 4 per cent), the police (36 per cent and 18 per cent). It is therefore not surprising to find that a larger proportion of young white people than older white people favour more effective enforcement, and extension, of the laws against discrimination. Fifty-seven per cent of young whites say they agree with more effective enforcement, compared with 48 per cent of older whites; the corresponding proportions agreeing with the suggestion that tougher laws should be introduced are 53 per cent and 40 per cent.

Awareness of the Commission of Racial Equality and the Community Relations Councils

We asked informants whether they knew of 'any organisation set up by Parliament to deal with race relations', and, if so, which these were. Those who did not mention the Commission for Racial Equality were then asked directly whether they had heard of it; the same procedure was followed for the Community Relations Councils. The results are shown in Table 154. About 15 per cent of West Indians mention the CRE without a prompt, and there is little difference between men and women. Asian men are far more likely than Asian women to mention the CRE: the figures are 20 per cent and eight per cent respectively. The figures for whites are even lower, at nine per cent for men and three per cent for women. A further 50 per cent of West Indians and whites say they have heard of the CRE; for Asian men this figure is 42 per cent and for Asian women 25 per cent. This leaves a substantial group in each sample who say they have not heard of the CRE when prompted: about 30 per cent of West Indians, 35 per cent of Asian and white men, and over half of Asian and white women. A small percentage of black informants mentioned other bodies spontaneously, as did 13 per cent of white men and six per cent of white women; the favourite of these other bodies was the Race Relations Board, a body which ceased to exist five years before the survey was carried out. The proportions of informants mentioning the CRCs without prompt and saying they have heard of them are lower still, and follow the same pattern of variation between ethnic groups and between men and women.

There is not much difference between younger and older informants in their awareness of the CRE and CRCs, but young West Indians and whites more often say they have not heard of them (36 and 49 per cent respectively, compared with 27 and 42 per cent of the older groups).

A comparison with the equivalent results from the 1974 survey shows that ignorance of the CRE is greater now than ignorance of the Race Relations Board was at that time. At least a third of white, West Indian and Asian men in 1974 mentioned the RRB spontaneously, and the proportion of men who had not heard of it was only ten per cent among whites and West Indians, and 26 per cent among Asians. The extent of awareness among Asians has declined less dramatically than among whites and West Indians, but this is because of the much lower level from which it started in 1974, particularly among women.

Table 138:	Asians and West Indians: Beliefs about treatment of Asians and West Indians

(See also Tables 53, 119, 129 and 132 for other items from this question, concerning council housing departments, estate agents, building societies, banks, employers, DHSS offices and hospitals)

Column percentages

	West Indian	Asian
Are people of Asian/West Indian origin treated the same, better or worse than white people by...		
The Police		
Same	16	41
Better	1	3
Worse	64	30
DK	19	26
The Courts		
Same	23	42
Better	1	2
Worse	38	9
DK	38	47
Schools		
Same	44	67
Better	2	4
Worse	36	12
DK	18	17
Trade Unions		
Same	49	40
Better	*	3
Worse	9	7
DK	42	50
Insurance Companies		
Same	48	48
Better	2	2
Worse	10	5
DK	40	45
Pubs		
Same	40	21
Better	2	1
Worse	18	15
DK	40	64
Base: Adults		
(weighted)	1843	3471
(unweighted)	894	1688

Table 139: Asians and West Indians has life in Britain improved for own ethnic group over last 5 years?

Column percentages

	West Indian	Asian	Indian	Paki- stani	Bangla- deshi	African Asian
In general, do you think life in Britain is now better for people of Asian/West Indian origin than it was five years ago, is it worse or has there been no change?						
Better	20	15	16	12	4	21
Worse	53	51	50	54	53	47
No change	19	17	17	17	16	18
Don't know	8	17	16	17	26	14
Base: Adults						
(weighted)	1843	3471	1349	940	313	804
(unweighted)	894	1688	633	476	173	372
Same question in 1974 survey						
Better	54	35	40	31		32
Worse	16	18	17	21		18
No change	20	32	31	36		31
Don't know	9	14	12	12		19

Asians and West Indians: Reasons given for saying life has become worse over last five years

Column percentages

	West Indian	Asian
Recession, Unemployment etc.	50	53
Inflation, Other Economic Pressures	29	32
Violence or Other Trouble Caused by Unemployment	6	3
Any General Mention of Recession	**67**	**67**
Unemployment Worse Among Blacks	17	11
Discrimination	10	13
Racialism, National Front	14	21
Racial Attacks	5	10
Any mention of racialism, racial disadvantage	**41**	**49**
General Violence in Society	9	14
Housing Has Become Worse	7	4
Base: Adults who say life has become worse		
(weighted)	985	1767
(unweighted)	481	854

Note: More than one response was sometimes given to this question, and the percentages therefore add up to more than 100.

278

Table 141:   Asians and West Indians: Reasons given for saying
               life has improved over last five years

Column percentages

	West Indian	Asian
Housing Better	13	8
Living Standards Better	20	47
Better Opportunities for Black People	19	15
More Facilities and Amenities for Black People	3	13
Black People More Established/More of them	12	14
Race Relations Laws	8	2
Black People Know their Rights	4	2
Black People More Accepted	44	14
Base: Adults who say life has got better		
(weighted)	368	517
(unweighted)	171	226

Note: More than one response was sometimes given to this
        question, and the percentages therefore add up to more
        than 100.

279

Table 142:   Asians and West Indians: Views on trend in racial
              discrimination

Column percentages

	West Indian	Asian
Would you say there is about the same amount of racial discrimination in Britain as there was five years ago, less discrimination today or more discrimination today?		
Same	24	24
Less	21	7
More	43	45
Don't know	13	24
Base: Adults		
(weighted)	1843	3471
(unweighted)	894	1688

Table 143: Asians and West Indians: Attitudes towards laws against racial discrimination

Column percentages

	West Indian	Asian
'The present laws against racial discrimination should be enforced more effectively'		
Agree strongly	46	39
Agree	34	47
Neither agree nor disagree	13	10
Disagree	5	2
Disagree strongly	1	1
'There should be new and stricter laws against racial discrimination'		
Agree strongly	44	34
Agree	31	41
Neither agree nor disagree	15	15
Disagree	6	6
Disagree strongly	3	3
Base: Adults		
(weighted)	1843	3471
(unweighted)	894	1688

Table 144: Asians and West Indians: Attitudes towards multi-racial life in Britain

Column percentages

	West Indian	Asian
'People of Asian/West Indian origin should have white friends they see outside of the workplace'		
Agree	88	87
Disagree	3	3
'People of Asian/West Indian origin should join political organisations alongside white people'		
Agree	80	84
Disagree	7	4
'People of Asian/West Indian origin should join trade unions alongside white people'		
Agree	86	85
Disagree	4	3
'People of Asian/West Indian origin should keep themselves apart from white people'		
Agree	4	5
Disagree	92	83
'People of Asian/West Indian origin should avoid living in mainly white areas'		
Agree	8	7
Disagree	92	83
Base: Adults		
(weighted)	1843	3471
(unweighted)	894	1688

Table 145: Asian and West Indians: Attitudes towards preservation of culture and cultural assimilation

Column percentages

	West Indian	Asian
'People of Asian/West Indian origin should try to preserve as much of their own way of life and culture as possible'		
Agree	80	88
Neither agree nor disagree	10	6
Disagree	8	5
'It is a good thing to be able to speak the language (Asian) dialect or patois (West Indian) of your family's area of origin'		
Agree	62	95
Neither agree nor disagree	14	2
Disagree	22	2
'People of Asian/West Indian origin should try to adopt the way of life and culture of white people'		
Agree	34	39
Neither agree or disagree	19	18
Disagree	45	42
Base: Adults		
(weighted)	1843	3471
(unweighted)	894	1688

<u>Table 146:</u>   Acceptance and understanding by white people: beliefs of West Indians and Asians

Row percentages

	Defin-itely true	Prob-ably true	Prob-ably not true	Defin-itely not true	Don't know
'White people have now accepted people of Asian/ West Indian origin as part of British Society'					
West Indian informants	9	42	16	26	7
Asian informants	6	40	25	19	10
'White people do not understand the way of life or culture of Asian/ West Indian people'					
West Indian informants	38	36	12	8	6
Asian informants	25	45	15	8	8

Base: Adults

	West Indian	Asian
(weighted)	1843	3471
(unweighted)	894	1688

Table 147:   Whites: Beliefs about treatment of Asians and West Indians
(see also Tables 53, 119, 129 and 132 for other items from this question, concerning council housing departments, estate agents, building societies, banks, employers, DHSS offices and hospitals)

Column percentages

Are people of Asian and West Indian origin treated the same, better or worse than white people by...

	The Police	The Courts	Schools	Trade Unions	Insurance Companies	Pubs
Same	65	71	73	70	60	51
Better	4	6	6	2	1	1
Worse	21	8	8	7	8	26
DK	10	14	13	22	32	22

Base: Adults
   (weighted)   5375
   (unweighted)   2265

285

Whites: Belief about trend in racial discrimination
and attitudes towards laws against discrimination

Column percentages

Would you say there is about the same amount of racial discrimination in Britain as there was five years ago, less discrimination or more discrimination today?	
Same	18
Less	33
More	39
Don't know	10
'The present laws against racial discrimination should be enforced more effectively'	
Agree	50
Neither agree nor disagree	18
Disagree	31
'There should be new and stricter laws against racial discrimination'	
Agree	43
Neither agree nor disagree	16
Disagree	41
Base: Adults	
(weighted)	5375
(unweighted)	2265

Table 149: White men and women: Views on treatment of black people, by view of trend in racial discrimination

Column percentages

	There is more discrimination	There is less discrimination
Those who say:		
Employers treat blacks worse than whites	28	25
Council housing depts. treat blacks worse than whites	15	12
Police treat blacks worse than whites	23	21
Employers treat blacks better than whites	5	3
Council housing depts. treat blacks better than whites	17	13
Police treat blacks better than whites	5	3
Employers treat black same as whites	54	64
Council Housing dept. treat blacks same as whites	49	61
Police treat blacks same as whites	64	69
Base: Adults		
(weighted)	2089	1795
(unweighted)	873	758

Table 150: White men and women: Views on treatment of black people, by attitude towards more effective enforcement of laws against discrimination

Column percentages

	'The present laws against racial discrimination should be enforced more effectively'	
	Agree	Disagree
Those who say:		
Employers treat blacks worse than whites	31	22
Council Housing depts. treat blacks worse than whites	17	10
Police treat blacks worse than whites	27	17
Employers treat blacks better than whites	3	5
Council Housing depts. treat blacks better than whites	11	21
Police treat blacks better than whites	2	7
Employers treat blacks same as whites	57	65
Council housing depts. treat blacks same as whites	56	53
Police treat blacks same as whites	64	70
Base: Adults		
(weighted)	2677	1691
(unweighted)	1184	698

288

Table 151:   Whites: Attitudes to life in multi-racial Britain

Column percentages

'People of Asian and West Indian origin should keep themselves apart from white people'	
Agree	8
Disagree	87
'People of Asian and West Indian origin should avoid living in mainly white areas'	
Agree	18
Disagree	72
'People of Asian and West Indian origin should try to preserve as much of their own culture as possible'	
Agree	50
Disagree	40
Base: Adults	
(weighted)	5375
(unweighted)	2265

Acceptance and understanding by white people: Beliefs of white people

Row Percentages

	Defin- itely true	Prob- ably true	Prob- ably not true	Defin- itely not true	Don't know
'White people have now accepted people of West Indian origin...	16	48	18	13	6
'White people have now accepted people of Asian origin...	12	46	19	17	5
'White people do not understand the way of life... of West Indian people'	31	44	15	6	4
'White people do not understand the way of life... of Asian people'	38	41	10	7	4

Base: Adults
    (weighted)   5375
    (unweighted)   2265

Table 153:   Changes in life over last five years by age group

Column percentages

	West Indian		Asian	
	Aged 16-24	Aged over 24	Aged 16-24	Aged over 24
In general do you think life in Britain is now better for people of Asian/West Indian origin than it was five years ago, is it worse or has there been no change? (Base = All)				
Better	22	19	21	13
Worse	45	57	40	53
No change	21	18	16	18
Don't know	13	5	23	16
If life is worse, why? (Base = Those who say life is worse)				
Any general mention of recession	**54**	**71**	**58**	**68**
Unemployment worse among blacks	21	15	17	10
Discrimination	12	10	9	13
Racialism, National Front	23	12	20	21
Racial Attacks	4	5	8	10
Any mention of racialism, racial disadvantage	**57**	**36**	**48**	**49**

Awareness of Commission for Racial Equality and Community Relations Councils

Column percentages

	White		West Indian		Asian	
	Men	Women	Men	Women	Men	Women
Spontaneously mentioned CRE	9	3	17	14	20	8
Heard of CRE, when prompted	56	44	51	53	42	25
Not heard of CRE	34	52	28	31	35	56
Spontaneously mentioned CRCs	2	2	9	8	13	6
Heard of CRCs, when prompted	43	35	45	43	39	22
Not heard of CRCs	54	62	42	46	44	64
Mentioned other body (e.g. 'Race Relations Board')	13	6	3	3	4	2
Base: Adults						
(weighted)	2567	2802	1630	1790	3870	3013
(unweighted)	1001	1262	781	876	1836	1484

1974 Survey:

	White		West Indian		Asian	
	Men	Women	Men	Women	Men	Women
Spontaneously mentioned Race Relations Board	34		40	25	33	7
Heard of RRB, when prompted	57		51	58	41	35
Not heard of RRB	9		11	17	26	58

292

XI Conclusions

Black people in the British labour market

The survey gives us a depressing picture of the economic lives of people of Asian and West Indian origin in Britain today. They are more likely than white people to be unemployed, and those who are in work tend to have jobs with lower pay and lower status than those of white workers. Examination of the changes in the employment patterns of white, Asian and West Indian people over the eight years between 1974 and 1982 shows that there has been little convergence of the types of job done by the majority and minority ethnic groups, while their unemployment rates have sharply diverged.

Our analysis suggests that the tenacity of the pattern of poor jobs among black workers is due to a number of factors. In particular, we have seen that each of the following is partly responsible: the different educational backgrounds of workers from different ethnic groups; the frequent lack of fluency in English among Asian workers; the different residential locations of the majorities of white and black workers; an ethnic minority labour market which seems to be in some respects quite different from that of white workers; and racial discrimination, both direct and indirect. Although it may be helpful at first to discuss these factors separately, we shall see that none of them can be treated in isolation from the others.

The variations between the job levels of the different ethnic minorities are important. While West Indian men and Asian men of all origins have a larger proportion of semi-skilled and unskilled manual workers among them than do white men, the size of this difference and the job distribution of the remaining workers are not the same. Among West Indians and Sikhs we find there is a large proportion of skilled manual workers and a relatively small proportion of non-manual workers; among African Asians we find relatively large proportions of non-manual workers, at senior and junior levels; among Bangladeshis we find very few men working in skilled manual jobs, and very many in semi-skilled work. Variations can also be seen in the comparisons of the jobs of women: while, overall, a smaller proportion of blacks have non-manual jobs than whites, this difference is by far the strongest when the comparison involves Sikhs, and weakest when it involves Hindus. It is quite correct to talk about generally lower job levels, for the overall distribution of jobs is worse for blacks than for whites; but in addition there is, for each ethnic group, a particular way in which the distribution is inferior.

When the job levels of white, Asian and West Indian employees with the same levels of qualifications are compared, some of the differences between the ethnic groups are reduced. This shows that the very large differences between the job levels of white and black workers are attributable in part to differences in their formal qualifications. But the gap between them is not removed entirely by these like-for-like comparisons: there is still a large difference between white and black job levels among those with and without qualifications. And we have to be careful not to overstate the differences of qualifications: although over half of the black employees (57 per cent) have no academic or vocational qualifications, the proportion of white employees without qualifications is nearly a half (44 per cent). There is, therefore, a considerable portion of the labour market where formal qualifications are not a major determinant of job level. Previous work experience is important, and this must be especially true for vacancies where formal qualifications are not essential; we might, therefore, expect immigrant workers to be at a disadvantage when competing with the indigenous population because their experience of work in the UK is limited. In fact, this explanation loses a lot of its appeal when we consider that the immigration of West Indians reached a peak over twenty years ago, and has been very limited since then; furthermore, only one in ten of the Asian workers in the survey came to Britain after 1974, and their pattern of job levels is identical to that of those who arrived earlier. Thus the lack of British work experience cannot be seen as an explanation of the low job levels of blacks.

For Asian workers there is a specific aspect of their newness to Britain that undoubtedly has an effect on their job levels, and this is the lack of fluency in English. Only half of the Asian men and less than half of the Asian women interviewed were assessed by the Asian interviewers as speaking English fluently; a fifth of the men and half of the women speak English 'slightly or not at all'. As might be expected, the level of fluency among workers is related very strongly to job level. Even so, comparison of the job levels of those men who are fluent in English with white workers of equivalent qualifications still shows a larger proportion doing semi-skilled and unskilled manual work. The balance of manual to non-manual workers in this group of Asians is, however, the same as among whites, so in this respect Asians fluent in English have achieved a measure of equality with white workers. This finding could be seen as a hopeful sign for the future, but other survey results indicate that Asians are not treated the same as other British workers with the same qualifications. The position of Asians fluent in English is a particular illustration of a general point about the position of Asians and West Indians in the labour market: they are found disproportionately in specific occupations with specific employers, and, perhaps most importantly, often have Asian managers and employers. In other words, they have succeeded mainly with employers that traditionally employ Asians (such as the NHS and the catering industry) and in 'ethnic business', and there appears to be only a small movement towards the wider distribution across the labour market that is found among white people. In short, a poor command of English among Asians is very strongly related to job level and is clearly an impediment to individual job mobility, but it does not fully explain the differences between the types of jobs held by whites and Asians with similar qualifications.

In this report we have explained at some length the different residential distributions of white, West Indian and Asian people in this country. The different industrial make-up of the areas in which we find a majority of each ethnic group would be expected to affect their job distributions, but the survey shows that these regional differences actually dilute the contrast between the job levels of blacks and whites, rather than helping to explain it away. This is principally because of the concentration of non-manual jobs in London: a relatively large proportion of black employees are found in the capital (in the survey, 53 per cent of West Indians and 35 per cent of Asians, compared with 12 per cent of whites). At a more local level, there is evidence that the white people living in those census enumeration districts identified as areas of ethnic minority settlement are economically disadvantaged when compared to other whites, so it can be argued that at a micro level of geographical analysis black people are found in localities where people tend to have jobs at a generally lower level. This fits with our knowledge of the original settlement of immigrants in areas of manual labour shortage. But job mobility could take place while workers were living in such an area. Deprived areas in cities are often close to areas of relative affluence, where residents have very high job levels, and it is clear that 'travel-to-work areas' are more important than immediate residential neighbourhood. We are unable to organise the survey data to make an analysis on this basis, but the data on job levels in inner and outer London shows little evidence that the broad area of residence helps to explain the persistence of the gap between white and black workers.

295

The extent to which Asian and West Indian employees are found in different occupations is only partly shown by the comparison of job levels. The classification of each job into one of five groups, as in many tables in this report, makes survey data manageable but it omits a lot of detail, and a closer look reveals that within these categories there are further orders of difference between white and black jobs. Indications that this is so come from the fact that within each category blacks tend to work shifts more commonly, supervise others less commonly, and, among men, receive lower wages. But the nature of the differences become clearer when the jobs are also classified by industrial sector and by whether they are in public or private enterprises. This more detailed occupational breakdown reveals that the distribution of Asians and West Indians in the employment structure is heavily distorted by the existence of traditional channels of black employment opportunity and by minimal penetration of other types of work. For example, among workers in the transport and communications, 11 per cent of West Indian men have non-manual jobs, not far short of the 16 per cent figure for white men, but in manufacturing industry only one in twenty West Indian men has a non-manual job, compared with nearly one in three white men. Again, in the private sector, the proportion of white men who are non-manual workers is twice as high as the proportion of Asian men, while in the public sector the two are the same; in manufacturing, 82 per cent of Asian women are semi-skilled or unskilled workers, compared to 38 per cent of white women, while in the professional and scientific sector the situation is reversed, the proportions being 15 and 28 per cent respectively. Although there are many complexities, it is clear that the types of jobs in which black people are well represented are those which they filled when they first moved to this country and, among Asians, those jobs related to the development of Asian businesses; the occupations in which they are least well represented are the non-manual jobs and manual supervisors' jobs in the private sector, particularly in manufacturing. Although Asian men and women and West Indian women are well represented in non-manual jobs in the public sector, these jobs are again rather different from those of the same level among whites: medical and ancillary staff in the NHS and public transport staff make up large numbers among them. West Indian men working in the public sector have a far lower percentage of non-manual workers among them than other groups of blacks.

Far from showing any convergence of white and black job patterns, our analysis has instead revealed that there is an imbalance in the distribution of occupations which is likely to inhibit such convergence. The result is that it is very difficult for blacks to break out of that section of the labour market that we could either label 'multi-racial' or 'for blacks and poor whites only' and into the section that is now the preserve of white workers. This is not simply to say that racial discrimination by employers in their recruitment and promotion practices confines black people to the part of the job market they have traditionally occupied; it is also clear that other factors have become intertwined with discrimination to reinforce its effect.

To begin with, the expectations of black workers must be affected by the fact that some types of job have been more open than others to them, and this must in turn affect their job-seeking activity. At its simplest level, this means that black people are likely to increase their chances of getting jobs by applying for those posts for which blacks are known to be accepted and avoiding those which seem to be white bastions. But the complex cultural and psychological processes that also limit expectations may be just as powerful as this rational assessment of the chances of getting various jobs. For people to see their relatives, friends and other members of their ethnic group working in jobs that are quite different from those done by white people, and to know that this has been the case for tens of years, cannot but affect their perception of their own place in the economy. Both these factors limit the practical expectations of black people in the job market (and note that we are talking of expectations, not aspirations) and thereby reduce any pressure there might otherwise be to move into new areas of employment. Shiftwork has a similar reinforcing effect: we have seen how the overall wages differential between black and white men is reduced by the greater proportion of blacks working shifts, and it is therefore easy to understand how the types of jobs that involve shift premiums can become valued as reducing economic inequality. But this type of work is located disproportionately at the foot of the occupational ladder, and it therefore constitutes a trap. Moreover, the association of shiftwork with poor English fluency points to another way in which the pattern of poor jobs, and shiftwork itself, are reproduced: language has been shown to be related to occupational position in several ways in this report, and the existence of shift teams that are relatively homogeneous in terms of an ethnic minority language are at one and the same time a source of economic strength for the Asian community and a major block to the advancement of those workers, in terms of both occupational mobility and English fluency. There is a further mechanism by which the job patterns of Asians in Britain is reproduced through differences of language: because English language skills are less important for the execution of the work involved in semi-skilled and unskilled manual jobs, there is little in the nature of the work to help people improve their English and no pressure on them to do so. In other words, if the work can be carried out with minimal English fluency, neither

297

the employee nor the employer have an immediate incentive to change things. But in maintaining the low level of English fluency this process prevents the employee from being able to move beyond this type of work. Thus the language problem and the job problem maintain each other.

Although the position of black employees relative to that of white employees has remained static in terms of the jobs they do, the same cannot be said for the proportion who are out of work. The rise in the unemployment rate has been larger for blacks than for whites, and this compounds the economic disadvantage of black people. As with our analysis of occupations, no single factor is entirely responsible for the different unemployment rates. All of the problems that lead to the perpetuation of the low job levels among blacks also tend to push their unemployment rate up higher than that of whites, although geographical variations bear a much stronger relationship to ethnic differences in the case of unemployment rates than in the case of job levels. Additionally, it has been the lower-level jobs that have been lost in greatest numbers during the recession, and so the impact on black people has been even greater than would otherwise be expected. That is to say the sectors of the labour market in which blacks tend to be found have been eroded by unemployment more than other sectors, and this process is quite separate from the effects of discrimination and of educational and language differences: it is a feature of their position in the occupational class structure. And just as lower job levels have been associated with greater job loss, so unemployment further hinders any chances of job mobility. Thus, unemployment will play its own part in maintaining the distinct and inferior occupational patterns among black workers.

The survey shows that proportionally more Asians than whites stay on in full-time education beyond the age of 16 and the overall level of self-employment is now higher among Asians than among whites. While neither of these need be the result of conscious attempts to avoid competing with whites in the restricted job market, the result is the same: for those remaining at school or college, entry to that market is postponed, and for those starting their own business, it is left behind. The trend towards self-employment is very strong among British Asians: the self-employed as a proportion of all working Asians has nearly doubled since 1974 and nearly one in ten of the Asian men in the survey who worked in Britain in 1974 moved by 1982 from being an employee to being self-employed. Self-employment is not a guarantee of economic success, indeed for some individuals it leads to financial ruin, but it has an overwhelming appeal when compared to ordinary employment in a labour market that is hostile to the advancement of black people, and that appeal is the chance of real success by one's own efforts and talents. In other words, for many

298

Asians the possibilities of advancement offered by self-employment are greater than those available as an employee; and the perils of self-employment are likely to be preferable to the despair of unemployment. However, there may be a danger of overstating the argument that Asians have moved into self-employment as a strategy to avoid competing with white people for jobs. There is within the Asian communities a strong historical and cultural tradition favouring self-reliance and self-employment, and it could be argued that, with the passing of the time required to build up capital in Britain, this development would have occurred anyway. It seems likely, however, that what has happened is the result of the combination of these factors: self-employment is regarded as desirable, while opportunities in employment are limited, and these 'pull' and 'push' factors operate in the same direction.

On balance, we conclude from our comparison of the 1974 and 1982 surveys and our analysis of individual jobs and job movements that the British job market has changed little in its hostility to black workers, except that it now excludes more of them from work altogether. The few changes for the better have been largely the result of a consolidation of the original immigrant position within the labour force (for example, in the health service and in the transport services) or have been the result of the development of black businesses. Furthermore, the factors that perpetuate the pattern of disadvantage are strengthened by the pattern itself; the impact of racial discrimination is therefore increased by this circle of causes and effects, and we are left with a rigid pattern that not only has survived through the 1970s, but also shows no signs of breaking down in the near future.

Household income

Among men, one of the most important consequences of black workers' inferior position in the labour market is their low level of wages. The median weekly earnings of full-time white employees in the survey are £129, compared with £109 for West Indians and £111 for Asians. Among women, who as a group have a disadvantaged position in the labour market irrespective of their ethnic origin, there is no clear gap of this kind: if anything, West Indian women have slightly higher overall earnings than white women. This, we argued earlier, is due partly to the very low earnings of women generally, (there being as a result little room for a further dimension of disadvantage along ethnic lines), partly to the tendency for West Indian women workers to be in unionised workplaces, which generally have higher rates of pay, and partly to the presence of black women in large firms and public-sector organisations, which generally have higher rates of pay than smaller firms in the private sector. There is some evidence that Asian women, whose jobs are located in the private sector more

299

often than those of West Indian women, have a lower overall wage level than white or West Indian women, but the differences are not of the same scale as those between men of different ethnic origins.

The low level of individual male earnings among black workers has the effect of lowering the household incomes of black families relative to those of white families; but this effect is reinforced by other differences between whites, Asians and West Indians. Because a relatively large proportion of West Indian workers are women, West Indian households are reliant on income from women's wages to a greater extent than are white households and, as women's wages are generally lower than men's, this tends to further depress household incomes. A different factor exacerbates the effect of low earnings on the household incomes of Asians: in their case, larger average household sizes mean that more people depend on the earnings of each worker than in white or West Indian households. In other words, the earnings of Asian workers would have to be on average higher than those of white workers if their families were to enjoy the same standards of living, while in fact their earnings are lower.

Higher unemployment rates also affect the household incomes of black people. Because of their already high ratio of dependants to earners, Asian households are particularly badly hit by the loss of wage-earners through unemployment. Nearly one in five Asian nuclear families have no wage-earner, compared with one in twelve white nuclear families; within the families that do have at least one earner, each Asian worker supports 2.8 other people on average, while each white worker supports 1.8 other people. The impact of unemployment on West Indian families is less obvious at first sight, for the proportions of households lacking an earner and the dependency ratios are similar for whites and West Indians. But again we have to take into account the higher overall economic activity rate of West Indians resulting from the larger proportion of working women. The higher activity rates of West Indians should mean their households lack an earner less frequently and have lower overall ratios of dependants to earners than whites, and if this were true it would help to offset the effect of West Indians' lower individual earnings; the fact that whites and West Indians have instead very similar dependency ratios and proportions of wageless households is the result of the higher unemployment rates of West Indians, and it is not therefore an indicator of economic equality, but a further demonstration of the way the operation of the labour market thwarts the attempts of West Indians to achieve equality of earned household income.

The higher levels of unemployment among black people result in greater proportions of their household incomes coming from unemployment benefit, rather than wages. Any tendency for the unemployed not to claim the benefit to which they are entitled would make the effects of joblessness even more harsh, and it is therefore not surprising to see that the level of unregistered unemployment among black people is for the most part no higher than among white people. There is, however, a significant proportion of West Indian women who are seeking work but are not registered as unemployed. The reasons they give for non-registration are varied, but there is one group among them to whom we shall return later: these are lone parents who are seeking work but have not registered, either because their past national insurance contributions are insufficient to entitle them to benefits or because they expect to have difficulties with child care if offered most kinds of work.

As regards the contribution of other state benefits to household incomes, the differences between the ethnic groups are largely determined by differences of age and household type. For example, relatively few black households are in receipt of income from retirement pensions while a relatively large proportion receive child benefit, and this is because black households are young and are often in the child-rearing phase of their life. Supplementary Allowances are more commonly claimed by West Indian households than white or Asian households, and this is partly because of the larger proportion of lone-parent households among West Indians; lone parents are, for all ethnic groups, the households that are most commonly in receipt of supplementary allowances. The proportion of other families receiving supplementary allowances is a little higher among West Indians than among whites, and although this is not surprising because of the higher level of unemployment among West Indians, it is noteworthy that the proportion of Asian families claiming is about the same as that of white families. Although 19 per cent of Asian nuclear families lack a wage-earner, and the same proportion are in receipt of unemployment benefit, only eight per cent of households report that they are receiving Supplementary Allowances. Since the rules governing entitlement are complex and we cannot within this survey tell who should and should not be claiming, this finding does not necessarily imply that a greater proportion of Asian families are failing to receive benefits to which they are legally entitled; however, it should be of concern that, for whatever reason, proportionally fewer wageless families have their income boosted by supplementary allowances in the Asian community than in the rest of the population.

A similar finding suggests that Asian families that do contain wage-earners are not as often in receipt of Family Income Supplement as might be expected from their low earnings and large household sizes. Among West Indians, the proportion of households receiving FIS is higher than among whites, and this reflects their low earnings; among Asians, however, this proportion is the same as among whites. As in the case of supplementary allowance it is not possible to assess directly the entitlement of each family in the survey to FIS, but these overall figures do suggest that some Asian households do not receive it when they ought to. FIS is a benefit that is applied for postally, rather than administered as part of other official processes (as in the case of child benefit, for which there seems to be no under-claiming) and this could lead to underclaiming, given that many Asians are not literate in English.

The position of lone-parent households demands our special attention within this general discussion of the household incomes within the different ethnic groups. Eighteen per cent of the West Indian households in the survey are lone parents living with at least one child aged under 16, compared with three and four per cent of Asian and white households respectively. Nearly all of these West Indian lone parents are women. Half of them have no earned income, and only 13 per cent receive any income from a person outside the household; exactly one half of West Indian lone parents receive supplementary allowance. Where lone parents are working (or an older child is working) the number of dependants for each earner is higher than for other household types, and this, in combination with the low level of women's wages and often the part-time nature of their work, results in the earned income per household member being lower than for other types of family. The survey shows that lone parent households are economically the most disadvantaged families, and this must be a matter of concern because the numbers of lone parents among the West Indian population grew considerably over the period between the 1974 and 1982 surveys, and this suggests that the lone parent family has become established as an important, viable household type among West Indians in Britain. Perhaps it is useful here to point out that although from a sociological viewpoint the lone-parent household seems now to be a permanent feature of West Indian life in Britain, from the viewpoint of the individual it may be far from being a permanent state, and single parenthood may be best viewed from this perspective, as a stage in the life-cycle: a lone parent will often become a partner in a married couple at a later date. However, this does not reduce the economic vulnerability of lone parents when they are on their own.

There is a final point we should make about the household incomes of Asian and West Indian people. Forty per cent of West Indian households and 30 per cent of Asian households send money occasionally or regularly to dependants outside the household. Most of this is sent to relatives in the family's country of origin. About a third of these households are sending the money regularly, and the amounts average about £17 per month per household from West Indians and £26 per month from Asians. The fact that many black people are giving some financial support to members of their

302

families elsewhere demonstrates the strength of family bonds among the minority ethnic groups, especially when it is remembered that their incomes are lower than those of whites; it also demonstrates another way in which cultural differences between white and black people make the lower earnings of blacks an even greater hardship than might be expected at first sight.

Access to housing and housing quality

The housing circumstances of British black people are extra-ordinary. Asians and West Indians have tenure patterns that are quite distinct from each other and from that of white people; the same applies to the types of property each ethnic group occupies, and to the size and quality of the property. Furthermore, these variations of type, size and quality are not fully explained by the different tenure distributions, nor by the geographical locations of the property. Finally, the straightforward relationship between occupational class and housing tenure that exists among the general population is almost completly absent among black people. To understand the reasons for these bewildering differences between the housing of Asians, West Indians and whites we have to look back to the periods of primary immigration in the 1950s and 1960s, when the initial patterns of ethnic minority housing were established.

On arrival in Britain the immigrants from the West Indies and the Indian sub-continent found accommodation in the only part of the housing market that was open to newcomers with limited capital, the private renting sector. At that time the availability of lodgings, rooms and whole properties to let was greater than it is today, and much of it was concentrated in the major cities where the immigrants first settled in search of jobs in the industries that were short of workers. Conditions in these privately rented properties were often very poor, and tenancies were insecure, so with the arrival of dependants and the establishment of family-centred households, movement to larger, better and more secure accommodation became a priority. At first, access to council accommodation was barred because the immigrants had not been in the country long enough to have the required residential or waiting-time qualifications (irrespective of any other indirect or direct racial discrimination on the part of the housing departments or staff). The only viable option for escape from the private rented sector was house purchase, although most immigrants taking this step could only afford cheap properties which were often in a poor state of repair. Naturally the housing conditions in the privately rented sector were worst for those with lower incomes, and the incentive to buy houses when wives and children came to this country was therefore greatest among the lower occupational groups. By hard work, determined saving and mutual support, even very poor Asians managed to buy their own houses or at least become a partner in the joint purchase of a house. By 1974, when the PEP survey was carried out, nearly three-quarters of Asian households owned or were buying their homes. The movement by West Indian households towards house purchase was not as marked, but, within equivalent occupational classes, there were larger proportions of West Indian households than of white households in owner-occupied property in 1974.

Although the rapid growth of owner-occupation among Asian and West Indian immigrants seems to have been against all the odds, it should be remembered that just as the jobs that were available to black people were those not wanted by white people, so the areas in which black people worked and lived tended to be those that white people were already moving away from. Migration away from inner-city areas has been very heavy over the last 20 years, so the availability of property for purchase has been relatively good. The worst of this property has of course been the cheapest, and therefore the black owner-occupiers have tended to take on the property with the worst problems. Thus the original pattern of owner-occupation among black people in Britain was associated neither with affluence, nor with particularly good property, and was therefore unlike the pattern among white people.

Once sufficient time passed to enable West Indian immigrants to qualify for council housing, many applied. By the time of the 1974 PEP survey, the proportions of West Indian households in council dwellings were approaching those of white households in the same occupational class groups. But the properties West Indians found themselves in were among the worst of the council stock, and this state of affairs could not be explained by financial imperatives as in the case of the houses that black people had bought, because the quality of property allocated in the public sector is meant to be independent of the tenants' incomes. Part of the problem was that before they moved into the council sector, West Indians lived in local authority areas with council dwellings that were relatively poor: more of the properties were flats in urban settings, rather than cottage estates in the suburbs. But other factors also ensured that the black families were given the worst of the property even within these local authority areas: indirect racial discrimination built into the allocation procedures and direct discrimination by housing staff accounted in part for this inequality of treatment.

Movement by Asian families into council housing began later and was much slower. The main periods of Asian immigration came after that of the West Indian immigration, and as a consequence their housing eligibility, in terms of length of time in an area and time on the waiting list, developed that much later. However, the subsequently very slow rate of entry to council housing among Asians could not be explained by the different timing of the migration periods; by 1974, fewer than five in a hundred Asian households had a council dwelling. One reason for this was that the council properties available were often too small for Asian households. Another was that the direct and indirect discrimination encountered by all black people was particularly acute in the case of Asian families. But there was also a strong cultural preference for home ownership among Asian immigrants, and a desire to remain geographically within or close to the established Asian communities. For Asians, council housing was therefore hard to get and not very desirable, and was seldom a viable alternative to the now relatively familiar private housing market. In fact, nearly half of the Asian families housed by councils up to 1974 were allocated a house or flat because their previous dwelling was to be demolished, and a further quarter because of homelessness or some other emergency. Fewer than one in five Asian council tenants had come through the waiting list.

Throughout the 1970s the privately rented sector continued to decline in importance for the housing of black and white people alike, but the general move into the two main housing sectors has brought only limited convergence of the tenure patterns of Asian, West Indian and white families, and in some respects the patterns have become even more ethnically polarised. Asians have begun to enter the council sector, but this has not affected the high level of Asian home ownership, which remains at over 70 per cent. The proportion of West Indian households in council accommodation has continued to rise, as has the proportion in housing associations, while the proportion of owner-occupiers has remained steady. Among whites, owner-occupation has become more common as the privately rented sector has shrunk, and council tenancy has remained level. The relationships between occupational class and housing tenure among blacks have become more like those among whites, but the legacy of the early patterns of ethnic minority housing is very strong, and many of the causes of those patterns persist to this day, with the result that there is still no straight-forward correspondence between occupational level and housing tenure among Asians or West Indians.

The tenure patterns that now exist among black households are therefore quite distinctive: Asians are found more commonly than whites in owner-occupied property, and West Indians are found more commonly in council property and housing association property. Examination of the tenure patterns of recently-formed households suggests that the ethnic differences are unlikely to be eroded in the near future, and are possibly becoming stronger. Considered overall, the quality of the housing of black people is much worse than the quality of housing in general in this country. Blacks are more often found in flats, and those in flats are more often at higher floor levels, and those with houses are less likely to have detached or semi-detached property; black families have smaller property on average, and, with larger household sizes, their density of occupation is much higher; black households more often share rooms or amenities with other households; the properties black families own or rent are older; and they are less likely to have a garden. These differences are not the product of the different ethnic tenure patterns: they remain when the comparison is restricted to council housing or to owner-occupied property.

It is not difficult to understand the reasons for the inferior quality of the dwellings bought by Asian and West Indian families. It has already been pointed out that black people often embarked on house-purchase with much lower incomes than white purchasers, and consequently bought much cheaper property. The jobs that were available to them were close to areas of poor housing that were being vacated by white people in their exodus to the suburbs. At the same time, racial discrimination on the part of vendors and estate agents discouraged any settlement in areas of better housing that were exclusively white. These factors acted together to locate ethnic minority communities in localities of poor housing, and to ensure that even in these areas the poorest quality dwellings were purchased by black people. The geographical integrity of these communities was also strengthened by the natural tendency of immigrants to settle near other members of their ethnic group for support. Recent years have seen considerable house movement among black owner-occupiers, and this has resulted in a great overall improvement in the quality of their properties. Very few black families are now sharing with other households or lack the use of a bath, hot water or an inside WC. But in terms of property type, age and size there is still a large gap between the quality of dwellings owned by white and black families: over two-thirds of white owners live in detached or semi-detached houses, compared with one third of black owners; the proportion of white owners with post-war properties is more than twice that among blacks; and, on average, the dwellings of white owners are half a room larger than those of blacks. Because of the larger average family sizes among blacks the effect of the smaller size of their houses is disproportionate: twenty-seven per cent of black owners have densities of occupation of more than one person per room, compared with only two per cent of white owners. ▸

The superiority of the dwellings of white council tenants over those of black tenants is even more marked than is the case for owner-occupiers. As explained above, black applicants for council property have been often located in areas where the available housing stock is less desirable than in other areas, and therefore the standard of their present accommodation reflects the general housing problems of the areas of original immigrant settlement.

However, we have shown in this report that differences between the properties of black and white tenants remain even when this factor is taken into account. The most glaring overall differences are those of dwelling type: blacks are found in flats far more commonly than the rest of the population, their flats are located more frequently on the upper floors, and the relatively small proportion of council houses allocated to black tenants tend to be the less desirable properties. Only one in ten black tenants has a detached or semi-detached house, compared with more than one in three white tenants, while over a third of black tenants live in flats with entrances above ground-floor level, twice the proportion found among whites. Despite the fact that black tenants are disproportionately located in blocks of flats, they also have a larger than average share of property built before the first world war, and this demonstrates further that the houses allocated to them tend to be of inferior quality. The properties allocated to black tenants (taking houses and flats together) are smaller than those allocated to white tenants by an average of half a room, and as in the case of owner-occupied dwellings, this means there are considerably more black households with high densities of persons per room.

Between the surveys in 1974 and 1982 the proportions of black council tenants sharing rooms or facilities with another household, or lacking basic amenities, fell considerably, as did the proportion living in properties built before the first world war. But even these improvements have not enabled the black tenants to 'catch up' with white tenants, partly because of the size of the original gap between them, and partly because of parallel improvements among the white tenants. The disparity between the dwelling types allocated to white and black tenants actually grew in this period: there are now proportionately fewer black tenants in houses, especially detached and semi-detached houses, than in the mid-70s. This is partly because the growth of the council sector among blacks in this period raised the proportion of new tenants among them (there is a relationship between length of tenancy and type of dwelling, because tenants in flats often apply for transfers to houses and if they are successful it is usually after a waiting period) and partly because the mix of properties let by councils to new tenants changed in this period: new tenants were more likely to be given a flat than they would have been in previous years.

Three other factors are important to the discussion of the poor quality of council properties allocated to black people: the first concerns the different household types found in the different ethnic groups, the second concerns the effects of the differing channels of access to council housing, and the third is racial discrimination.

307

One of the aims of housing management in the public sector is to match the needs of households with the various types of property in each local authority area. It might be expected, therefore, that the different balance of household types in the white, Asian and West Indian populations would explain the differences between the types of council property in which they live. We have seen in the report that the smaller household types (such as lone parents and lone adults) are more likely to be found in flats than larger households, and this contributes to the differences between the property types allocated to whites and West Indians: although the average household size is larger in the West Indian population, there is among West Indian council tenants a relatively high percentage of lone parent and lone adult households. But if comparisons are made holding household type constant there is still a big difference between the properties of whites and West Indians. Among Asians these smaller households are less common than in the population generally, and this should increase the proportion of houses rather than flats. Variations in household type therefore provide no help in explaining the present differences between the properties of whites and Asians, and in fact lead them to be understated. Returning to the special case of lone parents, we should be cautious of treating their inferior council housing simply as an explanatory factor in our overall analysis of ethnic differences: the frequent location of these households in blocks of flats must be a source of extra difficulties to them, especially as they are often on the upper floors, and it must be a matter of concern that these least desirable properties are disproportionately allocated to people who are already disadvantaged in other ways.

The circumstances in which a person or family comes to be given a council tenancy can affect the type of dwelling allocated, and, as these circumstances vary between ethnic groups, this relationship also helps to explain the ethnic variations in dwelling type. Tenants housed because they were homeless tend to have property inferior to that of other tenants; this is for a number of reasons, the most important being the lack of scope for choice of property in the urgent circumstances of the allocation. Over a quarter of Asian and West Indian tenants were first housed by the council because they were homeless or because of some other emergency, compared with less than a tenth of white tenants, and this may tend to depress the average quality of property allocated to the black tenants. Among West Indians this relationship is tangled with the pattern of housing allocations among different household types, for lone parents tend to be housed for reasons of homelessness more often than others.

The final factor we have to take into account is racial discrimination. There is a number of ways in which the mechanism of the local authority housing system can work, or be worked, to the detriment of black applicants and black tenants. We shall give here two examples identified by other research studies. The first example involves direct discrimination: often the reports of housing visitors play a part in determining the property allocated to a household, and their reports can be influenced by racial prejudice and cultural stereotypes, with the result that the chances of ethnic minority families receiving good quality accommodation are unfairly reduced. The second example is one of indirect discrimination, for it is the result of allocation rules established for reasons that had nothing at all to do with the ethnic origin of applicants. The allocation systems of many local authorities give very low priority to applicants who are presently owner-occupiers; this is because owner-occupiers are generally housed more adequately than people in privately rented or shared accommodation. But because of the special nature of the private housing market among black people, this ruling makes no sense in their case: many black applicants for council housing who are owner-occupiers are in fact in houses of very poor quality.

Geography, concentration and dispersal

Throughout this report we have seen how the characteristics of the survey informants are strongly related to the area in which they live: within each ethnic group there are large variations between the housing, employment and other aspects of the lives of people living in different regions of the country, different towns and cities, and different types of area within them. For this reason the distinctive geographical patterns of ethnic minority residence in this country have to be taken into account when making overall comparisons of the characteristics of the white population and the populations of Asian and West Indian origin.

In Chapters II and IV we discussed in some detail the residential patterns of black people. The London and West Midlands conurbations contain more than half of Britain's black population, compared with less than a fifth of the white population, and within these two conurbations the black population is concentrated in the inner areas more than the white population. There are also concentrations of black people in urban areas in other parts of the country: in the East Midlands, in Manchester, and in West and South Yorkshire, for example. It would be a mistake, however, to describe the residential patterns of the British black population as exclusively inner-urban, for many ethnic minority communities have grown up in suburban areas and in smaller towns; the point is that the part of the black population living in these areas is proportionately much smaller than it is in the general population, not absent altogether.

In the towns and cities where there are significant numbers of black people there is a further level of geographical clustering.

309

Black households are not scattered evenly throughout these areas, but tend instead to be found in a number of small districts within them. About half of the black population lives within census enumeration districts having local concentrations of ethnic minority households over 12 per cent, and a fifth lives in enumeration districts having concentrations over 30 per cent. But although these figures demonstrate a high degree of geographical clustering by the black population, it should be noted that the great majority of Asians and West Indians live in enumeration districts with predominantly white populations. Even those enumeration districts where half or more of the households are black are usually surrounded by others that are mainly white, and therefore at a level of geographical analysis any larger than one or two streets (the average enumeration district contains about 165 households) nearly all 'ethnic minority areas' have a majority white population.

In this chapter we have already discussed briefly the forces that moulded the pattern of immigrant settlement in the 1950s and 1960s. Because the migration was primarily a response to the availability of work, employment factors were largely responsible for determining the broad patterns of settlement close to the industries recruiting black workers, mainly in London, the West Midlands, the North-West and the East Midlands. The links between early migrants and their countries of origin meant that the first areas of settlement were the obvious destinations for those who followed, and thus the pattern became reinforced. At the very local level, we have described how the position of black immigrants in the housing market played a large part in determining their actual residential locations within the towns and parts of cities to which they had come to work. Of course, even at this level the social networks of black migrants were very important and they reinforced the pattern of local concentration; in a new country, faced by racial hostility on the part of many individuals and organisations around them, and with limited financial resources, the migrants, particularly those for whom English was not their first language, derived much support from their own local ethnic community. Thus the initial, distinctive geographical distribution of black people in Britain was the result of a combination of the position of colonial immigrants within the British labour market, their limited access to housing, and the internal dynamics of migrant settlement and mutual support.

The census gives us a good source of data on the way this pattern had developed by 1971, and because the sample structure for the PSI survey was based on the 1971 census areas we have been able to examine the changes that occurred between 1971 and 1982. In this period the black population in Britain grew by about 60 per cent, by immigration and by natural increase, and it might be expected that this major demographic change, along with the

310

passing of eleven years, would have been accompanied by a substantial change in geographical distribution. In fact there has been very little change, except for a movement within areas of established ethnic minority residence that has reduced the very sharp localisation of minority communities. Seen in comparison with the geographical spread of the white population, the distribution of black people has hardly changed at all. To those who have observed a growth in the numbers of black people in areas that are almost exclusively white, this finding may seem at odds with their own experience. But there is no parodox here. The absolute numbers of black people living in traditionally white areas have increased, but only in line with the overall increase in the black population; the dispersed households therefore form about the same small percentage of the total black population as they did in 1971. The corollary of this is that in the more concentrated areas the absolute numbers of black people have also grown, and therefore the local densities of black residence have grown, although in some districts the movement of black households from areas of high density to nearby areas of lower density will have limited this effect.

Thus, although there has been some change in the residential pattern of Asian and West Indian households, this has taken place within the confines of local authorities and electoral wards previously identifiable as areas of immigrant settlement. Here we can see an important parallel with the developments in the labour market over the same period: the jobs of Asians and West Indians have largely remained within the employment sectors that originally accepted immigrant workers, and at the same occupational levels. Given the high level of geographical mobility among Asians and West Indians (46 per cent moved house in the five years preceding the survey) and the length of time that most Asian and West Indian workers have been in Britain, it is remarkable that the position of black people in British society, in terms of both their place in the labour market and their residential location, has changed so little.

Because the overall geographical distribution of the black population has been very stable, many of the poor districts where the first immigrants settled have continued to have the highest densities of black residence. We therefore find that the areas of high density tend to be those which have the worst housing and employment problems. Households moving away from these areas are those able to afford better housing and those who do not need the support of their own ethnic community as much as others, and therefore any outward movement tends to strengthen the association between disadvantage and local density. This association is notably stronger among Asians than among West Indians, and there are three explanations for this. First, the reliance by Asians on private-sector housing means that market forces have a greater impact on their residential location than is the case among West Indians, who are more reliant on local authority housing. Secondly, there is the connection between disadvantage and poor English fluency: those with more limited English tend to have the worst employment, but, because they are the group that is most dependent on the ethnic facilities and support available in the more concentrated Asian communities, they are also the group least likely to move elsewhere. Thirdly, the traditionally strong patterns of Asian kinship support and reciprocal obligation tend to maintain the association between disadvantage and concentration in a similar way, by protecting the more vulnerable households within the community, irrespective of language difficulties.

It is important to note that while the geographical distribution of Asians and West Indians has changed little in terms of the districts in which they live, there have been important changes in their housing circumstances within those areas. In the owner-occupied sector, house moves have brought about considerable improvements in housing conditions. Residential mobility among black owner-occupiers over the period we have examined can therefore be characterised as movement to upgrade rather than as movement to disperse. In the local authority sector the picture is harder to interpret because of the contrast between transfers and new allocations: transfers of tenants between properties are usually to improve their conditions, but the recent allocations to new tenants have been properties that are in some respects worse than those allocated to black tenants in the past, for, although they are newer and better equipped, they are also more likely to be flats rather than houses. Nevertheless, the move into council tenancy has meant an upgrading of property for many of these new tenants because a large number of them were previously in privately rented and shared dwellings, where conditions were much worse. In this sense it can be said that the moves into and between council properties have, like the moves in the owner-occupied market, involved an upgrading of accommodation for most households, despite the fact that they have taken place largely within the established areas of ethnic minority residence.

Educational background

Nearly all Asian adults and three-quarters of West Indian adults in the UK are immigrants, and therefore many of them have educational backgrounds that are different from those of white adults. As the proportions of British black people born and educated in this country increases, so these differences diminish, but at present they are large enough to have a substantial overall effect on the relative job levels of black workers. Generally, people of Asian and West Indian origin are less likely than whites to have formal qualifications of an academic or vocational nature, but because of the broad range of countries, regions and cultures from which the immigrants come, there are some complex variations between different groups.

Among people aged over 25 there are two particular features of interest within the overall pattern. The first is the fact that Asians, and Asian men especially, are educationally very heterogeneous: there is a sizable group of them with very little formal education, and another, equally large group with a very high level of education and qualifications. A fifth of Asians aged over 25 left full-time education before they were ten years old, but another fifth stayed on beyond their nineteenth birthday; for whites, the first of these groups is almost non-existent, and the second accounts for less than a tenth of the population aged over 25. The second feature is the different balance of academic and vocational qualifications held by Asians and West Indians. The proportions of Asian men with various academic qualifications are similar to those of white men, but far fewer have formal vocational qualifications; when West Indian men are compared to white men they are seen to have fewer qualifications of both types, but compared to Asian men they more commonly hold qualifications for skilled manual work. Among women, the levels of academic qualifications of Asians and West Indians are closer together than among men, but the gap between their levels of vocational qualifications is wider: very few Asian women aged over 25 have any formal vocational qualifications.

Younger black people have levels of qualifications that are much more like those of whites, but they are not identical. Although in our sample the levels of qualifications are on balance lower among young black adults than among young white adults, the differences between Asians and West Indians, and between men and women, are substantial and have something of the character of those described among older people. The most striking finding is the fact that a half of Asian young women have no qualifications, vocational or academic, compared with only a fifth of white and West Indian young women. However, the proportion with A-levels and degrees is similar for Asians and whites, suggesting a polarisation between young Asian women with good academic qualifications and those with none at all; there is also evidence in the survey that the pattern is rapidly changing, with many more young Asian women gaining academic qualifications.

The growth of the UK-educated section of the black population is not the only source of change in the proportion with formal qualifications. We find that a larger proportion of black people than white people now stay in full-time education after the ages of 16 and 20, and as a consequence the trend towards an overall increase in the proportion with academic qualifications must be

313

even stronger than would be inferred from the demographic changes. West Indian young men are an exception to this, although they are as likely as young white men to stay on. There is also a significant group of black women who are studying part-time for qualifications: nine per cent among West Indians and five per cent among Asians, compared with two per cent among whites. The effects of these two factors in raising the 'average qualifications' of the black population have been hidden to some extent by the recent immigration of female and elderly male dependants who have few qualifications. This is a further demonstration of something that is clear from the rest of the analysis of ethnic differences in educational background: the white, Asian and West Indian populations are all made up of groups that have widely differing educational experiences and formal qualifications, and it is not very useful to think in terms of 'average levels', which fall unhappily between the real situations of these different groups and give rise to misleading stereotypes.

Language

In this report we have repeatedly shown the extent to which poor English fluency is linked with other forms of disadvantage among people of Asian origin. It is therefore of great concern that a substantial proportion of the adult Asian population have limited English, and that this is improving only slowly. Overall, about half of Asian men and a third of Asian women speak English fluently, according to the interviewers' assessments, while a fifth of Asian men and nearly half of Asian women speak English 'slightly or not at all'.

As in the case of educational background, levels of fluency differ between the various Asian ethnic groups as well as between men and women: people of Indian and African Asian origin are more likely to be fluent than people of Pakistani and Bangladeshi origin. The two ends of the spectrum are Bangladeshi women, three-quarters of whom have little or no English, and African Asian men, two-thirds of whom are fluent in English. There is a very strong relationship with age (over half of Asian adults under 25, and over 90 per cent of those born in the UK, speak English fluently) and as young British Asians grow up the proportion of fluent adults rises, but there is little evidence of other factors additionally working in this direction. Between 1974 and 1982 the size of the group with little or no English fell from 42 per cent to 36 per cent in the areas common to both surveys, a change mainly accounted for by the fluency of young adults. One reason for the apparently slow change is the arrival in this period of new immigrants, who are unlikely to have fluent English. But our analysis shows that there is no uniform relationship between length of time in Britain and English fluency: for example, almost as many of the Asian men who came to this country between 1977 and 1982 have fluent English as those who came in the early 1960s. Thus any assumption that the adult immigrant population will develop fluency in English just as a result of living and working in Britain is incorrect, and there are clear reasons for this. The development of Asian communities has removed many of the immediate day-to-day problems encountered by people with a different language: the availability of facilities where Asian languages are spoken has been of great benefit, but inevitably has reduced the pressure to learn English. Also the tendency for Asian workers to be with employers that traditionally take on Asians and to work in shift teams with others of their ethnic group limits the necessity of spoken exchanges with white people. When we asked Asian workers whether they felt they experienced difficulties because of language when they tried to obtain a job, or had any language difficulties at work, less than one in ten said they had. The Asian community provides a buffer against the problems of English fluency, and this is further demonstrated by the very strong relationship between local Asian density and individual level of English.

It is very important to consider this problem in the light of the fact that multi-lingualism among Asians is the norm rather than the exception. Most Asian people have some fluency in at least one Asian language other than their own, as well as English. There is also a large group among those without fluent English who record interest in facilities for learning English: over a third say they would like the opportunity to improve their English, and about ten per cent have attended special classes of some kind. Considering the extent to which the perceived personal disadvantage of poor English is minimised as a result of the cultural solidarity of Asians and their position in the labour market, these findings show a major - but untapped - interest in the further learning of English. It is equally clear that the positive commitment that Asians have towards their own languages does not itself constitute a barrier to their further learning of English. Young people with very good English feel as strongly as others about the importance of Asian languages and as this view is essentially multi-lingual it is entirely compatible with any movement towards more widespread fluency and literacy in English.

The persistence of inequality
As we systematically compare the jobs, incomes, unemployment rates, private housing, local authority housing, local environments and other aspects of the lives of people with different ethnic origins, a single argument emerges in respect of the way the circumstances of black people came to be and continue to be worse than those of white people. In its most general form, the argument runs as follows. Asian and West Indian immigrants came to Britain

315

not as a result of a spontaneous migratory fervour, but as a result of the availability of jobs that offered rates of pay that were higher than those that could be obtained by the migrants in their countries of origin. There were openings for immigrants because the expanding economy of the 1950s and early 1960s created demands for labour that could not be satisfied from within the indigenous workforce. However, these openings were located at the lower levels of the job market, in jobs left behind by white workers who could in this period more easily become upwardly mobile. The result was that even highly qualified immigrants found themselves doing manual work, while those without qualifications were given the very worst jobs. The same mechanism operated with regard to housing and residential area. Asians and West Indians settled in the areas that white people were leaving, and in the poor housing stock no longer wanted by whites who could afford to move on or who were housed by the council. Black people came from the former colonies into this country to a position of ready-made disadvantage; their entry to British society was as a replacement for the lost battalions of urban manual workers, not, as it might have been, as a group of newcomers with a varied range of qualifications, skills and abilities who could make contributions at all levels of society. And perhaps the most serious aspect of this movement of immigrant workers into the unwanted jobs and housing at the foot of the social pyramid was that the patterns of disadvantage were bound to reproduce themselves rather than gradually disappear: many of the forces that initially prevented immigrants obtaining better jobs and housing continued to act in this way, and were augmented by new forces that emerged from the reaction of the white population and the adaptation of the black newcomers. Built into the circumstances of the immigration were factors which would inhibit the breakdown of the 'coloured immigrant' status of black workers settled in Britain. Additionally, the position of black newcomers was worsened by the inflexibility of British institutions when they were confronted with differences of family structure and language and with other cultural differences; in many cases even the response of white people who recognised these problems has been to wait for and to promote the erosion of these cultural differences, to wait for black families to become more like whites.

The patterns of disadvantage were therefore set early in the history of Britain's present black population and became in many respects self-sustaining. The processes of direct and indirect racial discrimination in employment operate as if to recognise the legitimacy of recruitment of black workers to some jobs but their exclusion from others, while a variety of factors maintain the geographical distribution of black families in the areas of original immigrant settlement. The movement of the economy into recession has also had a grave impact on the circumstances of black people because it has eaten away part of the narrow foothold on which many immigrant workers are forced to rest: unemployment has disproportionately affected lower-paid manual jobs and those in the older manufacturing industries in the conurbations. Thus, although the conditions of black people in this country are still moulded by the historical circumstances of their settlement here, the economic imperatives that established those circumstances have disappeared. But the collapse of the demand for labour has not only created higher rates of unemployment among blacks: it has also provided extra fuel for racialism and discrimination among whites. We therefore find that many Asian and West Indian people feel that these problems have worsened, while in the 1974 survey they were outnumbered by those who felt things were getting better.

Some things, as we have seen, really have got better. Overall housing conditions among black people have improved because of movement away from privately rented and shared dwellings and because of movements by owner-occupiers to better houses. But there are still severe inequalities between the housing of black and white families, not least because of the limited geographical spread of ethnic minority residence. The jobs of young people who are lucky enough to have work are closer than before to the jobs of young white workers; but many young blacks are outside employment, either because they are unemployed, staying on at school or college, or, in the case of women, remaining in the home, and there must therefore be doubt as to whether this indicates any real improvement in the opportunities for black workers. The massive move into self-employment by Asian workers will certainly bring economic betterment for some, and has certainly meant an escape from discrimination in recruitment and promotion; what the long-term effects of this move will be we cannot tell. It is perhaps significant that this avenue of potential upward mobility involves a step out of the normal channels of job recruitment and a reliance on the individual's own enterprise, and this can be seen partly as a response to the barriers to advancement that exist for black employees.

If this analysis of the changes in the inequalities between white and black people in Britain over the past decade seems in the main pessimistic and negative, it should be noted that before the survey was carried out there were reasons to have higher hopes. The 1976 Race Relations Act made indirect discrimination unlawful, gave individuals access to courts and tribunals to individually pursue discrimination cases, and set up the Commission for Racial Equality with its strategic role to identify areas of discrimination and work to eradicate them. The black communities themselves have become more established, and any disadvantages flowing

317

specifically from the unfamiliarity of immigrants with the employment and housing markets should have diminished now that such a large proportion of black people have been in this country for over ten years. Over the past few years the profile of racial discrimination and racial disadvantage as issues has been raised by a number of public policy initiatives, at a local level and at a national level, and these range from the ethnic minorities units and positive action schemes set up by some local authorities through to the extensive reporting by the House of Commons Home Affairs Committee and its predecessors. There has been considerable activity by members of the ethnic minority communities to organise facilities for themselves, both for fighting racialism, legally and politically, and for self-help, in areas such as child-care and supplementary schooling. Programmes of government aid in urban areas, particularly the areas that have relatively large ethnic minority populations, have existed in various forms since 1969. Our expectation when embarking on this study was that we would find a substantial reduction in the levels of inequality and that there would be pointers towards the way these changes might be further encouraged. Instead we find a complex jumble of old and new inequalities, rooted in three linked problems. First, it is clear that racialism and direct racial discrimination continue to have a powerful impact on the lives of black people. Second, the position of the black citizens of Britain largely remains, geographically and economically, that allocated to them as immigrant workers in the 1950s and 1960s. Third, it is still the case that the organisations and institutions of British society have policies and practices that additionally disadvantage black people because they frequently take no account of the cultural differences between groups with different ethnic origins.

It is outside the scope of this report to propose detailed policies that might be adopted by central and local government, by employers, by trade unions and by other bodies in order to break this continuing pattern of inequality. It is right, however, that we should draw public attention, and the attention of these organisations, to a number of issues, some broad and some narrow, which the survey results suggest to be of direct relevance to this endeavour.

(1) Vigorous positive action will be necessary to prevent racial inequality from persisting.
The fact that the mechanisms of racial inequality have become entrenched and self-sustaining means that it is not enough to establish a formal legal framework of equality by outlawing racial discrimination. The separateness of the jobs and the residential locations of British people of Asian and West Indian origin is so firmly established that it generates among both whites and blacks assumptions, expectations and

318

behaviour that perpetuate it; only if these impediments are systematically challenged at every level, whenever they might arise, will there be a chance to move away from the present situation.

(2)   A particular effort is needed in the private sector of industry.
The job levels of black workers, relative to those of whites, are lower in the private sector than in the public sector, and are lowest in manufacturing industry. Among men, non-manual and supervisory jobs remain almost exclusively white in this area of the economy, and, among women, blacks are severely under-represented in non-manual jobs. Removing the barriers that prevent the recruitment of blacks to these jobs is a matter of urgency if inequality in the labour market as a whole is to be tackled. This does not mean that the public sector and the service sector have a clean bill of health in this respect: although historically black people have obtained employment more freely within these sectors (and this is reflected in the survey findings), a substantial degree of inequality exists there, and this is particularly visible in the case of West Indian men.

(3)   Limited fluency in English continues to be strongly associated with economic disadvantage; and vice-versa. The circle needs to be broken.
Problems of English fluency have become part of the spiral of inequality because the limited space occupied by people of Asian origin in British society limits the need and the opportunities for learning English, and the resulting lack of fluency plays a part in preventing many Asians from breaking out of the manual jobs traditionally allocated to them. Problems of fluency for the present generation will not therefore melt away, and will continue to affect the quality of life for many families, unless concerted action is taken to make available and encourage the use of facilities for learning English. The tradition of multi-lingualism in the Asian community and the size of the proportion in the survey who expressed interest in facilities to learn more English both suggest that this action would stand a good chance of success.

(4)   The move among Asian workers to self-employment is not taking place among West Indians. If there are particular obstacles that explain this, they should be tackled.
Whilst it has to be regarded as secondary to the issue of establishing real equality of opportunity in the job market, differential access to the finance and advice necessary for setting up a business could be an important source of disadvantage. Self-employment can be a means of economic

319

advancement and it erodes the traditional role of black workers as low-status employees. Our survey provides no information on the difficulties people face when attempting to set up their own businesses, but other studies have shown that West Indians face particular problems in respect of finance and advice(1).

(5) There is still a mismatch between the needs of Asian and West Indian council tenants and types of property allocated to them.

Asian and West Indian families are on average larger than white families and more frequently have children. It is therefore a major source of disadvantage that they are housed in properties that are on average smaller, more likely to be flats than houses, and less likely to have access to gardens. In particular the council housing system deals inadequately with large Asian households, for whom the property is generally too small, and West Indian lone-parent households, many of whom are housed in blocks of flats.

(6) The council property allocated to black tenants is generally worse than that allocated to white tenants; this is the result of a number of factors, including discrimination.

Irrespective of the differing needs of white, Asian and West Indian households, there is a considerable gap between the quality of black and white tenants' properties. We have discussed a number of ways in which this comes about as a result of the areas of residence and the workings of the allocation systems. Direct and indirect discrimination has played a part in this process, and continues to do so, as the recent Commission for Racial Equality report on housing in Hackney has demonstrated(2). The reviews of procedures that some local authorities have begun should be continued and extended, to identify the ways in which the procedures work to reduce the quality of black tenants' housing and the ways in which the system is vulnerable to individual prejudice and discrimination.

(7) Local authority boundaries tend to preserve the geographical distribution and the housing disadvantage of black council tenants.

Allocations and transfers in the council sector are carried out by local authorities within their own boundaries and there is little administrative scope for mobility of tenants between them. This locks council tenants - and applicants - within their present areas of residence, particularly within London; but because of the variations in the quality of housing stock between local authorities, and because black people tend to be located in the areas with worse stock, this limit on mobility holds together part of the overall pattern of racial

320

disadvantage in housing. The issues of cross-boundary allocation, transfer and exchange may in fact deserve attention in their own right, but their relevance to the continuing geographical concentration of black households in poor housing makes them particularly important.

(8) Although racial inequality cannot be explained as merely a product of different residential locations, it is the case that the problems of our inner cities have a grave effect on the circumstances of the population of Asian and West Indian origin.

Too often in the past the recognition of racial inequality has been subverted by an insistence that all disadvantage is geographically-based, and, as we have seen in this report, this is simply not the case. But there can be no doubt that residential location has a very strong relationship with the availability of jobs, the types of jobs available, the type of housing available, facilities for shopping and other domestic tasks, the general quality of the local environment in terms of traffic and health risks, and numerous other aspects of the quality of life. The fact that such a large part of the black population lives in the decayed inner areas of Britain's cities, as a result of the changes within British society that accompanied and promoted their immigration, makes the problems of these areas an important element of racial disadvantage.

(9) The relatively large proportion of lone-parent households of West Indian origin should be taken into account in planning local services.

The emergence of the lone parent households as relatively common among West Indians raises questions about housing and employment that need some thought. We have seen how at present lone parents are not well-housed, nor are they as often in full-time or part-time work as they might be if childcare facilities were better developed. Careful attention to these problems is needed if we are not to witness the growth of multiple disadvantage within this group.

(10) There is a lack of confidence in the protection offered by the police against the serious problem of racial attacks.

The survey not only shows that violent racially-motivated attacks on black people are a common and frightening aspect of racialism in Britain, but also that only half of Asian men and women, and less than a third of West Indian men and women felt that their ethnic group could rely on the protection of the police against them. This was backed up by a surprisingly high level of support for the idea of organising self-defence groups. Our analysis suggests that the 1981 Home Office Report Racial Attacks did not overestimate the numbers of racial attacks that become known to the police, and suggests that many more of these incidents go unreported.

(11) <u>Within the black communities there is overwhelming support for the notion of 'integration' in its basic sense of working and living alongside white people, but there is also a strong commitment to preserving ethnic minority culture.</u>
The attitudes of black people regarding their position in British society stand in marked contrast to the place that they have come to occupy: support for ideas about residence in areas separate to whites and avoidance of white people generally is very weak indeed, and is arguably even weaker than one would expect as a result of the problem of racial attacks, while ideas to the contrary, about having white colleagues and friends, receive the support of nearly nine out of ten survey informants. The residential and occupational segregation of black people is not, therefore, a product of any fundamental desire to avoid whites. A large majority of Asians and West Indians also express views, not surprisingly, in support of the survival of their ethnic culture and way of life.

(12) <u>While black people - and Asians in particular - are cautious of accusing white people and institutions of discrimination, there is a body of concern over the actions of employers, landlords and the police. A majority support the ideas of further enforcing and extending the laws against discrimination.</u>
The attitude questions reveal little evidence of any generalised resentment among black people over their position in British society. Although over 40 per cent say that discrimination has worsened in recent years, a series of questions on whether specific bodies discriminate against blacks received a very cautious response overall, and the proportion saying that there was discrimination was for most examples less than a majority. Several bodies stand out from the others, however, with a significant proportion of Asians and West Indians claiming they discriminated: those were employers, private landlords and the police. Among West Indians, concern is also expressed, though to a lesser extent, about the courts, housing departments and schools. When asked whether they agreed or disagreed that the present anti-discrimination laws should be more effectively enforced, over 80 per cent agreed, and 75 per cent said there should be new, harder laws in this area.

At the beginning of this report we said that the focus of the PEP/PSI studies over the past 18 years has shifted from the treatment of immigrant workers to the circumstances of the

322

British black population. This third study shows that the occupational and geographical position of black people in Britain is still largely shaped by the conditions of the original migration. The early immigrants fitted into specific localities, parts of the housing stock and corners of the economy that had been vacated by sections of the white working class who had moved on to better things. They tended to remain within these specific sectors because of racial discrimination and because of the mutual reinforcement of a network of interlocking disadvantages. The present findings show that the more recent migrants and the children of the earlier migrants are still confined, for the most part, to these same areas and sectors of the economy, while the signs of economic regeneration are elsewhere.

For the most part, therefore, Britain's well-established black population is still occupying the precarious and unattractive position of the earlier immigrants. We have moved, over a period of 18 years, from studying the circumstances of immigrants to studying the black population of Britain only to find that we are still looking at the same thing. There is just the same need now as in 1976 for action to give black people access to widening economic opportunities and life chances; and there is just the same need to pursue equality between racial groups in Britain.

Notes
1.   See, for instance:
     West Indian Business in Britain: Research commissioned from the SSRC Research Unit on Ethnic Relations. Memorandum to House of Commons Home Affairs Committee, HMSO, 1980; Black Business in Lambeth, Research Memorandum 20, London Borough of Lambeth, 1982; Peter E. Wilson, Black Business Enterprise in Britain, Runnymede Trust, 1983.
2.   Race and Council Housing in Hackney. Report of a Formal Investigation. CRE, January 1984.

APPENDIX 1   DEFINITIONS

(a)   Inner areas
      The definitions of the inner areas of the three main
      conurbations used in this report are as follows:

Inner London: All the 'Group A' Boroughs, i.e.
                       City of London
                       Camden
                       Hackney
                       Hammersmith & Fulham
                       Haringey
                       Islington
                       Kensington & Chelsea
                       Lambeth
                       Lewisham
                       Newham
                       Southwark
                       Tower Hamlets
                       Wandworth
                       Westminister

Inner Birmingham: Birmingham 'Core Area', i.e. these
                       electoral wards (1971 areas):

Handsworth	Sparkbrook
Soho	Sparkhill
Newton	Saltley
Aston	Washwood Heath
Duddeston	Moseley (part)
All Saints	Acock's Green (part)
Rotton Park	Gravelly Hill (part)
Ladywood	Sandwell (part)
Deritend	

Inner Manchester: Manchester-Salford 'Special Area', i.e.
                       these electoral wards (1971 areas):

Manchester	Salford
Alexandra Park	Weaste
St. Luke's	Seedley
All Saints	Langworthy
Ardwick	St. Paul's
St. Mark's	Docks
Longsight	Ordsall Park
Beswick	Regent

Manchester	Salford
Bradford	Crescent
Miles Platting	Trinity
New Cross	St. Matthias
Newton Heath	St. Thomas's
Openshaw	Albert Park
Gorton North	Charlestown
Gorton South	Mandley Park
Rusholme	
Moss Side East	
Moss Side West	
St. George's	
St. Peter's	
Hugh Oldham	
Collegiate Church	
Blackley (part)	
Moston (part)	
Chorlton cum Hardy (part)	
Old Moat (part)	
Crumpsal (part)	
Levenshulme (part)	
Harpurhey (part)	
Lightbowne (part)	
Cheetham (part)	

It should be noted that inner Birmingham and inner Manchester areas are as defined for administration of part of the Government's inner-city policy (the 'partnership scheme') and the lists of wards given above are complete: the PSI survey covered only a sample of wards within each area, not all of them. We cannot (for reasons of confidentiality) specify the wards covered; there were four in inner Birmingham and three in inner Manchester. In London the survey covered all boroughs.

(b) Coding of occupations
Job levels were coded according to the 1971 Census classification of socio-economic groups (see Classification of Occupations 1970, HMSO, 1970):

SEG Code

1.   Employers and managers in central and local government, industry, commerce etc. (large establishments)

2.   Employers and managers in central and local government, industry, commerce etc. (small establishments)

325

3.	Professional workers (self-employed)
4.	Professional workers (employed)
5.1.	Intermediate non-manual workers (ancillary workers and artists)
5.2.	Intermediate non-manual workers (foremen and supervisors, non-manual)
6.	Junior non-manual workers
7.	Personal service workers
8.	Foremen and supervisors, manual
9.	Skilled manual workers
10.	Semi-skilled manual workers
11.	Unskilled manual workers
12.	Own account workers (other than professional)
13.	Farmers - employers and managers
14.	Farmers - own account
15.	Agricultural workers
16.	Members of armed forces

For most of the analysis these categories were grouped under these headings:

	SEG Codes
Professional/Employer/Manager	1,2,3,4,13
Other non-manual	5.1, 5.2, 6
Skilled manual & Foreman	8, 9, 12, 14
Semi-skilled manual	7, 10, 15
Unskilled manual	11

Industry sectors were coded twice, first according to the 1971 Census Industry Order Minimum List Headings and secondly according to the Industrial Division Classification used in the 1981 Census. In the report we use the Industry Order Headings for employees and the Industrial Divisions for the self-employed.

(c)   Qualifications
It is impossible to arrive at a completely satisfactory way of comparing the qualifications of different groups of people because the value put on each type of qualification varies with the circumstances in which it is assessed or needed. In the very simplest example of this, it is clearly not worth applying for a skilled manual job on the basis of a university degree, but, equally clearly, there is a sense in which a graduate is better educated than a person with an apprenticeship. Nevertheless we cannot simply compare the proportions of each group holding each type of qualification

326

since it is the 'highest' qualifications held by the individual that are the most important. Thus we need to put qualifications into a hierarchy, but we are unable to do this without giving relative values to vocational and academic qualifications which may often be inappropriate. In an attempt to get round these problems we have put informants' qualifications into two hierarchies, one covering academic qualifications and the other covering vocational and professional qualifications. Of course this distinction is itself rather artificial, as no academic pursuit is devoid of practical use and no vocational training is totally lackng in technical or theoretical study, and there are 'borderline' qualifications that force almost arbitrary choices upon us. Attention should be drawn to the particularly difficult cases of teaching, social work and nursing qualifications. All are professional/vocational qualifications, but as the context of the teaching profession is itself academic, we have classified teaching qualifications as academic rather than vocational. Thus, all those with a teaching qualification will appear in the 'A level or above (no degree)' category, unless they also have a degree; those with social work or nursing qualifications will appear in the 'professional or clerical qualification' category on the vocational scale and will be classed on the academic scale according to their highest other qualification. Other difficulties are presented by the fact that some qualifications were obtained overseas, and therefore are not strictly comparable to British qualifications. This is not to say they will necessarily be of any less educational value, rather that they are difficult for British people, and employers in particular, to assess. Close inspection of the actual qualifications involved shows that this problem is less severe than it might have been, partly because of the broadness of the categories used, but also because an aspect of the relationship between Britain and the New Commonwealth is the practice of taking British GCE examinations abroad. These are clearly of equivalent value to British GCEs. In addition, very few Asian or West Indian men have degrees only from overseas, and very few Asians and West Indians only have academic qualifications from overseas that are not degrees or GCE's; we have therefore classed all degrees together, and omitted all 'other' qualifications taken overseas entirely. The broadness of the top category of the vocational qualification scale means that we need not make a fine distinction between the British and overseas origins of the qualifications, particularly as most of them are in fact British. A very small number of apprenticeships were served overseas.

327

The classification of qualifications was made as follows.

Highest Academic Qualification

1. Degree or Higher Degree: Any degree or higher degree, British or non-British

2. GCE 'A' Level, HND/C or above (no degree): Any GCE 'A' Level or SCE 'Higher' level, Higher National Diploma or Certificate, teaching qualification

3. GCE 'O' Level, ONC/D: Any GCE 'O' Level, Ordinary National Certificate or Diploma

4. CSE or other academic qualification below 'O' Level: Any CSE or British equivalent (e.g. Matriculation)

Highest Vocational Qualification

1. Professional or Clerical: Any Professional, clerical, social work or nursing qualification

2. Apprenticeship: Any completed trade apprenticeship

3. City & Guilds: Any City and Guilds qualifications

APPENDIX 2 EARNINGS DIFFERENTIALS AND NON-RESPONSE

A proportion of the informants did not give a figure for their earnings, either because they did not know themselves or because they did not wish to give this information.   Among black informants the level of non-response was higher than among white informants, as can be seen below:

Non-response rate (full-time employees)

Men
White	4%
West Indian	16%
Asian	16%

Women
White	6%
West Indian	16%
Asian	16%

It is possible that those refusing to give a figure for their earnings tended to be those in the upper earnings groups, and that the larger non-response among the blacks has therefore artificially lowered the black earnings medians given in this report. This suggestion is supported by the fact that non-response tends to be more common in the higher SEG groups among both whites and blacks, although the tendency is stronger among whites.

	Non-response rate (Full-time employees)	
	White Men	Black Men
Professional/Employer/Manager	9%	24%
Other non-manual	4%	19%
Skilled Manual/Foreman	3%	17%
Semi-skilled Manual	1%	11%
Unskilled	–	18%

This could have serious implications for the reliability of the estimated differential between black and white earnings. The most severe test we can give to our data is to assume that <u>all</u> of the missing cases are in the two highest earnings bands used in the survey (over £143 per week) and recalculate the earnings medians. If we do this for men, we find that the overall earnings gap between white and black employees closes by almost a half: our original figures show that black men have an earnings median which is 85 per cent of the white median, while the adjusted black median is 92 per cent of the adjusted white median. Given that only 17 per cent of the known black men's earnings are in the two highest bands, the assumption that every one of the missing cases would be in this category is unlikely to accord with reality. If we make a less severe test based on the more reasonable assumption that half the missing cases are in the two highest bands (over £143), a quarter are in the band below (£117-£143) and a quarter in the band below that (£92-£116), we find that the black median is 88 per cent of the white median.

Gross weekly earnings of full-time employees
Median to nearest pound

	Based on known earnings	Assuming all missing earnings over £143	Assumng half missing earnings over £143
White	£129	£131	£130
Black	£110	£120	£115

Thus we see that the 15 per cent overall differential may be an overestimate, but the true figure is unlikely to be less than ten per cent, and that even if we make the most extreme assumption concerning the missing data the differential is reduced to a minimum of eight per cent.

APPENDIX 3 QUESTIONNAIRE

The questionnaire is divided into three parts called the household module, the individual module and the alternate module. The use of these modules is described in Chapter I. The questionnaire shown is the version used for the interviews with black informants; the white schedule contained fewer questions, but the wordings were the same.

The questionnaire was printed in an English version and five bilingual Asian language versions. To illustrate how the Asian language translations were included on the schedule, the first seven pages of the questionnaire printed here are taken from the Punjabi/English version.

RESEARCH SERVICES LTD.

Station House, Harrow Road, Stonebridge Park, Wembley, Middlesex. HA9 6DE

P

J.2775/AK

SURVEY OF RACIAL MINORITIES

February 1982

HOUSEHOLD MODULE

Time started_____

O U O	SERIAL	C C	S R	E D	PER. NO.
(1-3)	(4-9)	0 1 (10-11)	(12-13)	(14-16)	(17)

INTERVIEWER FILL IN SERIAL, ED AND PERSON NUMBER

HOUSEHOLD COMPOSITION

For general background information, I would first like to ask you about the people who live here with you as members of your own household. By your household I mean people who live here regularly and with whom you share basic food and catering arrangements.

ਆਮ ਪਿਛੋਕੜ ਜਾਣਕਾਰੀ ਲਈ ਪਹਿਲਾਂ ਮੈਂ ਤੁਹਾਡੇ ਕੋਲੋਂ ਉਨ੍ਹਾਂ ਲੋਕਾਂ ਦੇ ਬਾਰੇ ਸਵਾਲ ਪੁੱਛਾਂਗਾ/ ਪੁੱਛਾਂਗੀ ਜੋ ਇਥੇ ਤੁਹਾਡੇ ਨਾਲ ਤੁਹਾਡੇ ਪਰਿਵਾਰ ਦੇ ਜੀਆਂ ਦੇ ਤੌਰ ਤੇ ਰਹਿੰਦੇ ਹਨ। ਤੁਹਾਡੇ ਪਰਿਵਾਰ ਤੋਂ ਮੇਰਾ ਮਤਲਬ ਹੈ ਉਹ ਲੋਕ ਜੋ ਇਥੇ ਬਾਕਾਇਦਾ ਰਹਿੰਦੇ ਹਨ ਤੇ ਜੋ ਤੁਹਾਡੇ ਨਾਲ ਖਾਣ ਖੁਆਉਣ ਹਨ।

LIST HOUSEHOLD MEMBERS, STARTING WITH THE PERSON IN WHOSE NAME THE HOUSE OR FLAT IS HELD (THE HEAD OF HOUSEHOLD).
LIST ALL AGED 16+ FIRST.   CODE ON PAGE 2/3

ASK FOR EACH PERSON:

1(a) Is .... male or female?

... ਪੁਰਸ਼ ਹੈ ਜਾਂ ਇਸਤਰੀ ?

1(b) How is ... related to (the head of household)?

ਪਰਿਵਾਰ ਦੇ ਮੁੱਖੀ ਨਾਲ ... ਦਾ ਕੀ ਰਿਸ਼ਤਾ ਹੈ ?

1(c) Is ... married, living as married, single, widowed, divorced or separated?

ਉਹ ਸ਼ਾਦੀਸ਼ੁਦਾ ਹੈ, ਸ਼ਾਦੀਸ਼ੁਦਾ ਵਾਂਗ ਰਹਿੰਦੇ/ਰਹਿੰਦੀ ਹੈ, ਛੰਦਾ/ਛੰਦੀ ਹੈ, ਰੰਡਾ/ਰੰਡੀ ਹੈ, ਤਲਾਕਸ਼ੁਦਾ ਹੈ ਜਾਂ ਪਤੀ/ਪਤਨੀ ਤੋਂ ਆਲਹਿਦਾ ਰਹਿੰਦਾ/ਰਹਿੰਦੀ ਹੈ ?

1(d) What was the age of ... on their last birthday?

ਪਿਛਲੇ ਜਨਮ-ਦਿਨ ਤੇ ... ਦੀ ਉਮਰ ਕਿੰਨੀ ਸੀ ?

1(e) In what country was ... born?
IF UK, AFRICA OR OTHER

... ਕਿਸ ਦੇਸ ਵਿੱਚ ਪੈਦਾ ਹੋਇਆ/ਹੋਈ ਸੀ ?

1(f) What country did his/her family come from originally?
IF IN DOUBT CODE ORIGIN OF FATHER'S FATHER

ਉਸਦਾ ਪਰਿਵਾਰ ਅਸਲੋਂ ਕਿਸ ਦੇਸ ਵਿੱਚ ਆਇਆ ਸੀ ?

ASK IF PERSON IS OVER 16

1(g) Was ... working full-time or working part-time last week? By part-time we mean from 8 to 30 hours per week.

ਹੁ ਪਿਛਲੇ ਹਫਤੇ ਫੁਲ-ਟਾਇਮ ਕੰਮ ਤੇ ਸੀ ਜਾਂ ਪਾਰਟ-ਟਾਇਮ ਕੰਮ ਤੇ ? ਪਾਰਟ-ਟਾਇਮ ਕੰਮ ਤੇ ਸਾਡਾ ਮਤਲਬ ਹੈ 8 ਤੋਂ 30 ਘੰਟੇ।

IF NO : Was he/she seeking work, off sick, retired, keeping house, or still in full-time education?

ਕੀ ਉਹ ਕੰਮ ਲੱਭ ਰਿਹਾ/ਰਹੀ ਸੀ, ਬੀਮਾਰ ਸੀ, ਰਿਟਾਇਰ ਸੀ, ਘਰ ਸਾਂਭਦਾ/ਸਾਂਭਦੀ ਸੀ ਜਾਂ ਹਾਲੇ ਤਕ ਪੂਰੇ ਸਮੇਂ ਲਈ ਪੜ੍ਹਾਈ ਕਰ ਰਿਹਾ/ਰਹੀ ਸੀ ?

ASK IF WORKING FULL OR PART-TIME

1(h) Was ...working at home or outside the home?
IF BOTH, CODE WHERE WORKED MOST

ਉਹ ਘਰ ਕੰਮ ਕਰ ਰਿਹਾ/ਰਹੀ ਸੀ ਜਾਂ ਘਰੋਂ ਬਾਹਰ ?

Was he/she working as an employee or self-employed?

ਉਹ ਕਿਸੇ ਦੀ ਨੌਕਰੀ ਕਰਦਾ/ਕਰਦੀ ਹੈ ਜਾਂ ਆਪਣਾ ਧੰਦਾ ਕਰਦਾ/ਚਲਾਉਂਦੀ ਹੈ ?

	HEAD OF HOUSEHOLD PERSON No.1	OTHER PERSONS IN HOUSEHOLD NUMBER:				
		2	3	4	5	6

1(a) Sex:

	(18)	(28)	(39)	(50)	(61)	(18)
Male	1	1	1	1	1	1
Female	2	2	2	2	2	2

1(b) Relationship to Head of Household:

		(29)	(40)	(51)	(62)	(19)
Husband/wife of head . .		1	1	1	1	1
Mother/father of head		2	2	2	2	2
Brother/sister of head		3	3	3	3	3
Daughter/son of head . .		4	4	4	4	4
Grandparent of head . .		5	5	5	5	5
Other relation of head		6	6	6	6	6
Not related to head . .		7	7	7	7	7

1(c) Marital Status:

	(19)	(30)	(41)	(52)	(63)	(20)
Married	1	1	1	1	1	1
Living as married . . .	2	2	2	2	2	2
Single	3	3	3	3	3	3
Widowed	4	4	4	4	4	4
Divorced/separated . . .	5	5	5	5	5	5

	(20)	(31)	(42)	(53)	(64)	(21)
Family Unit						

	(21-22)	(32-33)	(43-44)	(54-55)	(65-66)	(22-23)

1(d) Age:

1(e) Country born in:

	Born	Fam	Born	Fam	Born	Fam	Born	Fam	Born	Fam	Born	Fam
	(23)	(24)	(34)	(35)	(45)	(46)	(56)	(57)	(67)	(68)	(24)	(25)

1(f) Country of Family:

	Born	Fam	Born	Fam	Born	Fam	Born	Fam	Born	Fam	Born	Fam
United Kingdom	1	1	1	1	1	1	1	1	1	1	1	1
West Indies/Guyana . . .	2	2	2	2	2	2	2	2	2	2	2	2
India	3	3	3	3	3	3	3	3	3	3	3	3
Pakistan	4	4	4	4	4	4	4	4	4	4	4	4
Bangladesh/E.Pakistan. .	5	5	5	5	5	5	5	5	5	5	5	5
Africa (Asian origin) . .	6	6	6	6	6	6	6	6	6	6	6	6
Africa (other)	7	7	7	7	7	7	7	7	7	7	7	7
Other (WRITE IN)	8	8	8	8	8	8	8	8	8	8	8	8
DK.	9	9	9	9	9	9	9	9	9	9	9	9

1(g) Activity status:

	(25)	(36)	(47)	(58)	(69)	(26)
Working full-time . . .	1	1	1	1	1	1
Working part-time . . .	2	2	2	2	2	2
Seeking work/unemployed	3	3	3	3	3	3
Off sick/on holiday . .	4	4	4	4	4	4
Retired	5	5	5	5	5	5
Keeping house	6	6	6	6	6	6
Full-time student . . .	7	7	7	7	7	7
Government scheme . . .	8	8	8	8	8	8
Other	9	9	9	9	9	9
DK	0	0	0	0	0	0

1(h) Work type:

	(26)	(37)	(48)	(59)	(70)	(27)
Works at home	1	1	1	1	1	1
Works outside home . . .	2	2	2	2	2	2

	(27)	(38)	(49)	(60)	(71)	(28)
Employee	1	1	1	1	1	1
Self-employed	2	2	2	2	2	2
DK	3	3	3	3	3	3

(72-76) blank   (01-09) Serial
(77-80) J.2775   (10-11) 02
(12-17) Serial

HOUSEHOLD CONTINUATION:	OTHER PERSONS IN HOUSEHOLD NUMBER:					
	7	8	9	10	11	12
	(29)	(40)	(51)	(62)	(18)	(29)

1(a) Sex:

	(30)	(41)	(52)	(63)	(19)	(30)
Male	1	1	1	1	1	1
Female	2	2	2	2	2	2

1(b) Relationship to Head of Household:

	(30)	(41)	(52)	(63)	(19)	(30)
Husband/wife of head . .	1	1	1	1	1	1
Mother/father of head	2	2	2	2	2	2
Brother/sister of head	3	3	3	3	3	3
Daughter/son of head . .	4	4	4	4	4	4
Grandparent of head . .	5	5	5	5	5	5
Other relation of head	6	6	6	6	6	6
Not related to head . .	7	7	7	7	7	7

1(c) Marital Status:

	(31)	(42)	(53)	'(64)	(20)	(31)
Married	1	1	1	1	1	1
Living as married . . .	2	2	2	2	2	2
Single	3	3	3	3	3	3
Widowed	4	4	4	4	4	4
Divorced/separated . . .	5	5	5	5	5	5

	(32)	(43)	(54)	(65)	(21)	(32)
Family Unit						

1(d) Age:

	(33-34)	(44-45)	(55-56)	(66-67)	(22-23)	(33-34)
	|	|	|	|	|	|

1(e) Country born in:

	Born	Fam	Born	Fam	Born	Fam	Born	Fam	Born	Fam	Born	Fam
	(35)	(36)	(46)	(47)	(57)	(58)	(68)	(69)	(24)	(25)	(35)	(36)
United Kingdom	1	1	1	1	1	1	1	1	1	1	1	1
West Indies/Guyana . . .	2	2	2	2	2	2	2	2	2	2	2	2
India	3	3	3	3	3	3	3	3	3	3	3	3
Pakistan	4	4	4	4	4	4	4	4	4	4	4	4
Bangladesh/E.Pakistan. .	5	5	5	5	5	5	5	5	5	5	5	5
Africa (Asian origin). .	6	6	6	6	6	6	6	6	6	6	6	6
Africa (other)	7	7	7	7	7	7	7	7	7	7	7	7
Other (WRITE IN)	8	8	8	8	8	8	8	8	8	8	8	8
DK	9	9	9	9	9	9	9	9	9	9	9	9

1(f) Country of Family: (applies to 1(e) second column "Fam")

1(g) Activity status:

	(37)	(48)	(59)	(70)	(26)	(37)
Working full-time . . .	1	1	1	1	1	1
Working part-time . . .	2	2	2	2	2	2
Seeking work/unemployed	3	3	3	3	3	3
Off sick/on holiday . .	4	4	4	4	4	4
Retired	5	5	5	5	5	5
Keeping house	6	6	6	6	6	6
Full-time student . . .	7	7	7	7	7	7
Government scheme . . .	8	8	8	8	8	8
Other	9	9	9	9	9	9
DK	0	0	0	0	0	0

1(h) Work type:

	(38)	(49)	(60)	(71)	(27)	(38)
Works at home	1	1	1	1	1	1
Works outside home . . .	2	2	2	2	2	2

	(39)	(50)	(61)	(72)	(28)	(39)
Employee	1	1	1	1	1	1
Self-employed	2	2	2	2	2	2
DK	3	3	3	3	3	3

IF MORE THAN 12 HOUSEHOLD MEMBERS,
CONTINUE ON SEPARATE SHEET.

(73-76) blank   (01-09) Serial
(77-80) J.2775   (10-11) 03
                 (12-17) Serial

CC3

	CODE	ROUTE

1(i) Does anyone in this household have any children under 16 who do not live here?

ਕੀ ਇਸ ਪਰਿਵਾਰ ਵਿੱਚ ਕਿਸੇ ਦੇ 16 ਸਾਲ ਤੋਂ ਘੱਟ ਉਮਰ ਦੇ ਬੱਚੇ ਹਨ ਜੋ ਇਥੇ ਨਹੀਂ ਰਹਿੰਦੇ ?

(40)

Yes   1 ——) Q.1(j)
No   2 ——) Q.2a
DK   3

IF "YES", ASK:

(41)M

1(j) Where do(es) the child(ren) live?   PROMPT IF NECESSARY

ਦੇਸੋਂ ਬਾਹਰ
ਬਰਤਾਨਿਆ ਵਿੱਚ ਰਿਸ਼ਤੇਦਾਰਾਂ ਨਾਲ
ਬਰਤਾਨਿਆ ਵਿੱਚ ਬੋਰਡਿੰਗ ਸਕੂਲ ਵਿੱਚ
ਲੋਕਲ ਅਥਾਰਿਟੀ ਦੇ ਬਚਿਆਂ ਦੇ ਘਰ ਵਿੱਚ

ਕਿਸੇ ਹੋਰ ਬਚਿਆਂ ਦੇ ਘਰ ਵਿੱਚ
ਲੋਕਲ ਅਥਾਰਿਟੀ ਦੇ ਲੇ-ਪਾਲਕ ਮਾਪਿਆਂ ਨਾਲ

ਕਿਸੇ ਹੋਰ ਲੇ-ਪਾਲਕ ਮਾਪਿਆਂ ਨਾਲ
ਗੋਦੀ ਲੈ ਲਿਆ/ਲੈ ਲਏ ਗਏ
ਕਿਸੇ ਦੂਜੀ ਜਗਾ

Abroad 1
With relatives in UK 2
At boarding school in UK 3
In a local authority
   children's home 4
In another children's home . . . 5
With local authority
   foster parents 6
With any other foster parents . . 7
Adopted 8
Other (WRITE IN) 9

DK   0

(42)

Now I should like to ask you about your present accommodation.

ਹੁਣ ਮੈਂ ਤੁਹਾਡੀ ਮੌਜੂਦਾ ਰਿਹਾਇਸ਼ ਬਾਰੇ ਸਵਾਲ ਪੁੱਛਣੇ ਚਾਹੁੰਦਾਂਗਾ

2(a) Does your household <u>share</u> any rooms, including bathrooms, toilets and kitchens, with any other households? I mean with other people whose basic food and catering arrangements are quite separate from yours.

Yes   1 ——) Q.2b
No   2 ——) Q.4
DK   3

ਕੀ ਤੁਹਾਡਾ ਪਰਿਵਾਰ ਕਿਸੇ ਦੂਸਰੇ ਪਰਿਵਾਰ ਨਾਲ ਕੋਈ ਕਮਰੇ ਸਾਂਝੇ ਤੌਰ ਤੇ ਇਸਤੇਮਾਲ ਕਰਦਾ ਹੈ ? ਇਸ ਵਿੱਚ ਉਸੀ ਬਾਥਰੂਮ, ਟਾਏ ਲਿਟ ਤੇ ਕਿਚਿਨ ਦੀ ਸ਼ਾਮਲ ਕਰੋ । ਦੂਸਰੇ ਲੋਕਾਂ ਤੋਂ ਮੇਰਾ ਮਤਲਬ ਹੈ ਜਿਨ੍ਹਾਂ ਦਾ ਆਲੂ-ਖਾਣ ਦਾ ਪ੍ਰਬੰਧ ਤੁਹਾਡੇ ਨਾਲੋ ਬਿਲਕੁਲ ਵੱਖਰਾ ਹੈ ।

(43)

IF "YES" (Code 1 Q.2(a) ASK:

2(b) With how many other households do you share rooms?   WRITE IN NUMBER

ਕਿਨੇ ਹੋਰਨਾਂ ਪਰਿਵਾਰਾਂ ਨਾਲ ਤੁਹਾਡੀ ਕਮਰਿਆਂ ਦੀ ਸਾਂਝ ਹੈ ?

(44)   (45)

2(c) How many people altogether live in these other households?   WRITE IN NUMBER

ਇਨ੍ਹਾਂ ਦੂਸਰੇ ਪਰਿਵਾਰਾਂ ਦੇ ਕੁੱਲ ਕਿੰਨੇ ਜੀਆ ਹਨ ?

(46)

2(d) Do any of these other people pay any rent to you?

Yes   1
No   2
DK   3

ਕੀ ਇਨ੍ਹਾਂ ਦੂਸਰੇ ਲੋਕਾਂ ਵਿੱਚੋਂ ਕੋਈ ਤੁਹਾਨੂੰ ਕਿਰਾਇਆ ਦਿੰਦਾ ਹੈ ?

(47)

IF SHARING (Q.2(a) CODE 1) ASK:

3. Apart from bathrooms, toilets and kitchens less than 6 feet wide, how many rooms do you share with other households?   WRITE IN NUMBER

ਛੇ ਫੁੱਟ ਚੌੜਾਈ ਤੋਂ ਘੱਟ ਦੇ ਬਾਥਰੂਮ, ਕਿਚਿਨ ਤੇ ਟਾਏਲਿਟ ਨੂੰ ਛੱਡਕੇ ਦੂਜੇ ਪਰਿਵਾਰਾਂ ਨਾਲ ਤੁਹਾਡੇ ਕਿੰਨੇ ਕਮਰੇ ਸਾਂਝੇ ਹਨ ?

ASK ALL:

4. Do you have use of the following?

ਕੀ ਇਨ੍ਹਾਂ ਵਿਚੋਂ ਕੋਈ ਤੁਹਾਡੇ ਘਰ ਵਿਚ ਹੈ ?

IF "YES", AND SHARE IT AT Q.2(a) ASK:

Do you share it with any other household?

ਕੀ ਇਹ ਕਿਸੇ ਹੋਰ ਪਰਿਵਾਰ ਨਾਲ ਸਾਂਝਾ/ਸਾਂਝੀ ਹੈ ?

		Have, Not Shared	Have, Shared	Do not have	DK	ROUTE
ਬਾਥਰੂਮ	Bathroom	1	2	3	4	(48)
ਪੱਕਾ ਬਾਥ ਜਾਂ ਸ਼ਾਵਰ	Fixed bath or shower . .	1	2	3	4	(49)
ਕਿਸੇ ਦੀ ਸਾਈਜ਼ ਦੀ ਕਿਚਿਨ	A kitchen of any size . .	1	2	3	4	(50)
ਅੰਦਰਲਾ ਫਲੱਸ਼ ਟਾਇਲਿਟ	Inside flush toilet . . .	1	2	3	4	(51)

ASK ALL:

5. Does your household have ...

ਕੀ ਤੁਹਾਡੇ ਘਰ ਵਿਚ ... ਹੈ ?

		Yes	No	DK	
ਟੂਟੀ ਦਾ ਗਰਮ ਪਾਣੀ	Hot water from the tap	1	2	3	(52)
ਕਪੜੇ ਧੋਣ ਵਾਲੀ ਮਸ਼ੀਨ	A washing machine	1	2	3	(53)
ਕਲਰ ਟੈਲੀਵਿਜ਼ਨ	A colour television	1	2	3	(54)
ਫਰਿੱਜ	A fridge	1	2	3	(55)
ਡੀਪ ਫਰੀਜ਼ਰ/ਫਰੀਜ਼ਰ	A deep freeze/freezer	1	2	3	(56)
ਸੈਂਟਰ ਹੀਟਿੰਗ, ਪੂਰੀ ਜਾਂ ਅੱਧੀ	Central heating, full or part				
(ਸਟੋਰੇਜ਼ ਹੀਟਰਜ਼ ਦੀ ਸ਼ਮੂਲ ਕਰੋ)	(including storage heaters). .	1	2	3	(57)
ਕਾਰ ਜਾਂ ਵੈਨ (ਕੰਪਨੀ ਕਾਰ ਸਮੇਤ)	Use of a car or van (inc.'company car')	1	2	3	(58)

ASK ALL:

6(a) How many rooms do you and your household have for your own exclusive use? Do <u>not</u> include toilets, bathrooms or kitchens less than 6 feet wide.

WRITE IN NUMBER

(59-60)

ਤੁਹਾਡੇ ਕੋਲ ਕਿੰਨੇ ਕਮਰੇ ਤੁਹਾਡੀ ਤੇ ਤੁਹਾਡੇ ਪਰਿਵਾਰ ਦੀ ਇਕੱਲੀ ਵਰਤੋਂ ਲਈ ਹਨ? ਇਸ ਵਿਚ ਤੁਸੀ ਛੇ ਫੁੱਟ ਚੌੜਾਈ ਤੋਂ ਘੱਟ ਵਾਲੇ ਬਾਥਰੂਮ ਟਾਇਲਿਟ ਜਾਂ ਕਿਚਿਨ ਨਾ ਗਿਣੋ ।

6(b) And how many of these are used as bedrooms? (COUNT BEDSITTERS)

WRITE IN NUMBER

(61)

ਇਨ੍ਹਾਂ ਵਿਚੋਂ ਕਿੰਨੇ ਕਮਰੇ ਸੌਣ ਲਈ ਵਰਤੇ ਜਾਂਦੇ ਹਨ ?

6(c) Do you have the use of ...

ਕੀ ਤੁਹਾਡੇ ਕੋਲ ... ਹੈ ?

IF YES : Is it shared or unshared?

ਕੀ ਇਹ ਸਾਂਝਾ/ਸਾਂਝੀ ਹੈ ਜਾਂ ਇਕੱਲਿਆਂ ਦਾ/ਦੀ ?

		Have, Not Shared	Have, Shared	Do not have	DK	
ਬਾਗੀਚਾ ਜਾਂ ਵਿਹੜੀ (ਪੇਟਿਓ)	A garden or patio	1	2	3	4	(62)
ਟੈਲੀਫੋਨ	A telephone	1	2	3	4	(63)

7. When was your house/flat built?

ਤੁਹਾਡਾ ਘਰ/ਫਲੈਟ ਕਦੋਂ ਬਣਿਆ ਸੀ ?

IF RESPONDENT HAS DIFFICULTY, MAKE YOUR OWN ESTIMATE IF YOU CAN AND CODE 8:

(64)**M**

Before 1919	1
1919 - 1944	2
1945 - 1959	3
1960 - 1975	4
1976 - Now	5
Don't know, but before 1945	6
Don't know at all	7
Code if interviewer estimated	8

CC3

	CODE	ROUTE

8. Do you, or does someone in your household, own this dwelling or do you rent it?

(65)

ਇਹ ਘਰ ਤੁਹਾਡਾ ਜਾਂ ਤੁਹਾਡੇ ਪਰਿਵਾਰ ਦੇ ਕਿਸੇ ਜੀਅ ਦਾ ਹੈ ਜਾਂ ਤੁਸੀਂ ਇਸ ਵਿੱਚ ਕਿਰਾਏ ਤੇ ਰਹਿੰਦੇ ਹੋ ?

Own (inc. with mortgage or loan) . . . . 1 —) Q.14a
Rent (inc. from Housing Association) . . . . 2 ⎤
Rent free . . . . 3 ⎦ —) Q. 9a
Squatter . . . . 4 ⎤
Equity sharing/'rent and buy'. 5
Co-ownership Housing Assoc... 6 —) Q.14a
Other (WRITE IN) _ _ _ _ _ _ 7 ⎤
                          DK 8 ⎦

(66)

ASK IF RENT/RENT FREE (Q.8 Code 2 and 3)

9(a) Do you rent from ... READ OUT. PRIORITY CODING:

ਕੀ ਤੁਸੀਂ... ਤੋਂ ਕਿਰਾਏ ਤੇ ਲਿਆ ਹੈ ?
ਕਾਉਂਸਲ ਤੋਂ
ਹਾਊਸਿੰਗ ਅਸੋਸੀਏਸ਼ਨ / ਖੈਰਾਤੀ ਟਰੱਸਟ ਤੋਂ
ਇਸ ਬਿਲਡਿੰਗ ਵਿੱਚ ਰਹਿੰਦੇ ਇੱਕ ਵਿਅਕਤੀ ਤੋਂ
ਕਿਸੇ ਹੋਰ ਰਹਿੰਦੇ ਇੱਕ ਵਿਅਕਤੀ ਤੋਂ
ਨੌਕਰੀ ਦੇਣਦਾਰੇ ਤੋਂ
ਕੰਪਨੀ ਤੋਂ
ਕਿਸੇ ਹੋਰ ਤੋਂ

The Council . . . . 1 —) Q.11
A Housing Association/ Charitable Trust . . . . . . 2 —) Q.10
An individual living in this building . . . . . . 3 —) Q.9b
An individual living elsewhere . . . . 4 —) Q.9b
Your employer . . . . 5 ⎤
A company . . . . 6 ⎦ —) Q.10
Other (WRITE IN) _._._._._. 7 ⎤
                         DK 8 ⎦ —) Q.11

(67)

ASK IF LANDLORD IS AN INDIVIDUAL (Q.9(a) Codes 3 and 4)

9(b) Is your landlord white, of Asian origin or of West Indian origin?

ਤੁਹਾਡਾ ਮਾਲਕਮਕਾਨ ਗੋਰਾ ਹੈ, ਏਸ਼ੀਅਨ ਹੈ ਜਾਂ ਵੈਸਟ-ਇੰਡੀਅਨ?

Asian 1
West Indian _._. 2
White 3
Other (WRITE IN) _ 4
            DK 5

9(c) Is your landlord a relative of anyone in your household?

(68)

ਕੀ ਮਾਲਕਮਕਾਨ ਤੁਹਾਡੇ ਪਰਿਵਾਰ ਦੇ ਕਿਸੇ ਜੀਅ ਦਾ ਰਿਸ਼ਤੇਦਾਰ ਹੈ ?

Yes 1
No 2
DK 3

(69)

ASK IF PRIVATELY RENTED (Q.9(a) Codes 2 to 7)

10. Is this a furnished or an unfurnished tenancy?

ਕੀ ਇਹ ਕਿਰਾਏਦਾਰੀ ਸਾਮਾਨ ਸਮੇਤ ਹੈ ਜਾਂ ਸਾਮਾਨ ਤੋਂ ਬਿਨਾਂ ਹੈ ?

Partly furnished/furnished . . 1
Unfurnished 2
                          DK 3

J.2775   - 7 -

CC3/4

	CODE	ROUTE
	(70)	

ASK IF RENT/RENT FREE (Q.8 codes 2 and 3)

OTHERS GO TO Q.14a)

11(a) Do you pay rates separately from your rent?

ਕੀ ਤੁਸੀਂ ਰੇਟ ਕਿਰਾਏ ਤੋਂ ਵੱਖਰੇ ਦਿੰਦੇ ਹੋ ?

Yes — 1 —) Q.11b
No — 2] —) Q.12a
DK — 3]

ASK IF "YES":

(71)

11(b) Do you get a rate rebate?

ਕੀ ਤੁਹਾਨੂੰ ਰੇਟ ਵਿੱਚ ਛੋਟ ਮਿਲਦੀ ਹੈ ?

Yes — 1 —) Q.11c
No — 2] —) Q.11d
DK — 3]

ASK IF "YES":

(72) (73)

11(c) How much is the rebate? WRITE IN AMOUNT £_____ per_____

ਛੋਟ ਕਿੰਨੀ ਹੈ ?

ASK IF PAY RATES: (Q.11a) Code 1)

(74) (75)

11(d) How much are the rates paid by your household, without
       subtracting any rebate?
       Please include any recent supplements.

ਛੋਟ ਵਿੱਚ ਪਾ ਕੇ ਦੱਸੋ ਤੁਹਾਡੇ ਪਰਿਵਾਰ ਵੱਲੋਂ
ਕਿੰਨਾ ਰੇਟ ਦਿੱਤਾ ਜਾਂਦਾ ਹੈ । ਇਸ ਵਿੱਚ ਨਵੇਂ
ਨੇਵੇ ਵਾਧੇ ਵੀ ਪਾ ਕਰੋ ।

WRITE IN TO NEAREST 50p

£_____ per_____.

(76)	blank
(77-80)	J.2775
(01-09)	Serial
(10-11)	04
(12-17)	Serial

CC4

	CODE	ROUTE

ASK IF RENT/RENT FREE: (Q.8 codes 2 and 3)

OTHERS GO TO Q.14a)

(18)

12(a) Do you get a rent rebate or allowance?

Yes 1 ⟶) Q.12b
No 2
DK 3 ⟶) Q.13a

ASK IF "YES":

(19-20)

12(b) How much is the rebate or allowance?   WRITE IN AMOUNT

£ _____ per _____

12(c) How much rent does your household pay?   WRITE IN AMOUNT

(21-22)

£ _____ per _____

12(d) Does this include the heating costs?

(23)

Yes 1
No 2
DK 3

IF REBATE AT Q.12(a), ASK:

(24)

12(e) Is this the amount after taking off the rebate?

Yes 1
No 2
DK 3

(25)

ASK ALL COUNCIL TENANTS   (Q.9(a) Code 1)

OTHERS GO TO Q.14a)

13(a) When did you (or Head of Household) first
become a council tenant?

January – March 1
April   – June 2
July   – September 3
October – December 4
DK 5

(26-27)

YEAR: 19

13(b) How did you first come to be housed by the council? Were you:

(28)M

READ OUT:

... housed because your home
    was to be demolished 1
... housed because you were
    homeless 2
... housed from waiting list . . . 3
    housed on medical/
...   Social Services advice . . . 4
or housed for some other reason 5
    (WRITE IN)

13(c) Is this your first council dwelling, that is the
first for which you (or HoH) were responsible?

(29)

Yes 1
No 2
DK 3

CC4

	CODE	ROUTE

13(d)   **Have you ever applied to the council for a transfer or move from this address?**

(30)

Yes   1 ——→ Q.13e
No   2 ⎤
DK   3 ⎦ —→ Q.22

ASK IF "YES":

(31)

13(e)   **Are you still on the transfer waiting list?**

Yes   1 ——→ Q.13f
No   2 ⎤
DK   3 ⎦ —→ Q.22

ASK IF "YES":

(32-33)

13(f)   **How long have you been on the transfer waiting list?**   Years

(34-35)

Months

13(g)   **Why do you want a transfer?   PROBE:** _____

(36)M

(37)

ASK ALL WHO ARE NOT A COUNCIL TENANT:

14(a)   **Have you ever applied to a local council for accommodation to rent?**

Yes   1 ——→ Q.14c
No   2 ——→ Q.14b
DK   3 ——→ Q.14c

ASK IF "NO":

(38)M

14(b)   **Why is it that you haven't applied?**

No need/can buy   1
Don't want to live in
    council accommodation   . . .   2
Waiting lists too long   3
Other (WRITE IN)   4

ASK IF "YES":

(39)

14(c)   **Is your name on the waiting list now?**

Yes   1 ——→ Q.14d
No   2 ⎤
DK   3 ⎦ —→ Q.15a

ASK IF "YES" TO Q.14(c):

(40)

14(d)   **When did you put your name down?**

January - March   1
April   - June   2
July   - September   3
October - December   4
DK   5

(41-42)

YEAR: 19

CC4

	CODE	ROUTE

ASK ALL OWNERS   (Q.8 Code 1)   (43)

OTHERS GO TO Q.22

15(a) Is the property owned by one person or is it owned jointly?

One owner . . . .   1 ──) Q.16a
Jointly . . . .   2 ──) Q.15b
                         DK   3 ──) Q.16a

ASK IF JOINTLY OWNED: (44-45)

15(b) How many joint owners are there?   WRITE IN NUMBER . . . .

                                                                       (46)M

And are they?   READ OUT:

Husband and Wife (or couple
    living as husband and wife)   1
Brothers   2
Other combination of
    relations   3
Other combination of
    individuals (WRITE IN) . . .   4

                                                              DK   5
                                                                       (47)

16(a) Is the property owned outright, or is it
       being purchased with a mortgage or loan?

Outright . . . .   1 ──) Q.18a
Loan or mortgage . . . . . .   2 ──) Q.16b
                         DK   3 ──) Q.18a

ASK ALL WITH LOAN OR MORTGAGE:

16(b) How are you buying the property?
       Is it with a ....   READ OUT:

	Q.16b			Q.16c	
	Yes	No	DK		
Mortgage from a building society	1	2	3	4	(48)
Mortgage from a local authority (council) . .	1	2	3	4	(49)
Mortgage from employer . .	1	2	3	4	(50)
Mortgage from a bank . . .	1	2	3	4	(51)
Mortgage from insurance company . . .	1	2	3	4	(52)
Loan from a bank	1	2	3	4	(53)
Loan from a finance company	1	2	3	4	(54)
Loan from a relative or relatives	1	2	3	4	(55)
Loan from an unrelated individual	1	2	3	4	(56)

ASK IF MORE THAN ONE SOURCE OF FINANCE MENTIONED:

16(c) From which of these sources did you obtain the
       largest part of the money that you borrowed?

CODE ANSWER IN
LAST COLUMN ABOVE

CC4

| | CODE | ROUTE |

ASK IF LOAN OR MORTGAGE:

17(a) How much are your total mortgage/loan repayment costs per month?
If you have an endowment mortgage, please include the
policy payments **and** the interest payments.

(57-59)

Per month £

17(b) Does this figure include any house insurance
and mortgage protection insurance?

	(60)M
Yes, house insurance	1
Yes, mortgage protection	2
No	3
DK	4

17(c) How did you raise **most** of the money for
the **deposit** on this property?

	(61)M
No deposit - 100% mortgage ..	1
Sale of previous place	2
Bank loan	3
Relatives	4
Saving	5
Inheritance	6
Other (WRITE IN)	7
DK	8

ASK ALL OWNERS (Q.8 Code 1):

(62-63)

18(a) What was the purchase price of
the property, when you bought it?   WRITE IN: £ _____

(64-65)

When was this?   WRITE IN YEAR ONLY   19

18(b) Did you rent the property from
the council before you bought it?

	(66)
Yes	1
No	2
DK	3

18(c) Is the property freehold or leasehold?

	(67)	
Freehold	1	Q.19a
Leasehold	2	Q.18d
DK	3	Q.19a

ASK IF LEASEHOLD:

18(d) Will the lease expire within the next 20 years?

	(68)
Yes	1
No	2
DK	3

CC4/5

		CODE	ROUTE

ASK ALL OWNERS (Q.8 Code 1):

(69)

19(a)	Do you get a rate rebate?	Yes	1	) Q.19b
		No	2	
		DK	3	) Q.20

ASK IF "YES":

(70-71)

19(b)   How much is the rebate? WRITE IN AMOUNT £ _____ per _____

(72-73)

ASK ALL OWNERS (Q.8 Code 1):

20   How much are your rates, without subtracting any
        rebate, but including any recent supplements?

WRITE IN AMOUNT £ _____ per _____

(74-76) blank	(01-09) Serial
(77-80) J.2775	(10-11) 05
	(12-17) Serial

		CODE	ROUTE

21(a)	Since moving here, have you approached the council to see whether you are eligible for a grant to help with repairs or improvements?		(18)	
		Yes	1	) Q.21c
		No	2	) Q.21b
		DK	3	) Q.22

(19)M

21(b)   What are the reasons you have not
        approached the council for a grant?   DO NOT PROMPT

Don't know about grants . .	1	
Nothing needed fixing/ installing	2	
Already know not eligible	3	
Difficulty with/ dislike of forms	4	) Q.22
Other (WRITE IN)	5	
DK	6	

ASK IF "YES" AT Q.21a:

(20)

21(c)	Did you obtain a grant?	Yes	1	) Q.22a
		No	2	
		DK	3	) Q.21d

(21)

21(d)	Were you actually refused a grant?	Yes	1	) Q.21e
		No	2	
		DK	3	) Q.22a

ASK IF "YES:"

(22)M

21(e)   What reason was given to you for the grant being refused?

ASK ALL:

I'd like to ask you about state benefits:

22(a) **Are you, or is anyone in your household receiving any of the following state benefits?**

READ OUT AND CODE BELOW

ASK FOR EACH RECEIVED:

22(b) **Who receives that?**

22(c) **How much do they receive per week?**

		Q.22(a)			Q.22(b)		Q.22(c)	
	Benefit:	Yes	No	DK	Person (Relationship)	Person Number	Weekly Rate	
	Child benefit	1	2	3	(23)		£ _____	(32-33)н
	Family income supplement	1	2	3	(24)		£ _____	(34-35)н
	Unemployment benefit .	1	2	3	(25)		£ _____	(36-37)н
	Sickness benefit/ Industrial injury benefit	1	2	3	(26)		£ _____	(38-39)н
	Supplementary benefit or allowance / Supplementary pension	1	2	3	(27)		£ _____	(40-41)н
	Retirement pension, old age or widow's pension	1	2	3	(28)		£ _____	(42-43)н
	Other national insurance or state benefit (widow's benefit, disablement/invalidity pension of allowance; mobility allowance etc)							
	_____	1	2	3	(29)		£ _____	(44-45)н
	_____	1	2	3	(30)		£ _____	(46-47)н
	_____	1	2	3	(31)		£ _____	(48-49)н

(50)(51) (52)(53)(54)(55) (56) (57) (58)

	CODE	ROUTE

ASK ALL:

23(a) Do you (or any other members of your household) regularly
receive money from any person outside the household?
I don't mean any wages or rent they may pay you.

(59)

Yes, regularly .... 1 —) Q.23b
Yes, sometimes 2
No 3   -) Q.24
                    DK 4

ASK IF "YES, REGULARLY":

23(b) Is this money for any particular reason? RECORD ANSWER VERBATIM

(60)M

No reason 0

23(c) Approximately how much is
received per month in total?   WRITE IN AMOUNT

(61-62)

£ _____ per month

**ASK IF HOUSEHOLD CONTAINS PERSONS 16 OR OVER
OTHER THAN HEAD OF HOUSEHOLD OR SPOUSE:**

OTHERS GO TO Q.25

(63)

24(a) Does anyone in your household other than yourself (or your
spouse) make any financial contribution towards the cost of
this accommodation or its upkeep? I don't mean a contribution
just for food alone.

Yes 1 —) Q.24b
No 2
DK 3   -) Q.25

ASK IF "YES":

24(b) Who else makes a contribution?   ENTER PERSON
NUMBER

Person Number	(64-65)M

J.2775

ASK ALL:

CC5

	CODE (66)	ROUTE

25(a) Do you (or does anyone else in your household) regularly <u>send</u> money to other members of the family or to other dependents not living here?

Yes, regularly — 1 ⎤ → Q.25b
Yes, sometimes — 2 ⎦
No . . . . . . — 3 ⎤ → CLASSI-
DK — 4 ⎦ FICATION

(67)M

ASK IF "YES":

25(b) Is the money sent for any particular reason?

No particular reason . . . . . — 1
To support parent(s) . . . . . — 2
For school fees/expenses . . . — 3
To support own children . . . . — 4
To help unemployed (relations) — 5
For special occasions . . . . . — 6
To help them (unspecified) . . — 7
Other (WRITE IN) . . . . — 0

(68)M

25(c) Does this go to someone in this country, someone in your family's country of origin, or someone in another country?

This country . . . . — 1
Country of origin . . . . . . — 2
Other country . . . . — 3
DK — 4

(69-70)

25(d) Approximately how much is sent per month in total?

WRITE IN AMOUNT

£ _____ per month

CC5

	CODE	ROUTE

CLASSIFICATION

INTERVIEWER TO RECORD

Type of dwelling:

(71)

		CODE
Whole building:	Detached house	1
	Detached bungalow	2
	Semi-detached house	3
	Semi-detached bungalow	4
	Terraced house	5
Part of building:	Self-contained flat 5+ storeys in block	6
	Self-contained flat 4- storeys in block	7
	Other (WRITE IN)	8

_____

(72)

If part of building:	Purpose built	1
	A conversion	2
	Can't tell	3

(73)

Lowest floor of household's accommodation is ...	Below street level	1
	Ground floor	2
	1st floor	3
	2nd floor	4
	3rd floor	5
	4th - 9th floor	6
	10th+ floor	7

(74) (75) (76) (77-80) J.2775

DATE_____   TIME ENDED _____

Interviewer name:_____Number_____

RESEARCH SERVICES LTD.

Station House, Harrow Road, Stonebridge Park, Wembley, Middlesex. HA9 6DE

J.2775/AK   SURVEY OF RACIAL MINORITIES   February 1982

                              INDIVIDUAL MODULE   Time started_____

															PER NO.

O U O   SERIAL   CC   SR   ED   NO.
(1-3)   (4-9)   0   6   (12-13)   (14-16)   (17)
                      (10-11)

INTERVIEWER FILL IN SERIAL, ED AND PERSON NUMBER

I would like to start by asking about where you have lived.
Then we'll move on to housing and jobs.

		CODE (18)	ROUTE

1(a)   In what country were you born?

	CODE (18)	
West Indies/Guyana	1	
India	2	
(West) Pakistan	3	
Bangladesh/E. Pakistan . . .	4	
Kenya	5	⎤ Q.2a
Uganda	6	
Tanzania	7	
Zambia	8	
Malawi	9	
Other Africa	0	

	(19)	
Northern Ireland	1	
England, Wales	2	-) Q.1b
Scotland	3	
Other country (WRITE IN) . .	4	) Q.2a

IF BORN IN GREAT BRITAIN OR NORTHERN IRELAND, ASK:

1(b)   In what country were your parents born?

INTERVIEWER - CODE BOTH PARENTS

	Mother born (20)	Father born (22)
West Indies/Guyana . .	1	1
India	2	2
(West) Pakistan . . .	3	3
Bangladesh/E. Pakistan	4	4
Kenya	5	5
Uganda	6	6
Tanzania	7	7
Zambia	8	8
Malawi	9	9
Other Africa	0	0

	(21)	(23)
U K	1	1
Other country (WRITE IN)	2	2
DK	3	3

1(c)   In the three months before they came to Britain,
       in which country did they live?

	Mother lived (24)	Father lived (26)
West Indies/Guyana . .	1	1
India	2	2
(West) Pakistan . . .	3	3
Bangladesh/E. Pakistan	4	4
Kenya	5	5
Uganda	6	6
Tanzania	7	7
Zambia	8	8
Malawi	9	9
Other Africa	0	0

	(25)	(27)
U K	1	1
Other country (WRITE IN)	2	2
Father never came to UK	−	3
DK	4	4

ASK ALL NOT BORN IN GREAT BRITAIN OR NORTHERN IRELAND.OTHERS GO TO   CODE | ROUTE
                                                                  Q.3a

2(a)   In the three months before you came to Britain,
       in which country did you live?

OBTAIN AND WRITE IN EXACT DESCRIPTION OF COUNTRY AND
DISTRICT. ALSO RING CODE BELOW, IF APPROPRIATE

CARIBBEAN (28)	BANGLADESH/E.PAKISTAN (29)	AFRICA	(30)
. . . . . .	Border with Assam/	. . .	
Barbados 1	Sylhet 1	Malawi . . .	1
Guyana/Belize 2	Maritime Assam 2	Other Africa	2
Jamaica 3	Other Bangladesh . . . 3	Other Country	3
Trinidad/Tobago . . . 4			
Other Caribbean . . . 5	INDIA		
	Punjab 4		
(WEST) PAKISTAN	Gujarat 5		
North West Frontier . 6	Other India 6		
Mirpur and other			
parts of Kashmir . 7	AFRICA		
Punjab 8	Kenya 7		
Karachi 9	Uganda 8		
Other (West) Pakistan) 0	Tanzania 9		
	Zambia 0		
			(31)

2(b)   In what month and year did you move to Britain?

January − March	1	
April − June	2	
July − September . . .	3	
October − December	4	
DK month	5	
	(32-33)	

YEAR: 19

J.2775   - 3 -

		CODE	ROUTE

ASK ALL:

3(a)   In the past five years have you made any visits to your family's
        country of origin? (INCLUDE VISITS TO EAST AFRICA IF
        RESPONDENT'S FAMILY FROM THERE)

(34)

                                              Yes   1 ──→) Q.3b
                                              No   2
                                              DK   3 ──) Q.4

IF YES, ASK: (35-36)

3(b)   How many visits have you made in the past five years?

                                         WRITE IN
                                         NUMBER

3(c)   Thinking of your most recent visit to your family's   (37)
        country of origin, were you given any special leave by
        your employer for the visit - that is, either paid or
        unpaid leave in addition to your normal holiday
        entitlement?

                Yes   1
                No   2
                Not employed at the time . .   3
                Self-employed at the time .   4
                                         DK   5

                                                   (38)

ASK ALL: Moving on now to housing.

4.   Would you say you are satisfied or dissatisfied
        with this house/flat?

IF SATISFIED   : Just satisfied or very satisfied?

IF DISSATISFIED : Just dissatisfied or very dissatisfied?

                Very satisfied   1
                Just satisfied   2
                Just dissatisfied   3
                Very dissatisfied   4
                                         DK   5

J.2775 ASK ALL:

C C 6

	CODE	ROUTE

5(a) At how many addresses, including the present one, have you lived in the past five years?

(39-40)

WRITE IN BOX, EXCLUDE HOLIDAY ADDRESSES

5(b) Where did you live five years ago? That is, in the beginning of 1977. I don't need the actual address, just the town and the district.

(41-43)

(44)

Same house/flat as now . . .   1 —→) Q.7
Same district different
flat/house as now . . . .   2 ⎤
Different district (WRITE IN)   3 ⎦ —) Q.5c

(45)

5(c) Was that house or flat owner-occupied, rented from the council, or privately rented?

Owned/buying it   1
Private rent   2
Council rent   3
Other (WRITE IN)   4
DK   5

(46)

5(d) At that place, did you or your household share any rooms or facilities with another household?

Yes   1
No   2
DK   3

(47-48)

6(a) When did you move to this, your present address?

RECORD YEAR :   19

(49)

6(b) What was your main reason for moving from your last address to this one?

UNDERLINE MAIN IF MORE THAN ONE

	C C 6	
	CODE	ROUTE

ASK ALL

7. Would you say you are satisfied or dissatisfied
    with living in this neighbourhood?
    DO NOT DEFINE NEIGHBOURHOOD

(50)

IF SATISFIED   : Just satisfied or very satisfied?

IF DISSATISFIED : Just dissatisfied or very dissatisfied?

Very satisfied 1
Just satisfied 2
Just dissatisfied 3
Very dissatisfied 4
                        DK   5

ASK ALL:

8(a) Do you think there are private landlords in Britain who
     would refuse a person accommodation because of their
     race or colour?

(51)

Yes . . . . 1 ——) Q.8b
No . . . . 2 ┐
                        ⌐DK 3 ┘ —) Q.8e

IF YES, ASK:

8(b) Do you think this is true of most private landlords,
     about half, fewer than half, or hardly any?

(52)

Most 1
About half 2
Fewer than half 3
Hardly any 4
                        DK   5

8(c) Why do you think they would refuse a person
     accommodation because of their race or colour?

(53)M

WRITE IN: _____

(54)M

8(d) How do you know that private landlords refuse people
     accommodation because of their race or colour?

(55)M

WRITE IN: _____

	CODE	ROUTE

8(e) Do you, or does someone in <u>your</u> household, own this
      dwelling or do you rent it from the council or from
      some other organisation or person?

CODE (56)

Own . . . .   1 ⎤ →) Q.11a
Rent from council . . . . .   2 ⎦
Rent from other organisation
    or person . . . .   3 ⎤
Other (WRITE IN) . . . . . .   4 ⎦ →) Q.9
                                    DK   5

(57)

ASK ALL PRIVATE RENTERS AND 'OTHER' (Codes 3 & 4 at Q.8(e))

9.   Have you personally ever applied to rent a house or flat
      or rooms from a white landlord who was a complete stranger?

Yes . . . .   1 ⎯) Q.10a
No . . . .   2 ⎤ →) Q.11a
Other answer (WRITE IN) . .   3 ⎦
                                    DK   4

(58)

IF YES, ASK:

10(a) Have you yourself ever been refused accommodation for
       reasons which you think were to do with race or colour?

Yes . . . .   1 ⎯) Q.10b
No . . . .   2 ⎤ →) Q.11a
                                    DK   3 ⎦

(59-60)

IF YES, ASK:

10(b) Can you say on about how many separate occasions you
       have been refused private rented accommodation for
       reasons which you think were to do with race or colour?

WRITE IN
NUMBER

(61-62)

Now I would like to ask you about the (<u>last</u>) occasion
you were refused private rented accommodation for
reasons which you think were to do with race or colour.

10(c) When was this?   ENTER YEAR: 19

10(d) Was the landlord white, or of Asian, West Indian or
       some other origin?

	CODE (63)	ROUTE

White   1
Asian   2
West Indian   3
Other (WRITE IN) 4
                          DK   5

10(e) What reasons were given for the refusal?

       (64-65)

       WRITE IN: _____

       _____

       _____

10(f) Why in particular do you think it was to do
       with race or colour?

       ASK: "Any other reason?" UNTIL "No"   (66-67)

       WRITE IN: _____

       _____

       _____

       _____

       _____

10(g) When you were refused accommodation (on this occasion)
       did you go to anyone for advice or help about the
       laws against racial discrimination?   Yes   1   (68)
                                                         No   2
                                                         DK   3

       IF YES, ASK: (69)M

10(h) Who did you go to?   DO NOT PROMPT   Community Relations Council/
                                                Officer   1
                                              Commission for Racial
                                                Equality   2
                                              Citizens Advice Bureau . . . 3
                                              Legal Advice Centre   4
                                              Solicitor   5
                                              Friend 6
                                              Trade Union   7
                                              Police 8
                                              Job Centre/Employment Office 9
                                              Other (WRITE IN) 0

                                                                         (70)
                                                                    DK   1

10(i) What was the outcome?   OBTAIN FULL DETAILS:

	CODE	ROUTE
	(71)M	

_____

_____

_____

ASK ALL:

Moving on now to employment:

11(a) The government runs special schemes to help unemployed people
get jobs or training. Do you know of any such schemes?
Can you name any?

CODE ANY MENTIONED IN FIRST COLUMN BELOW.   DO NOT PROMPT.
CODE IF NAME MOSTLY CORRECT

11(b) I'm going to read out a list of schemes. Will you please tell
me for each one whether you have heard of it or not.

READ OUT LIST EXCEPT THOSE MENTIONED ABOVE
AND CODE IN COLUMNS 2 AND 3

11(c) Have you ever applied to go on any of
these schemes organised by the government?

CODE ALL THAT APPLY IN FOURTH COLUMN

	11a Mentioned	11b Heard of	11b Not heard of	11c Applied for
	(72)M	(73)M	(74)M	(75)M
Training Opportunities Scheme (TOPS), formerly Government Training Scheme	1	1	1	1
Community Enterprise Programme (CEP) or Special Temporary Employment Programme (STEP) . .	2	2	2	2
Youth Opportunities Programme (YOP), e.g. Work Experience, Community Industry, Training Workshops	3	3	3	3
(Other (WRITE IN))	4			4
None/DK	5	. . .		5 → Q.15a)

(76)   blank (01-09) Serial
(77-80) J.2775 (10-11) 07
               (12-17) Serial

	CODE	ROUTE

11(d) Have you ever applied for any schemes run by
       <u>anyone else</u> to help unemployed people to get
       jobs or training?

                                                    Yes   (18) 1 ┬─) Q.11e
                                                     No   2 ┐
                                                     DK   3 ┘├─) Q.12a

       IF YES, ASK: (19)M

11(e) What scheme(s) did you apply for?   WRITE IN

_____

_____

11(f) Who organised the scheme(s)?   (20)M
       Was it ...   READ OUT:

                              A local authority   1
                          or a voluntary group   2
                          or a private company   3
                          or someone else (WRITE IN) . .   4

                                                       DK   5

11(g) Did you actually start on the scheme/   (21)
       any of the schemes?

                                                    Yes   1 ┬─) Q.11h
                                                     No   2 ┐
                                                     DK   3 ┘├─) Q.11i

       IF YES, ASK: (22)

11(h) Did you complete the scheme/any of the schemes? Yes   1 ┬─) Q.11j
                                                     No   2 ┐
                                                     DK   3 ┘├─) Q.11i

       IF NO TO (g) OR (h), ASK: (23)M

11(i) Why didn't you go on/complete the scheme(s)?

       WRITE IN _____

_____

11(j) How soon after the end of the scheme   (24)
       (most recent of the schemes) did you get a job?

                          Still don't have job _ _ _ _ _   0

                          LESS than 1 month _ _ _ _ _ _   1

                                                       (25-26)

                 IF ONE MONTH OR MORE, WRITE IN   MONTHS

ASK Q.12-14 AS APPROPRIATE FOR THOSE WHO APPLIED FOR TOPS, CEP,   C C 7
STEP, YOP; OTHERS GO TO Q.15. IF APPLIED FOR A TOPS PLACE AT Q.11(c) CODE ROUTE

		CODE	ROUTE
12(a)	Thinking of the TOPS course you applied for, did you actually start the course?	(27)	
	Yes	1	—) Q.12b
	No	2	
	DK	3	—) Q.12c

IF YES, ASK: (28)

12(b)	Did you complete the course?		
	Yes	1	—) Q.12d
	No	2	
	DK	3	—) Q.12c

IF NO TO Q.12(a) OR Q.12(b), ASK: (29)M

12(c) Why didn't you go on/complete the course?

WRITE IN: _____

_____

IF YES TO Q.12(b), ASK: (30)

12(d) How soon after the end of the course did you get a job?

                          Still don't have job _ _ _ _ _ _   0
                          LESS than 1 month _ _ _ _ _ _ _ _   1

                                                    (31-32)

              IF ONE MONTH OR MORE, WRITE IN   MONTHS

12(e) In that job, how often did you use what you had   (33)
       learned on the course? Would you say ... READ OUT:

                          All or most of the time . .   1
                          Some of the time   2
                          Rarely or never   3
                                                    DK   4

                                                          (34)
IF YES TO Q.11(c) (i.e. APPLIED FOR A CEP/STEP PLACE), ASK:

13(a) Thinking of the CEP/STEP scheme you applied for,
       did you actually start on the scheme?
                                                    Yes   1   —) Q.13b
                                                    No   2
                                                    DK   3   —) Q.13c

IF YES, ASK: (35)

13(b)	Did you complete the scheme?		
	Yes	1	—) Q.13d
	No	2	
	DK	3	—) Q.13c

IF NO TO Q.13(a) OR Q.13(b), ASK: (36) M

13(c) Why didn't you go on/complete the scheme?

WRITE IN: _____

_____

C C 7

	CODE	ROUTE

IF YES TO Q.13(b), ASK:

13(d) How soon after the end of the scheme did you get a job?

	(37)	
Still don't have job	0	
LESS than 1 month	1	

(38-39)	
IF ONE MONTH OR MORE, WRITE IN		MONTHS

IF YES TO Q.11(c) (i.e. APPLIED FOR A YOP PLACE), ASK:

14(a) Thinking of the YOP scheme you applied for, did you actually start on the scheme?

	(40)	
Yes	1	—) Q.14b
No	2	—) Q.14c
DK	3	

IF YES, ASK:

14(b) Did you complete the scheme?

	(41)	
Yes	1	—) Q.14d
No	2	—) Q.14c
DK	3	

IF NO TO Q.14(a) OR Q.14(b), ASK:

14(c) Why didn't you go on/complete the scheme?

(42)M

WRITE IN: _____

IF YES TO Q.14(b), ASK:

14(d) How soon after the end of the scheme did you get a job?

	(43)	
Still don't have job _ _ _ _ _ _	0	
LESS than 1 month _ _ _ _ _ _ _	1	

(44-45)	
IF ONE MONTH OR MORE, WRITE IN		MONTHS

ASK ALL:

15(a) Did you have a full-time or part-time paid job last week, either as an employee or self-employed?

IF WORKING UNDER MSC SPECIAL SCHEMES - YOP, TOPS, CEP - DO NOT COUNT AS EMPLOYMENT HERE

	(46)	
Yes	1	—) Q.15b
No	2	—) Q.15c
DK	3	

IF YES, ASK:

15(b) Did you work at least 8 hours last week?

	(47)	
Yes, at least 8 hours . . .	1	—) Q.20a
No, less than 8 hours . . .	2	—) Q.15c
DK	3	—) Q.20a

	CODE	ROUTE

IF NO TO Q.15(a) OR Q.15(b), ASK:

15(c) Were you off sick or on holiday or leave from your normal job, or did you not have a regular job last week?

(48)

Sick . . . .   1 ⎤
Paid/unpaid/maternity/
   leave/holiday . . . . . .   2 ⎦ —) Q.20a
No regular job . . . .   3 —) Q.15d
No, other . . . .   4 —) Q.16a
             DK   5

IF NO REGULAR JOB AT Q.15(c), ASK:

(49)

15(d) For what reason were you not working last week?

CODE ALL THAT APPLY

Retired . . . .   1 —) Q.20a
Keeping house   2
Going to school or college   3
Permanently unable to work   4
Studying under Training
   Opportunities Scheme (TOPS)   5
Working under one of these
   special schemes:

   Youth Opportunities
     Programme (YOP) . . . . ⎤
                   —) Q.15e
   Community Enterprise
     Programme (CEP) . . . ⎦ ⊢ 6

Unemployed   7
Other/between jobs(WRITE IN)   8
             DK   9

ASK ALL WITH 'NO REGULAR JOB' AT Q.15(c), EXCEPT RETIRED:

(50)

15(e) Last week, did you help with a business run by a member of your family?

          Yes   1 —) Q.15f
          No   2 —) Q.16a
          DK   3

IF YES, ASK:

(51-52)

15(f) For how many hours did you help with this business last week?   WRITE IN

(53)

15(g) What kind of work were you doing?

(54)

WRITE IN: _____

(55)

15(h) What kind of business is it?

(56)

WRITE IN: _____

C C 7

	CODE	ROUTE

ASK ALL WITH 'NO REGULAR JOB' AT Q.15(c), EXCEPT RETIRED:

(57)

16(a) Are you looking for a job at present?

Yes 1 ——→) Q.16b
No   2 ⎤
DK   3 ⎦ ⊢) Q.17a

IF YES, ASK:

(58)

16(b) Are you looking for a full-time job or a part-time job?
       (Part-time is 8-30 hours, full-time 31 hours +)

Full 1
Part 2
Either 3
DK 4

(59)

ASK ALL WITH 'NO REGULAR JOB' AT Q.15(c), EXCEPT RETIRED:

17(a) Have you registered as unemployed at a government employment
       office, job centre or careers office?

IF NO, PROBE TO BE CERTAIN BEFORE CODING

Yes 1 ——→) Q.17c
No   2 ⎤
DK   3 ⎦ ⊢) Q.17b

IF NO, ASK:

(60)M

17(b) Why have you not registered?

       WRITE IN: _____

IF YES, ASK:

(61)

17(c) How long ago did you register as unemployed?

Up to 6 weeks 1
Over 6 weeks, up to
   8 weeks (2 months) 2
Over 2 months, up to 3 months 3
Over 3 months, up to 4 months 4
Over 4 months, up to 6 months 5
Over 6 months, up to 8 months 6
Over 8 months, up to 12 months 7
Over 12 months, up to 18 months 8
Over 18 months, up to 2 years   9

(62)

Over 2 years, up to 5 years   1
Over 5 years 2
DK 3

J.2775   - 14 -

C C 7/8

		CODE	ROUTE

IF YES TO Q.16(a) OR Q.17(a) (i.e. LOOKING FOR A JOB OR REGISTERED), ASK:

(63)**M**

OTHERS GO TO Q.20(a)

18(a) What sort of things have you done to try to find a job? PROMPT:

	CODE
Asked friends/relatives ..	1
Replied to advertisements .	2
Been to job centre/ employment office	3
Approached firms directly to see if they had vacancies	4
Been to local careers office	5
Been to a private employment agency	6
Contacted a trade union ..	7
Anything else(WRITE IN) ..	8
Nothing	9
DK	0

18(b) How many jobs have you applied for in the past 2 months, that is actual jobs not general applications?

(64-65)

WRITE IN NUMBER:

(66)

19(a) Are you getting National Insurance Unemployment Benefit or Supplementary Benefit?

Yes 1 —) Q.19b
No 2
DK 3 —) Q.19c

IF YES, ASK:

19(b) How much did this come to last week (Unemployment and Supplementary Benefit together)?

(67-68)

WRITE IN: £

19(c) When did you last have a regular job?

(69)

INCLUDE SELF-EMPLOYED:

January - March	1
April - June	2
July - September ...	3
October - December	4
DK Month	5

(70-71)

Year 19

(72)

Never had regular job ... 1 —) Q.19f
DK 2

(73-76) blank	(01-09) Serial
(77-80) J.2775	(10-11) 08
	(12-17) Serial

C C 8

	CODE	ROUTE

IF A DATE GIVEN AT Q.19(c), ASK:

19(d)   How did you come to leave your last job?   (18-19)

PROBE FULLY FOR DETAILS: _____

_____

_____

19(e)   What were the formal terms on which you left?   (20)
        Were you made redundant, dismissed, or did
        you retire or just leave?

Made redundant   1
Dismissed   2
Retired   3
Just left   4
Other (WRITE IN)   5

                                            DK   6

IF NO REGULAR JOB AT Q.15(c), ASK: (21)

19(f)   Have you had a paid job at any time in the last 10 years?

                                           Yes   1 —) Q.20a
                                           No   2 —) Q.32a
                                           DK   3

                                                              (22)

ASK ALL WORKING OR WHO WORKED IN LAST 10 YEARS ABOUT PRESENT
OR MOST RECENT JOB:

20(a)   Now I would like to ask you about your present job (last job)

        (IF 2 JOBS, ASK ABOUT MAIN JOB)

        Are you (were you) an employee or self-employed?

Employee . . . .   1 —) Q.20b
Self-employed . . . . . .   2 —) Q.24a
Other (WRITE IN) . . . . . .   3 —) Q.20b

                                            DK   4

IF EMPLOYEE OR OTHER (Code 1 or 3 at Q.20(a)) ASK: (23)

20(b)   Do you (did you) work in a business run by a member, or
        members, of your family?
                                           Yes   1
                                           No   2
                                           DK   3

C C 8

	CODE	ROUTE

IF EMPLOYEE OR OTHER AT Q.20(a), ASK:

21(a) What is (was) your occupation?

(24)

ENTER JOB TITLE AND DESCRIBE FULLY WORK DONE: _____

(25)

_____

_____

_____

(26)

21(b) What does (did) the firm or organisation you
       work (worked) for actually make or do?

(27)

PROBE WHETHER MANUFACTURING/PROCESSING AND
GIVE END PRODUCT OF FIRM. DESCRIBE FULLY:

(28)

_____

_____

_____

(29)

21(c) How many employees are (were) there at your place of work?

10 or less	1
11 - 25	2
26 - 50	3
51 - 100	4
101 - 250	5
251 - 500	6
501 - 1,000	7
Over 1,000	8
Can't say/DK	9

21(d) Out of every ten people employed at your place of work,
       how many are (were) of Asian or West Indian origin?

(30)

Fewer than 1 in 10	0
1 in 10 . .	1
2 in 10 . .	2
3 in 10 . .	3
4 in 10 . .	4
5 in 10 . .	5
6 in 10 . .	6
7 in 10 . .	7
8 in 10 . .	8
9 in 10 . .	9

(31)

Nearly all	0
DK	1

21(e) How long have you been working (did you work) for
       this firm/organisation?

                                                                        (32)

```
┌────────────────────────────────────┐
│                                    │
└────────────────────────────────────┘
```

                          Less than 1 month   1
                          1 but under   3 months   . . .   2
                          3 but under   6 months   . . .   3
                          6 but under 12 months   . . .   4
                                                      DK   5

       IF MORE THAN 1 YEAR, WRITE IN NUMBER OF YEARS   (33-34)
       (TO THE NEAREST YEAR) IN BOX:

                                                                        (35)

21(f) How did you first hear about the job?   CODE ONE ONLY

```
┌────────────────────────────────────┐
│                                    │
└────────────────────────────────────┘
```

                          Through friends   1
                          Through relatives   2

                          Direct application:
                          - by writing   3
                          - by telephone   4
                          - by calling in person . . .   5

                          Advertisement   6
                          Employment office   7
                          Job centre   8
                          Careers office   9
                          Private employment agency .   0
                                                                        (36)

                          Direct from employer   1
                          Through union   2
                          Other (WRITE IN)   3

                          ──────────────────────
                                                      DK   4

       IF THROUGH FRIENDS OR RELATIVES, ASK: (37)

21(g) Did your friend/relative speak to the employer for you,
       when you applied for the job?

```
┌────────────────────────────────────┐
│                                    │
└────────────────────────────────────┘
```

                                                      Yes   1
                                                      No   2
                                                      DK   3

                                                                        (38)

       ASK ALL WHO ARE OR HAVE BEEN AN EMPLOYEE IN LAST 10 YEARS
       ABOUT PRESENT OR MOST RECENT JOB

22(a) Are (were) there people working directly under you at present
       (in your last job)?

```
┌────────────────────────────────────┐
│                                    │
└────────────────────────────────────┘
```

                          Yes . . . .   1 ──) Q.22b
                          No   2
                          Other answer (WRITE IN) . .   3 ──) Q.23a

                          ──────────────────────
                                                      DK   4

	CODE	ROUTE

IF YES, ASK:

(39-40)

22(b)   How many people?

WRITE IN NUMBER:———)

(41-42)

22(c)   How many of these are (were) white?

WRITE IN NUMBER:———)

(43-44)

22(d)   And how many of the poeple working directly under
you are (were) of Asian or West Indian origin?

WRITE IN NUMBER:———)

(45)

23(a)   Is (was) your immediate boss white?

Yes, white . . . .   1 ——) Q.24a
No, not white . . . .   2 ——) Q.23b
Other answer (WRITE IN) . .   3⌉
) Q.24a
                              DK   4⌋

(46)

IF NOT WHITE, ASK:

23(b)   Is (was) he/she of Asian origin, West Indian origin,
or some other racial origin?

Asian   1
West Indian   2
Other   3
                              DK   4

(47)

ALL WHO ARE OR HAVE BEEN SELF-EMPLOYED IN LAST 10 YEARS, ASK:

OTHERS GO TO Q.25(a)

24(a)   What is (was) your business?

PROBE WHETHER MANUFACTURING/PROCESSING AND GIVE
END PRODUCT OF BUSINESS. DESCRIBE FULLY

(48)

(49)

24(b)   What is (was) your own position in the business,
and what are (were) your particular responsibilities?

(50)

DESCRIBE FULLY WORK DONE
ENTER FORMAL JOB TITLE IF ANY

(51)

C C 8

| | | CODE | ROUTE |

24(c) h   many paid employees are (were) there in this
       business including yourself?   (52-54)

WRITE IN NUMBER:

Can't say/DK   1

24(d) Can you estimate how many of the employees are   (55-57)
       (were) of West Indian or Asian origin
       (including yourself)?

WRITE IN NUMBER:

Can't say/DK   1

       ... and how many are (were) white?   (58-60)

WRITE IN NUMBER:

Can't say/DK   1

24(e) How long have you been (were you) working   (61)
       in this particular business?

                                   Up to 6 months   1
                                   7 - 12 months   2
                                                        DK   3

       IF MORE THAN 1 YEAR, WRITE NUMBER OF YEARS   (62-63)
       (TO NEAREST YEAR) IN BOX:

                                                                  (64)

       IF RESIDENT IN U.K. IN 1974 (SEE Q.2(b)), ASK:

       OTHERS GO TO Q.26(a)

25(a) What was your occupation eight years ago, in 1974?

       INTERVIEWER : REMIND RESPONDENT THIS WAS THE TIME
                     OF THE 3-DAY WEEK.
                                   Exactly same position in
                                     same organisation as
                                     job just described . . . .   1 ——›Q.27a
                                   Then in full-time education   2
                                   Unemployed . . . .   3 ——›Q.25c
                                   Not working - other reason   4
                                                        DK   5

       IF JOB DIFFERENT ENTER JOB TITLE AND
       DESCRIBE FULLY WORK DONE: (65-66)

                                                                  (67)

                                   Employee   1
                                   Self-employed   2

	CODE	ROUTE

IF WORKING, ASK:

(68)

25(b) And what did the firm, organisation or business
       actually make or do?

PROBE WHETHER MANUFACTURING/PROCESSING AND
GIVE END PRODUCT OF FIRM. DESCRIBE FULLY

(69)

IF RESIDENT IN UK IN   1974 BUT NOT IN EXACTLY SAME JOB AS NOW ASK: **(70)**

25(c) Have you been out of work and looking for a job for
       2 weeks or more since this time in 1974?

                                                  Yes   1 —) Q.25d
                                                  No   2 ⌉
                                                  DK   3 ⌡ —) Q.27a

IF YES, ASK: **(71-72)**

25(d) How many times have you been out of work for
       2 weeks or more since then?
                                         WRITE IN

                                                       (73)

IF STILL IN FULL-TIME EDUCATION IN 1974 (SEE Q.25(a)), ASK:

OTHERS GO TO Q.27(a)

26(a) What was the first regular job you had after
       you left full-time education?   Exactly same position   1
                                             in same organisation
ENTER JOB TITLE AND DESCRIBE FULLY WORK DONE as job described above   **(74)**

                                                                        (75)

      (76)   blank   (01-09) Serial
      (77-80) J.2775   (10-11) 09
                       (12-17) Serial

                                                  (18)

              Employee   1   ⌉
              Self-employed   2   ⌡ —) Q.26b
              Never had a job   3   —) Q.27a
                                        DK   4

	CODE	ROUTE

IF EVER HAD A JOB, ASK:

(19)

26(b) And what did the firm, organisation or business
actually make or do?

PROBE WHETHER MANUFACTURING/PROCESSING AND
GIVE END PRODUCT OF FIRM.   DESCRIBE FULLY

(20)

26(c) In which year did you start that job?

(21-22)

WRITE IN YEAR: 19

DK   0   0

ALL EMPLOYED OR SELF-EMPLOYED NOW, ASK:

(23)

OTHERS GO TO Q.32(a)

27(a) Are any of the employees in your workplace
members of a trade union?

Yes   1 —) Q.27b
No   2
DK   3 —) Q.28a

IF YES, ASK:

(24)

27(b) In your workplace does a trade union organise and
represent employees doing your kind of work?

Yes   1
No   2
DK   3

---

(25)

ASK ALL:

28(a) Are you a member of a trade union?

Yes . . . .   1 —) Q.28b
No   2
Other answer (WRITE IN) . .   3 —) Q.30a

DK   4

IF YES, ASK:

(26-27)

28(b) Which union do you belong to?

WRITE IN FULL NAME IF POSSIBLE:

(28)

28(c) Have you been to any meeting of your union
in the last 6 months?

Yes   1
No   2
DK   3

CC9

	CODE	ROUTE

29. Do you hold an elected post in your trade union?
     I mean, for example, are you a shop steward, a
     representative, or convenor or branch secretary?

(29)

Yes 1
No 2
DK 3

ALL WHO HAD A JOB OR WERE OFF SICK OR WERE
ON HOLIDAY/LEAVE LAST WEEK (SEE Q.15), ASK:

(30-31)

30(a) How many hours, including overtime but excluding meal
      breaks, did you work in the last week you were not
      off work for any reason?

WRITE IN NUMBER
OF HOURS

(32)

IF LESS THAN 35 HOURS, ASK:

30(b) Were you on short-time working during that week?

Yes 1
No 2
DK 3

---

(33)

IF WITH A JOB, OR OFF SICK OR ON HOLIDAY LAST WEEK, ASK:

31(a) Do you usually work shifts as part of this job?

Regularly 1
Sometimes 2 — Q.31b
Never 3 —
DK 4 — Q.32a

IF YES, ASK:

(34)M

31(b) What shift system do you work?

Double days 1
(e.g. 6 am - 2 pm; 2 pm - 10 pm)

Mornings (e.g. 6 am - 2 pm) 2
Evenings (e.g. 2 pm - 10 pm) 3
Nights (e.g. 2 am - 10 am) 4
Alternating shifts 5
Other (WRITE IN) 6

DK 7

---

(35)

ASK ALL ASIANS:

OTHERS GO TO Q.33(a)

32(a) Have you ever had any difficulties obtaining
      employment because of language problems?

Yes 1
No 2
Never tried to obtain
  employment 3
DK 4

C C 9

	CODE	ROUTE
	(36)	

32(b) And have you ever had any sorts of difficulty <u>at work</u>
because of English language problems, for example over
pay, health and safety or the union?

Yes   1 ——) Q.32c
No   2 ⌉
DK   3 ⌋ —) Q.33a

IF YES, ASK:

(37)M

32(c) What difficulties were these?

PROBE: _____

_____

_____

(38)

ASK ALL:

33(a) Do you think there are employers in Britain who would
refuse a job to a person because of their race or colour?

Yes . . . .   1 ——) Q.33b
No . . . .   2 ⌉
Other answer (WRITE IN) . .   3 ⌋ —) Q.35a

DK   4 ⌋

IF YES, ASK:

(39)

33(b) Do you think this is true of most employers,
about half, fewer than half or hardly any?

Most   1
About half   2
Fewer than half   3
Hardly any   4
Other answer (WRITE IN) . .   5

DK   6

33(c) Why do you think they would refuse a job to
a person because of their race or colour?

(40-41) M

WRITE IN _____

_____

_____

C C 9

	CODE	ROUTE

33(d) How do you know that employers refuse jobs to
people because of their race or colour?

(42)**M**

WRITE IN _____

---

(43)

34(a) Have you yourself ever been refused a job for reasons
which you think were to do with your race or colour?

Yes	1	—) Q.34b
No	2	
Other answer (WRITE IN) . .	3	—) Q.35a
DK	4	

IF YES, ASK:

34(b) On how many separate occasions have you
been refused a job for this reason?

WRITE
IN
NUMBER

(44-45)

DK	1	1

Now I would like to ask you about the last occasion
on which you were refused a job because of your
race or colour.

(46-47)

34(c) When was this?   WRITE IN YEAR: 19

34(d) What was the firm's business?

48-49)

WRITE IN _____

(50)

34(e) Did the firm employ under 20 people, between
20 and 150 or more than 150?

Under 20	1
20 - 150	2
150+	3
DK	4

34(f) How did you apply for this job?

(51)**M**

WRITE IN _____

C C 9

	CODE	ROUTE

34(g) Exactly what job did you apply for?

(52-53)

WRITE IN _____

_____

(54)

34(h) Did you personally see anyone from this firm?

Yes   1 ——) Q.34i
No   2 ⎤
DK   3 ⎦ —) Q.34j

IF YES, ASK:

(55-56) M

34(i) Who did you see?

WRITE IN TITLE OF PERSON SEEN:

_____

34(j) How did you learn you had been turned down?

(57-58) M

WRITE IN _____

_____

34(k) Why in particular do you think it was to do with
your race or colour?

(59-60) M

ASK : "Any other reason?" UNTIL "No"

_____

_____

_____

34(l) When you were turned down for the job, did you go to
anyone for advice or help about the laws against
racial discrimination?

(61)

Yes   1 ——) Q.34m
No   2 ⎤
DK   3 ⎦ —) Q.35a

J.2775   - 26 -

	CODE	ROUTE

(62)M

34(m)   Who did you go to?   DO NOT PROMPT

Community Relations Council/
    Officer   1
Commission for Racial
    Equality   2
Citizens Advice Bureau . . .   3
Legal Advice Centre   4
Solicitor   5
Friend   6
Trade Union   7
Police   8
Job Centre/Employment Office   9
Other (WRITE IN)   0

(63)

                    DK   1

(64)M

34(n)   What was the outcome?

OBTAIN FULL DETAILS _____

_____

(65)

35(a)   Do you believe there are firms or organisations in Britain where
promotion is less likely for Asian or West Indian
people than for white people, even though their
experience and qualifications are exactly the same?

Yes   1
No   2
Other answer (WRITE IN) . .   3

                    DK   4

(66)

35(b)   Have you ever been treated unfairly at work with
regard to promotion or a move to a better position,
for reasons which you think were to do with race or
colour? I don't mean when applying for a new job.

Yes . . . .   1 —) Q.35c
No   2
Other answer (WRITE IN) . .   3 —) Q.36a

                    DK   4

C C 9/10

	CODE	ROUTE

35(c)   On the last occasion when this happened, what was
        your position in the organisation at the time?

        (67-68)

        WRITE IN _____

        _____

35(d)   What was the position you wanted or failed to get?

        (69-70)

        WRITE IN _____

35(e)   What reasons were given for your treatment?

        (71-72) M

        ASK : "Any other reason?"   UNTIL "No"

        (73-74) M

35(f)   Did you take any action against the employer?

        (75)

        Yes, legal action   1 —┐
        Yes, other action   2 —┘→ Q.35g
                       NO   3 ——→ Q.36a
                       DK   4 —

        IF YES, ASK:

        (76)M

35(g)   What was the outcome?

        OBTAIN FULL DETAILS: _____

        _____

        _____

(77-80) J.2775
(01-09) Serial
(10-11) 10
(12-17) Serial

J.2775   - 28 -   C C 10

ASK ALL:

(18-19)

36(a)   What is or was your father's most recent
        full-time occupation?

┌───┐
│   │
│   │
└───┘

_____

_____   (20-21)

36(b)   What does or did the firm, organisation or business
        he works/worked in actually make or do?

┌───┐
│   │
│   │
└───┘

_____

_____

                                               (22)

ASK ALL:

I'd like to ask you now about education.

37(a)   At what ages did you start and finish full-time education?

┌───┐
│   │
└───┘

                    Age started   (WRITE IN):
                                               (23)
                Age finished: No full-time
                    education/under 10   1
                            10 - 12   2
                            13 - 15   3
                            16   4
                            17 - 19   5
                            20+   6
                Still in full-time education   7
                                       DK   8

37(b)   Do you have any academic qualifications such as CSE,   (24)
        'O' level and so on? Include non-British qualifications.

┌───┐
│   │   Yes   1 ──┼──) Q.37c
│   │ ──   No   2   │
└───┘   DK   3 ──┘ ─) Q.38a

C C 10

| | | CODE | ROUTE |

IF YES: ASK:

37(c) Can you tell me whether you have any of these
qualifications or have passed any of these exams?

	Brit-ish (25)M	Non-Brit-ish (27)M

SHOW CARD IF RESPONDENT CAN READ : CODE IN CORRECT COLUMN

	British (25)M	Non-British (27)M
C S E	1	1
G C E 'O' level or S C E 'ordinary' level or school certificate	2	2
Ordinary national certificate or diploma	3	3
G C E 'A' level or S C E 'higher' level	4	4
Higher national certificate or diploma	5	5
Degree	6	6
Teaching qualifications	7	7
Nursing qualifications	8	8
Social work qualifications . . .	9	9
Clerical and commercial qualifications	0	0

	(26)M	(28)M
Trade apprenticeship	1	1
City and Guilds	2	2
Membership of professional institution	3	3
Other (WRITE IN)	4	4
None	5	5
DK	6	6

(29)

ASK ALL:

38(a) Are you studying now either full-time or
part-time for further qualifications?

Yes, full-time	1	–) Q.38b
Yes, part-time	2	
No	3	–) Q.39a
DK	4	

IF YES, ASK: (30-31) M

38(b) What qualifications are you studying for?

USE TITLES LISTED ABOVE IF APPLICABLE

WRITE IN

	CODE	ROUTE

ASK ASIANS ONLY: ALL OTHERS GO TO Q.41

(32)

39(a) Have you ever attended any course of classes in this country designed to help your written or spoken English language? (I don't mean as part of your normal classes at school).

Yes, written . . . . 1 ⎤ ⊢) Q.39b
Yes, spoken . . . . 2 ⎦
No . . . . 3 ⎤ ⊢) Q.40
DK 4 ⎦

IF YES, ASK:

(33)M

39(b) Where did you attend the classes?

Were they ... READ OUT

Special classes at a school or college 1
Special classes at work or a Skill Centre 2
Part-time classes for adults at a local institute, college or centre 3
Part-time classes organised by an ethnic minority group 4
At home 5
Somewhere else (WRITE IN) 6

DK 7

(34)

ASK ASIANS ONLY:

ALL OTHERS GO TO Q.41

40(a) Would you like more opportunity to learn to improve your English language skills, either at work, at classes in your spare time, or through TV and radio?

Yes 1 ⊢) Q.40b
No 2 ⎤ ⊢) Q.41
DK 3 ⎦

IF YES, ASK:

(35)M

40(b) Would you prefer to do this ... READ OUT:

.. at work 1
.. at classes in your own time 2
.. through TV or radio 3
DK 4

(36)M

ASK ALL:
Now, can I just ask you about your family?
41. Do you have any children?

IF YES, how old is/are your child(ren) now?

0 - 5 1
6 - 11 2
12 - 15 3
16 4
17 - 20 5
21+ 6
None 7
DK . . 8

C C 10

		Yes	No	CODE DK	ROUTE

42(a)   Over the past year have you ....   READ OUT:

	Yes	No	DK	
.. attended any parent's meetings at your child's school . .	1	2	3	(37)
.. met any of your child's teachers at school	1	2	3	(38)
.. met any of their teachers at your home	1	2	3	(39)
.. had any other contact with your child's school (WRITE IN)	1	2	3	(40)

IF YES TO ANY MEETING, ASK: OTHERS GO TO Q.43(a)

42(b)   Did you ask for the meeting or was it suggested
        by the school or parent's group?

(41)M

I/we asked	1
Suggested by school or parents' group	2
DK	3

(42)

ASK ALL WITH SCHOOL-AGE CHILDREN: OTHERS GO TO Q.45(a)

43(a)   How do you feel about your children's education in this
        country to date? Would you say you were happy or
        unhappy with their education so far?

IF HAPPY   : Is that fairly happy or very happy?

IF UNHAPPY : Is that fairly unhappy or very unhappy?

IF MORE THAN ONE SCHOOL, MULTI-CODE IF
NECESSARY AND CODE 6

Very happy	1
Fairly happy	2
Fairly unhappy	3
Very unhappy	4
DK	5
More than 1 school	6

43(b)   (Even so) is there anything in particular that
        you are not happy about concerning your
        child's (children's) education?

(43-44)M

WRITE IN: _____

C C 10

	CODE	ROUTE

44(a) We have talked about the full-time schooling your child(ren) receive(s). Apart from this, do any of them receive any other schooling outside the home - for instance, to learn about their religion or language?

(45)

Yes . . . .   1 ——) Q.44b
No . . . .   2 ⎤
DK . . . .   3 ⎦ —) Q.45a

IF YES, ASK: (46)**M**

44(b) What things are they taught?

Asian language   1
Religion   2
Other (WRITE IN)   3

DK   4

44(c) Who organises these classes?   (47)**M**

The local authority   1
Commercial organisation . .   2
A religious body   3
A private individual   4
Other (WRITE IN)   5

DK   6

(48)

IF HAS ANY CHILDREN AGED 16 to 20 ASK:
OTHERS GO TO Q.46

45(a) Did any of your sons or daughters have any contact with the careers service before or after they left school?

Yes   1 ——) Q.45b
No   2 ⎤
DK   3 ⎦ —) Q.46

IF YES, ASK: (49)

45(b) Were you satisfied or dissatisfied with the help they were given by the careers service?

IF SATISFIED   : Just satisfied or very satisfied?

IF DISSATISFIED : Just dissatisfied or very dissatisfied?

Very satisfied   1
Just satisfied   2
Just dissatisfied   3
Very dissatisfied   4
DK   5

J.2775   - 33 -   C C 10

ASK ALL:

46.   If you need advice on difficulties with the following, who would you turn to ...

firstly, for advice on housing?   CODE IN FIRST COLUMN BELOW

and for advice on your employment?   CODE IN SECOND COLUMN BELOW

and for advice on legal matters?   CODE IN THIRD COLUMN BELOW

and for advice on claiming state cash benefits, that is, DHSS benefits such as
child benefit, pension and unemployment benefit?   CODE IN FOURTH COLUMN BELOW

	Hous-ing	Job	Legal	Bene-fits
	(50)M	(51)M	(52)M	(53)M
Someone in the household . . .	1	1	1	1
An advice centre	2	2	2	2
CRCs	3	3	3	3
Local council	4	4	4	4
Solicitor/lawyer	5	5	5	5
Citizens Advice Bureau (CAB)	6	6	6	6
Other (WRITE IN BELOW)	7	7	7	7
Don't need advice	8	8	8	8
DK	9	9	9	9

(WRITE IN:)

(WRITE IN:)

(WRITE IN:)

(WRITE IN:)

ASK ALL:

47.   Now I'd like to ask you about the health services.
Are you yourself registered with a doctor?

	CODE (54)	ROUTE
Yes	1	
No	2	
DK	3	

C C 10

	CODE	ROUTE
	(55)	

48(a) When you want a medical check-up or medical treatment because you are unwell or because you have hurt yourself, where do you normally go first? Do you go to ... READ OUT

Your local hospital . . . . 1 —→) Q.48b

Your local doctor, that is your general practitioner, GP (INCLUDES health centre/group practice) 2 ⌉

—) Q.49a

DK 3 ⌋

(56)

IF 'HOSPITAL', ASK:

48(b) Can I just check, do you usually go to the hospital for any medical problem, or just for emergencies?

Yes, any problem . . . . 1 —→) Q.48c

Emergencies only . . . . 2 ⌉

DK 3 ⌋ —) Q.49a

IF 'YES, HOSPITAL', ASK: (57 M)

48(c) Why do you go to the hospital rather than to your doctor?

WRITE IN _____

_____

ALL WOMEN WITH CHILDREN, ASK: (58-59)

OTHERS GO TO Q.53(a)

49(a) How many live children have you given birth to? WRITE IN NUMBER

(60-61)

49(b) How many of your children were born in this country? WRITE IN NUMBER

(62) M

49(c) Before your (last) child was born, did you attend an ante-natal clinic or have any ante-natal care?

Yes, clinic 1
Yes, other (WRITE IN). . . . 2
No 3
DK 4

49(d) After your (last) child was born, did you use the available post-natal services? (63)

Yes 1 —) Q.49f
No 2 ⌉
DK 3 ⌋ —) Q.49e

	CODE	ROUTE

IF 'NO' TO Q.49(c) (i.e. NOT ATTENDED ANTE-NATAL CLINIC), ASK:

(64)M

49(e) Were there any reasons why you did not attend an ante-natal clinic?

WRITE IN _____

(65)

IF WORKING MOTHERS OR LONE FATHERS WITH CHILDREN LIVING AT HOME AGED 0-5, ASK Q.50:   IF AGED 6-11 ASK Q.51(a):

(66)M

OTHERS GO TO Q.52

50   Who looks after your child(ren) too young for school, while you are at work?

CODE ALL THAT APPLY

Nursery school   1
Play group   2
Relative   3
Friend   4
Child minder   5
Other (WRITE IN)   6

_____ DK   7

IF WORKING MOTHERS OR LONE FATHERS WITH CHILDREN AGED 6-11 LIVING AT HOME, ASK:

(67)

OTHERS GO TO Q.52

51(a) Are you usually at home when your child(ren) leave(s) for school?

Yes   1
No   2
DK   3

(68)

51(b) Are you usually at home when your child(ren) return(s) from school?

Yes   1
No   2
DK   3

C C 10/11

		CODE	ROUTE

IF 'NO' AT EITHER Q.51(a) OR Q.51(b), ASK:

(69)

51(c) Does anyone look after the child(ren) before
       and after school?

                                                    Yes   1 ——) Q.51d
                                                    No   2 ⎤
                                                    DK   3 ⎦ —) Q.52

IF YES, ASK: (70) **M**

51(d) Who looks after the child(ren)? (MULTICODE)

                           Relative   1
                           Friend 2
                           Child minder 3
                           Other (WRITE IN) 4

                                                    DK   5

                                                   (71)

ASK ALL MOTHERS OR LONE FATHERS WITH CHILDREN UNDER AGE 12:

OTHERS GO TO Q.53(a)

52(a) Have any of your children attended nursery
       class or playgroup?
                                                    Yes   1 ——) Q.53
                                                    No   2 ⎤
                                                    DK   3 ⎦ —) Q.52b

IF 'NO', ASK: (72)

52(b) Did you try to arrange for any of them to
       attend nursery class or playgroup?
                                                    Yes   1 ——) Q.52c
                                                    No   2 ⎤
                                                    DK   3 ⎦ —) Q.53

IF 'YES' AT Q.52(b), ASK: (73) **M**

52(c) Why were they unable to go?

       WRITE IN   (74) **M**

C C 11

	CODE	ROUTE

ASK ALL:

53(a) I'd like to ask you now about race relations laws and organisations. Do you know of any organisations set up by Parliament to deal with race relations?

IF "YES": Which organisations are these? CODE IN FIRST COLUMN BELOW

IF CRE OR CRC NOT MENTIONED, ASK:

53(b) Have you heard of the Commission for Racial Equality, the CRE? CODE IN LAST 2 COLUMNS BELOW AS APPROPRIATE

Have you heard of the Community Relations Councils, CRCs? CODE IN LAST 2 COLUMNS BELOW AS APPROPRIATE

	Men-tioned	Heard of	Not heard of
	(18)M	(19)M	(20)M
Commission for Racial Equality (CRE)	1	1	1
Community Relations Councils (CRCs)	2	2	2
Other (WRITE IN)	3	–	–
None/DK	4	–	–

IF MENTIONED OR HEARD OF CRCs, ASK: OTHERS GO TO Q.54   (21)

53(c) Do you know of a Community Relations Council in this area?

Yes   1 —) Q.53d
No   2 ⌉
DK   3 ⌋ —) Q.54

IF YES, ASK: (22)

53(d) Have you ever been to its offices or met any of its officers or staff?

Yes   1 —) Q.53e
No   2 ⌉
DK   3 ⌋ —) Q.54

IF YES, ASK: (23)M

53(e) What was this in connection with?

WRITE IN _____   (24)M

C C 11

	CODE	ROUTE

ASK ALL:

54. Would you consider taking a person to court or an industrial tribunal if they discriminated against you on racial grounds?

(25)

No	1
Yes	2
I might/it depends	3
DK	4

(26)

55. If a person discriminated against you on racial grounds, would you consider contacting the Commission for Racial Equality or a Community Relations Council?

No	1
Yes	2
I might/it depends	3
DK	4

(27)

ASK ALL:

56(a) Can I ask, what is your religion or church?

Islam/Muslim	1	⟶) Q.56b
Sikhism	2	
Hinduism	3	
Church of England	4	
Roman Catholic	5	
Other (WRITE IN)	6	⟶) Q.57
None	7	
DK	8	

IF ISLAM, SIKHISM, HINDUISM AND WORKING, ASK: (28)

56(b) Does your employer allow you any time off work specially to attend religious meetings or ceremonies?

Yes	1
No	2
DK	3

56(c) Does your employer provide any facilities for prayer at work?

(29)

Yes	1	⟶) Q.56d
No	2	⟶) Q.57
DK	3	

IF YES, ASK: (30)M

56(d) What facilities are provided?

WRITE IN _____

C C 11

	CODE	ROUTE

INCOME SECTION

IF EMPLOYEE (SEE Q.20(a)), ASK: SELF-EMPLOYED GO TO Q.58(a)

SHOW INCOME CARD IF RESPONDENT CAN READ

57(a) Finally, the last time you were paid, what was your
       take-home wage or salary?
       (Please choose the code number on this card
       that comes nearest to the amount)

£ _____ per _____

OR CODE IN FIRST
COLUMN BELOW

57(b) And what was your gross pay, before
       tax or other deductions?
       (Please choose the code number on this card
       that comes nearest to the amount)

£ _____ per _____

OR CODE IN SECOND
COLUMN BELOW

(WEEKLY)	Take home (31)	Gross (33)
Up to £30	1	1
£31 - £37 . . .	2	2
£38 - £46 . . .	3	3
£47 - £59 . . .	4	4
£60 - £74 . . .	5	5
£75 - £91 . . .	6	6
£92 - £116 . . .	7	7
£117 - £143 . . .	8	8
£144 - £182 . . .	9	9
£183+	0	0
	(32)	(34)
DK	1	1
Refused	2	2	→ Q.60a

(35)

57(c) Is that your usual amount of pay or
       was it different for any reason?

Usual pay	1
Last time pay was less than	
usual - less overtime . .	2
- other reason . . .	3
(WRITE IN)	
Last time pay was more than	
usual - more overtime . .	4
- other reason . . .	5
(WRITE IN)	
Holiday pay, etc	6
Tax refund	7
Absent due to illness . . .	8
OTHER (WRITE IN).	9
DK	0

J.2775   - 40 -

C C 11

	CODE	ROUTE

IF SELF-EMPLOYED, ASK: OTHERS GO TO Q.60(a)

(36)

58(a)   Do you regularly draw sums of money or cheques from the business for your own use?

Yes . . . .   1 →) Q.58b
No . . . .   2 ⎤
Refused . . . .   3 ⎦ →) Q.59a

IF YES, ASK:

(37)

58(b)   How much do you usually take out, and how often?

WRITE IN: £ _____ per _____

(38)

Don't know   1
Varies   2
Refused   3

(39)

58(c)   After deducting the amount you withdraw and other expenses, how much profit did your share of the business yield in the most recent 12 months for which you have figures?   WRITE IN

£ _____

(40)

Don't know . . . .   1 ⎤→Q.58 d
Loss . . . .   2 ⎦ Q.59a
Refused . . . .   3 ⎦→

(41-42)

58(d)   What 12 month period was this?   Month _____ 19

TO

(43-44)

Month _____ 19

	CODE	ROUTE

IF SELF-EMPLOYED, ASK:

SHOW INCOME CARD IF RESPONDENT CAN READ

(45)

59(a) For the most recent 12 months for which you have figures, what was your total income from your business after <u>all</u> deductions, that is after tax, National Insurance and all expenses?
(Please choose the code number on this card that comes nearest to the amount)

£ _____ OR CODE:

Up to £1,560	1
£1,561 – £1,975 . . .	2
£1,976 – £2,443 . . .	3
£2,444 – £3,119 . . .	4
£3,120 – £3,899 . . .	5
£3,900 – £4,783 . . .	6
£4,784 – £6,083 . . .	7
£6,084 – £7,487 . . .	8
£7,488 – £9,515 . . .	9
£9,516+	0

(46)

DK	1	
Loss	2	
Refused	3	→Q.60a

59(b) What 12 month period was this?

(47-48)

Month _____ 19

TO

(49-50)

Month _____ 19

(51)

<u>ASK ALL IF MARRIED OR LIVING AS MARRIED IF SPOUSE IS NOT ALREADY INTERVIEWED ON INDIVIDUAL MODULE:</u> <u>OTHERS GO TO Q.61(a)</u>

60(a) Is you husband/wife currently in paid employment, either as an employee or self-employed?

Yes, employee	1	—) Q.60b
Yes, self-employed	2	—) Q.60c
No	3	—) Q.61a
DK	4	

C C 11

	CODE	ROUTE

IF SPOUSE IS EMPLOYEE, ASK:

SHOW INCOME CARD IF RESPONDENT CAN READ

60(b) The last time he/she was paid, what was
       his/her take home wage or salary?

       (Please choose the code number on this card
       that comes nearest to the amount)

       £_____ per_____

       OR CODE IN FIRST
       COLUMN BELOW

60(c) And what was his/her gross pay, before tax
       or other deductions?
       (Please choose the code number on this
       card that comes nearest to the amount)

       £_____ per_____

       OR CODE IN SECOND
       COLUMN BELOW

(WEEKLY)	Take home	Gross
	(52)	(54)
Up to £30	1	1
£31 – £37	2	2
£38 – £46	3	3
£47 – £59	4	4
£60 – £74	5	5
£75 – £91	6	6
£92 – £116	7	7
£117 – £143	8	8
£144 – £182	9	9
£183+	0	0
	(53)	(55)
DK	1	1
Refused	2	2

→ Q.61a

60(d) Was this the usual amount he/she is paid,
       or was it more or less than usual?

(56)

Usual amount	1
More than usual	2
Less than usual	3
DK	4

C C 11

	CODE	ROUTE
	(57)	

IF SPOUSE IS SELF-EMPLOYED, ASK:

SHOW INCOME CARD IF RESPONDENT CAN READ

60(e) For the most recent 12 months for which he/she has figures,
       what was his/her total income from the business after <u>all</u>
       deductions, that is after tax, National Insurance and all
       expenses?
       (Please choose the code number on this card
       that comes nearest to the amount)

£ _____ OR CODE:

Up to £1,560	1
£1,561 - £1,975	2
£1,976 - £2,443	3
£2,444 - £3,119	4
£3,120 - £3,899	5
£3,900 - £4,783	6
£4,784 - £6,083	7
£6,084 - £7,487	8
£7,488 - £9,515	9
£9,516+	0

(58)

DK	1
Loss	2
Refused	3

-) 0.61a

60(f) What 12 month period was this?

(59-60)

Month _____ 19

TO

(61-62)

Month _____ 19

ASK ALL:

(63)

61(a) Do <u>you</u> receive any other income from any sources we've not
       mentioned so far? For example, a second job, rent from
       property, interest on savings or dividends, etc.?
       I don't want you to include any State benefits –
       social securities, child benefit, and so on.

Yes	1	—) Q.61b
No	2	
DK	3	—) CLOSE

IF 'YES' AT Q.61(a), ASK:

61(b) What are these sources and how much do you receive?

CODE WHETHER BEFORE OR AFTER DEDUCTIONS

SOURCE	AMOUNT		DEDUCTIONS (tax, insurance, etc.)	
			Before	After
_____	£ _____ per _____		1	2
_____	£ _____ per _____		1	2
_____	£ _____ per _____		1	2
_____	£ _____ per _____		1	2

(64-70)

C C 11

	CODE	ROUTE
	(71)	

ASK ASIANS ONLY

ENGLISH LANGUAGE ASSESSMENT

IF INTERVIEW NOT CONDUCTED IN ENGLISH, ATTEMPT A
CONVERSATION IN ENGLISH WITH RESPONDENT IN ORDER
TO ASSESS ABILITY.

Speaks English:

Fluently	1	
Fairly well	2	
Slightly	3	
Not at all	4	
DK	5	

(72-76) blank
(77-80) J.2775

DECLARATION: I DECLARE THAT THE INFORMANT WAS UNKNOWN TO ME UNTIL THE
INTERVIEW TOOK PLACE, AND THAT THIS QUESTIONNAIRE HAS
BEEN CONDUCTED ACCORDING TO THE MANUAL AND HAS BEEN CHECKED.

Signed _____   Date _____

Name _____

Number _____   Time ended_____

RESEARCH SERVICES LTD.

Station House, Harrow Road, Stonebridge Park, Wembley, Middlesex. HA9 6DE

J.2775/AK **SURVEY OF RACIAL MINORITIES** February 1982

ALTERNATE MODULE Time started _____

O U O	SERIAL	C C	S R	E D	PER. NO.
(1-3)	(4-9)	1 2 (10-11)	(12-13)	(14-16)	(17)

INTERVIEWER FILL IN SERIAL, ED AND PERSON NUMBER

DO NOT ASK Q.1 AND 2 IF RESPONDENT ARRIVED IN UK
IN 1977-82 (SEE INDIVIDUAL MODULE Q.2b)

INTERVIEWER : ONLY READ WHICHEVER OF 'ASIAN' OR 'WEST INDIAN'
IS APPROPRIATE TO YOUR RESPONDENT.

C C 12

I would now like to ask you about some of
your attitudes and recent experiences.

		CODE (18)	

1(a) In general, do you think life in Britain is
now better for people of Asian / West Indian origin
than it was five years ago, is it worse
or has there been no change?

Better..........	1
Worse...........	2
No change.......	3
Other (WRITE IN)	4
_____ DK	5

1(b) Why do you say that?

ASK : "Any other reason" UNTIL NO

(19) M

_____

_____

(20) M

_____

_____

_____

_____

_____

_____

.2775   C C 12

	CODE
	(21)

2a) Would you say there is about the same amount of
     racial discrimination in Britain as there was
     five years ago, less discrimination today or
     more discrimination today?

                              More discrimination.   1
                              About the same......   2
                              Less discrimination.   3
                                              DK   4

2b) Would you say the following problems are
     now better than they were five years ago,
     about the same or would you say the situation
     has got worse?

READ OUT IN TURN	Better	About the same	Worse	DK	
Racialist insults directed at people of __Asian__ origin West Indian	1	2	3	4	(22)
Physical attacks for racial reasons on people of __Asian__ origin West Indian	1	2	3	4	(23)

J.2775   - 3 -

3. I am going to read out some statements and for each one I would
    like you to tell me whether you think it is true or not true.

                                                         C C 12

    IF TRUE: Would you say definitely true or probably true?
    IF UNTRUE: Would you say probably untrue or definitely untrue?

	Definitely true	Probably true	Probably not true	Definitely not true	DK	
(a) White people have now accepted people of (Asian/West Indian) origin as part of British society	1	2	3	4	5	(24)
(b) White people do not understand the way of life or culture of (Asian/West Indian) people	1	2	3	4	5	(25)
(c) People of (Asian/West Indian) origin can rely on the Police to protect them from racialist violence	1	2	3	4	5	(26)
(d) In the (Asian/West Indian) community there are large differences of views between young people and older people	1	2	3	4	5	(27)
(e) People of (Asian/West Indian) origin are seeing their way of life and culture being replaced by the culture of white people	1	2	3	4	5	(28)
(f) White people and people of (Asian/West Indian) origin can live in the same area without any problems of race relations	1	2	3	4	5	(29)
(g) People of (Asian/West Indian) origin have adopted many aspects of the way white people live	1	2,	3	4	5	(30)

4. Do you think people of (Asian/West Indian) origin are generally
    treated the same, better or worse than white people by:

    REPEAT QUESTION WHERE NECESSARY:

	Same	Better	Worse	DK	
(i) Employers	1	2	3	4	(31)
(ii) Schools	1	2	3	4	(32)
(iii) Building Societies	1	2	3	4	(33)
(iv) Banks	1	2	3	4	(34)
(v) Pubs	1	2	3	4	(35)
(vi) Council housing departments . . .	1	2	3	4	(36)
(vii) The police	1	2	3	4	(37)
(viii) The courts	1	2	3	4	(38)
(ix) Insurance companies	1	2	3	4	(39)
(x) Estate agents	1	2	3	4	(40)
(xi) Hospitals	1	2	3	4	(41)
(xii) Trade Unions	1	2	3	4	(42)
(xiii) Social Security Offices (DHSS)	1	2	3	4	(43)

5.   I am going to read out some things that people have said about race relations in
     this country. For each one, I would like you to tell me if you agree or disagree
     with it.

IF AGREE   : Would you say you agree
               or agree strongly?

IF DISAGREE : Would you say you disagree
               or disagree strongly?

C C 12

	Agree strongly	Agree	Neither agree nor disagree	Disagree	Disagree strongly	
(a) People of (Asian/West Indian) origin should be tolerant towards white people who are racially prejudiced	1	2	3	4	5	(44)
(b) People of (Asian/West Indian) origin should organise themselves politically to oppose racialism	1	2	3	4	5	(45)
(c) People of (Asian/West Indian) origin should if necessary organise self-defence groups to protect themselves from racialist violence	1	2	3	4	5	(46)
(d) People of (Asian/West Indian) origin should try to preserve as much of their own way of life and culture as possible	1	2	3	4	5	(47)
(e) People of (Asian/West Indian) origin should try to adopt the way of life and culture of white people	1	2	3	4	5	(48)
(f) It is a good thing to be able to speak the ((A) language/(WI) dialect or patios) of your family's area of origin	1	2	3	4	5	(49)
(g) Children should be taught the ((A) language/(WI) dialect or patios) of their family's area or origin	1	2	3	4	5	(50)
(h) People of (Asian/West Indian) origin should keep themselves apart from white people	1	2	3	4	5	(51)
(i) People of (Asian/West Indian) origin should avoid living in mainly white areas	1	2	3	4	5	(52)
(j) People of (Asian/West Indian) origin should join political organisations alongside white people	1	2	3	4	5	(53)
(k) People of (Asian/West Indian) origin should join trade unions alongside white people	1	2	3	4	5	(54)
(l) People of (Asian/West Indian) origin should have white friends who they see outside of the workplace	1	2	3	4	5	(55)

(m) continued on next page (5)

Question 5 continued:

		Agree strongly	Agree	Neither agree nor disagree	Disagree	Disagree strongly	
				C C 12			
(m)	Everybody should oppose racial prejudice whenever it occurs	1	2	3	4	5	(56)
(n)	The present laws against racial discrimination should be enforced more effectively	1	2	3	4	5	(57)
(o)	There should be new and stricter laws against racial discrimination	1	2	3	4	5	(58)
(p)	People of (Asian/West Indian) origin should just ignore prejudice	1	2	3	4	5	(59)

		CODE	ROUTE

6 (a) In the past two years, has your family had any contact with the British Immigration Services or the Home Office over any matter concerning immigration?

(60)

Yes   1 ——) Q.6b
No   2
DK   3 —) Q.7a

ASK IF "YES":

(61)M

(b) What was this concerning?

   (WRITE IN) _____

_____

(62)

(c) Overall, would you say you were satisfied or dissatisfied with the way the immigration services or the Home Office dealt with this matter/these matters?

IF SATISFIED   : Would that be just satisfied or very satisfied?

IF DISSATISFIED : Would that be just dissatisfied or very dissatisfied?

Very satisfied   1
Just satisfied . . . .   2 —) Q.7a
Just dissatisfied   3
Very dissatisfied . . . . . .   4 —) Q.6d
DK   5 ——) Q.7a

ASK IF JUST OF VERY DISSATISFIED:

(63)M

6 (d) Why were you dissatisfied?

   (WRITE IN) _____

J.2775

C C 12/13

	CODE	ROUTE

ASK ALL:

(64)

7(a) The next few questions are about things that may have happened to you since 1 January 1981 — that is since the beginning of <u>last</u> year. <u>During that time</u>, has anyone burgled or broken into your house/flat without permission, or tried to do so?

Yes   1 ——) Q.7b
No   2]
DK   3] —) Q.7d

(65-66)

ASK IF "YES":

7(b) How many times has your house/flat <u>actually</u> been burgled or broken into since the beginning of last year? Don't include <u>attempted</u> break-ins.

WRITE IN NUMBER:

(67-68)

7(c) How many times have you found anything that showed that someone had tried to break in, without actually getting in, since the beginning of last year?

WRITE IN NUMBER:

(69)

7(d) (Apart from this/these incidents) During that time has anyone deliberately damaged any property that belonged to you?

Yes   1 ——) Q.7e
No   2]
DK   3] —) Q.7f

(70-71)

ASK IF "YES":

7(e) How many times has this happened since   **WRITE IN NUMBER:** the beginning of 1981?

(72)

7(f) Since 1 January 1981, that is since the beginning of last year, has anyone physically attacked or assaulted you or molested you in any way?

Yes   1 ——) Q.7g
No   2
DK   3 —) Q.8a

(73-74)

ASK IF "YES":

7(g) How many times has this happened since   **WRITE IN NUMBER:** the beginning of 1981?

IF NO BURGLARY, DAMAGED <u>PROPERTY OR PHYSICAL ASSAULT, ETC.</u> <u>CLOSE.</u>

(75-76) blank   (01-09) blank
(77-80) J.2775   (10-11) 13
  (12-17) serial

C C 13

	CODE	ROUTE
	(18)M	

ASK IF "YES" AT Q.7(a)

OTHERS GO TO Q.9(a)

8(a) About your burglary/break in ...
      Can you tell me, briefly, what happened (in the most serious case
      since the beginning of last year)?

      PROBE FOR OUTLINE DETAILS OF NATURE AND CIRCUMSTANCES OF
      (MOST SERIOUS) INCIDENT.   RECORD RELEVANT DETAILS ONLY

_____

_____

_____

(19)

8(b) Was anything actually taken?

Yes	1
No	2
DK	3

8(c) Was anything damaged?   (20)

Yes	1
No	2
DK	3

ASK IF "YES" AT Q.8(b) or (c):

8(d) Approximately what was the value of the items taken?

	Items taken	Cost of damage
	(21)	(22)
Under £20	1	1
£20 - £50	2	2
£51 - £100	3	3
£101 - £200	4	4
£201 - £500	5	5
£501 - £1,000	6	6
£1,001 - £2,000	7	7
£2,001 - £5,000	8	8
£5,001+	9	9
DK	0	0

CODE IN FIRST COLUMN (at "Under £20" row)

8(e) Approximately what was the cost of
      the damage?

CODE IN SECOND COLUMN (at "£2,001 - £5,000" row)

8(f) Do you know for sure who did it?   (23)

Yes	1	-) Q.8g
No	2	
DK	3	-) Q.8h

ASK IF "YES" AT Q.8(f):   (24)

8(g) Was it someone or some people you knew before it happened?

Yes	1	
No	2	
Several offenders - knew some	3	-) Q.8i
DK	4	

C C 13

	CODE	ROUTE

ASK IF "NO"/"DK" AT Q.8(f):   (25)

8(h) Do you know anything about who did it or can you give
      any description(s) at all?

                                              Yes   1 ——→ Q.8i
                                              No   2 ⎤ ⟶ Q.8l
                                              DK   3 ——⎦

ASK Q.8(i) IF OFFENDER KNOWN OR CAN GIVE DESCRIPTION   (26-27)
i.e. "YES" at Q.8(f) or Q.8(h).

8(i) How many were there?   WRITE IN NUMBER

                                                             (28)M

8(j) How old was the person/were the people who did it?
      Would you say:
                              READ OUT:

                              A child/children of
                                school age   1
                              OR a young person/young people
                                between 16 and 25   2
                              OR an older person/older people 3
                              (Mixed ages)   4
                                                       DK   5

                                                             (29)

8(k) Was the person/were the people who did it white or
      Asian or West Indian or of some other origin?

                              White   1
                              Asian   2
                              West Indian   3
                              Other (WRITE IN)   4

                              _____

                              Different races   5
                                                       DK   6

8(l) Did you report this burglary/break in to the police?   (30)

                                              Yes   1 ——) Q.8m
                                              No   2 ⎤
                                              DK   3 ⎦) Q.9a

                                                             (31)
ASK IF "YES":

8(m) And overall, were you satisfied or dissatisfied with the
      way the police dealt with the matter?

      IF SATISFIED   : Is that just satisfied or very satisfied?

      IF DISSATISFIED : Is that just dissatisfied or very dissatisfied?

                              Very satisfied   1
                              Just satisfied   2
                              Just dissatisfied   3
                              Very dissatisfied   4
                                                       DK   5

J.2775   - 9 -

ASK IF "YES" AT Q.7(d) (HAS HAD PROPERTY DAMAGED)

OTHERS GO TO Q.10(a)

9(a)   About the time your property was damaged ...
       Can you tell me, briefly, what happened (in the most serious case
       since the beginning of last year)?

       PROBE FOR OUTLINE DETAILS OF NATURE AND CIRCUMSTANCES OF
       (MOST SERIOUS) INCIDENT.   RECORD RELEVANT DETAILS ONLY

9(b)   Approximately what was the cost of the damage?

Under £20	1
£20 − £50	2
£51 − £100	3
£101 − £200	4
£201 − £500	5
£501 − £1,000	6
£1,001 − £2,000	7
£2,001 − £5,000	8
£5,001+	9
DK	0

9(c)   Do you know for sure who did it?

Yes	1	Q.9d
No	2	Q.9e
DK	3	

       ASK IF "YES" AT Q.9(c):

9(d)   Was it someone or some people you knew before it happened?

Yes	1	
No	2	
Several offenders − knew some	3	Q.9f
DK	4	

       ASK IF "NO"/"DK" AT Q.9(c):

9(e)   Do you know anything about who did it or can you give
       any description(s) at all?

Yes	1	Q.9f
No	2	
DK	3	Q.9i

C C 13

CODE	ROUTE
(32)	
(33)	
(34)	
(35)	
(36)	

C C 13

	CODE	ROUTE

ASK Q.9(f) IF OFFENDER KNOWN OR CAN GIVE DESCRIPTION
i.e. "YES" AT Q.9(c) or Q.9(e). OTHERS GO TO Q.9(i)   (37-38)

9(f) How many were there?   WRITE IN NUMBER

(39)M

9(g) How old was the person/were the people who did it?
Would you say:

READ OUT:

A child/children of
  school age   1
OR a young person/young people
  between 16 and 25   2
OR an older person/older people   3
  (Mixed ages)   4
                            DK   5

9(h) Was the person/were the people who did it white or   (40)
Asian or West Indian or of some other origin?

White   1
Asian   2
West Indian   3
Other (WRITE IN)   4

_____

Different races   5
                            DK   6

9(i) Did you report this incident to the police?   (41)

Yes   1 → Q.9j
No   2 →Q.10a
DK   3

ASK IF "YES":   (42)

9(j) And overall, were you satisfied or dissatisfied with the
way the police dealt with the matter?

IF SATISFIED   : Is that just satisfied or very satisfied?

IF DISSATISFIED : Is that just dissatisfied or very dissatisfied?

Very satisfied   1
Just satisfied   2
Just dissatisfied   3
Very dissatisfied   4
                            DK   5

                                                                    C C 13

ASK IF "YES" AT Q.7(d)   (HAS BEEN ATTACKED/ASSAULTED/MOLESTED):   (43)M

OTHERS CLOSE

10(a) About the time you were attacked or molested ...
       Can you tell me, briefly, what happened (in the most serious case
       since the beginning of last year)?

       PROBE FOR OUTLINE DETAILS OF NATURE AND CIRCUMSTANCES OF
       (MOST SERIOUS) INCIDENT.   RECORD RELEVANT DETAILS ONLY

       _____

       _____

       _____

       _____   (44)

10(b) Did you see a doctor or have medical treatment of any
       sort as a result of what happened?

                                                      Yes   1 ——) Q.10c
                                                       No   2]
                                                       DK   3] —) Q.10d

       ASK IF "YES" AT Q.10(b):   (45)

10(c) Did you have to stay in hospital overnight?

       ASK IF "YES": For how many nights?

                            No   1
                            Yes: 1 night   2
                                 2 - 3 nights   3
                                 4 - 6 nights   4
                                 1 week or more   5
                                                     DK   6
10(d) Do you know for sure who did it?   (46)

                                                      Yes   1 ——) Q.10e
                                                       No   2]
                                                       DK   3] —) Q.10f

       ASK IF "YES" AT Q.10(d):   (47)

10(e) Was it someone or some people you knew before it happened?

                            Yes   1
                            No   2
                            Several offenders - knew some 3 —) Q.10g
                                                     DK   4

       ASK IF "NO"/"DK" AT Q.10(d):   (48)

10(f) Do you know anything about who did it or can you give   Yes   1 —> Q.10g
       any description(s) at all?   No   2]
                                                               DK   3] —> Q.10j

J.2775   - 12 -

	CODE	ROUTE

ASK Q.10(g) IF OFFENDER KNOWN OR CAN GIVE DESCRIPTION
i.e. "YES" AT Q.10(d) or Q.10(f):

(49-50)

10(g) How many were there?   WRITE IN NUMBER

(51)M

10(h) How old was the person/were the people who did it?
       Would you say:

                              READ OUT:

                              A child/children of
                                 school age   1
                              OR a young person/young people
                                 between 16 and 25   2
                              OR an older person/older people   3
                                 (Mixed ages)   4
                                               DK   5

(52)

10(i) Was the person/were the people who did it white or
       Asian or West Indian or of some other origin?

                              White   1
                              Asian   2
                              West Indian   3
                              Other (WRITE IN)   4

                              _____

                              Different races   5
                                               DK   6

(53)

10(j) Did you report the attack/assault to the police?

                                          Yes   1 ——→ Q.10k
                                          No   2 ——┐
                                          DK   3 ——┘→CLOSE

(54)

       ASK IF "YES":

10(k) And overall, were you satisfied or dissatisfied with the
       way the police dealt with the matter?

       IF SATISFIED   : Is that just satisfied or very satisfied?

       IF DISSATISFIED : Is that just dissatisfied or very dissatisfied?

                              Very satisfied   1
                              Just satisfied   2
                              Just dissatisfied   3
                              Very dissatisfied   4
                                               DK   5

_____

                              Time ended_____ __

Date_____

Interviewer name_____number_____

(55-76) blank
(77-80) J.2775